# Humor 2.0

## How the Internet Changed Humor

Salvatore Attardo

ANTHEM PRESS

Anthem Press
An imprint of Wimbledon Publishing Company
www.anthempress.com

This edition first published in UK and USA 2024
by ANTHEM PRESS
75–76 Blackfriars Road, London SE1 8HA, UK
or PO Box 9779, London SW19 7ZG, UK
and
244 Madison Ave #116, New York, NY 10016, USA

First published in the UK and USA by Anthem Press in 2023

© 2024 Salvatore Attardo

The author asserts the moral right to be identified as the author of this work.

All rights reserved. Without limiting the rights under copyright reserved above, no part of this publication may be reproduced, stored or introduced into a retrieval system, or transmitted, in any form or by any means (electronic, mechanical, photocopying, recording or otherwise), without the prior written permission of both the copyright owner and the above publisher of this book.

*British Library Cataloguing-in-Publication Data*
A catalogue record for this book is available from the British Library.

*Library of Congress Control Number: 2024943660*
A catalog record for this book has been requested.

ISBN-13: 978-1-83999-362-6 (Pbk)
ISBN-10: 1-83999-362-6 (Pbk)

This title is also available as an e-book.

# CONTENTS

| | | |
|---|---|---|
| *Introduction* | | 1 |
| 1. | Humor and the Internet | 7 |
| 2. | Memetics | 23 |
| 3. | Humor Theory | 39 |

**Part 1.  NEW GENRES**

| | | |
|---|---|---|
| 4. | The New Language of Humor | 51 |
| 5. | The Compilation | 63 |
| 6. | Internet Cartoons | 71 |
| 7. | Stuff White People Like | 77 |
| 8. | Dogecoin, the Joke Currency | 85 |
| 9. | The Spoiler Alert | 93 |
| 10. | Satirical News Websites and Fake News | 99 |

**Part 2.  MEMES AND MORE MEMES**

| | | |
|---|---|---|
| 11. | Memetic Drift or The Alliteration Arsonist | 111 |
| 12. | The Saga of Boaty McBoatface | 123 |
| 13. | A General Theory of Grumpy Cats | 131 |
| 14. | The Pastafarian Memeplex: Joke Religion as a System | 139 |
| 15. | When Chuck Norris Is Waiting, Godot Comes | 151 |
| 16. | The Half-life of a Meme: The Rise and Fall of Memes | 161 |

## Part 3.  MULTIMODALITY

17. Hitler's Opinion on the Parking Situation in Tel Aviv — 175
18. Photobombing as Figure Ground Reversal — 183
19. "Hard to Watch": Cringe and Embarrassment Humor — 189
20. Humor Videos — 197
21. Reaction Videos — 207

## Part 4.  THE DARK SIDE OF INTERNET HUMOR

22. The Use of Humor by the Alt-Right — 219
23. 4chan, Trolls and Lulz: Fascists at Play — 225
24. Pepe, Kek and Friends — 239

*Conclusion: Plus ça change…* — 249

*Bibliography* — 253

*Author Index* — 271

*Subject Index* — 275

# INTRODUCTION

This book grew on me. I started out with the observation that classical humor theory, in which I have played a small but not insignificant role, was still relevant in analyzing the new humor on the internet. The occasion was a request to participate to a conference held in St. Petersburg in 2019. The presentation developed into a paper. I was originally interested only in memes, but I soon realized that really interesting comedic innovations were to be found in the videos, the satirical news and even in the cryptocurrency space. I also became interested in the mechanisms of virality and in what made memes "cool" mostly as a result of a collaboration with Anthony Dion Mitzel. Then in 2020, I had the opportunity to teach a course for the University of Shanghai, in which I was able to explore these topics more in detail. Because I wanted to give the students a good idea of what all was happening on the internet, the class was quite broad and ranged widely. This is directly reflected in this book. Also around that time, I became aware of disturbing trends that connected trolling and the use of humor by the alt-right to disseminate its fascist propaganda. All of this eventually led me to write this book. Thus, the focus had shifted from a straight application of humor theory to internet humor to a more "cultural" approach, of trying to map some of the forms of humor on the internet and what had happened that changed the "ethos" of the internet itself and humor with it. Before proceeding with the task at hand, a few concerns need to be discussed.

## US Centrism

The coverage of this book is clearly US-centric. This is due largely to the fact that this is where I happen to be located. In some respects, this is not a problem, because the United States have been on the forefront of the developments of new media. However, especially in my discussion of the alt-right use of humor, the reader should keep in mind that the situation in other countries may be different (and I briefly address this in the text). I welcome discussion and contributions showing how the situation in other countries is different or similar to the United States, along the lines of Denisova (2019) and Gal (2019), for example. More on that below.

**Expertise**

I do not claim to be an expert about 4chan or Twitch. I often have had to resort to informants to understand what I was looking at. I used extensively Know Your Meme, Urban Dictionary and Wikipedia. I definitely did not do a participant-observer ethnographic study. In fact, from reading some of the studies that did use this methodology, I believe that there is such a thing as being too close to one's subject of research. However, I did do my due diligence, with visits to Twitter, Tumblr, Reddit, 4chan and many other websites which quite frankly I am happy to say I will most likely never visit again. I think that my outsider's perspective is an advantage, rather than a limitation, in this case. I am no anthropologist, folklorist or sociologist. I claim my intellectual heritage in linguistics and semiotics and the likes of Umberto Eco and Roland Barthes (*si parva licet componere magnis*).

I am also not a historian. While I do discuss, briefly and without any hope of depth, the historical development of the internet, I have generally elected to stay away from the morass of discussions of how a given genre of memes or a given platform have changed through time. This is not to say that a history of, say, Tumblr going from an independent platform, to being acquired by Yahoo in 2013 and by Verizon in 2017, only to be resold in 2019 to Automattic [*sic*], the company that owns WordPress (the blogging site), or of Musk's acquisition and gutting of Twitter would not be interesting and worthwhile. However, what interests me is how humor is presented or available on a platform. How it works on it. In some cases, the historical aspect is central to understanding how a meme works and then I have tackled it, but generally speaking my work is not concerned specifically with the historical context of the internet, as is for example Donovan et al. (2022), which I recommend for that perspective.

**Authenticity**

In what follows, I will assume, unless there is reason to question it, that the videos or memes posted are "authentic" meaning that they have been produced by people to achieve some goal that is not producing an example for an academic discussion of humor, the internet, etc. Obviously, I have no way of knowing whether a given meme was produced by a linguist and what their intention was, given that memes are mostly anonymous. Nonetheless, once a video, for example, has gone viral at least to the extent that it has been catalogued in Know Your Meme or appeared on YouTube and gathered more than a handful of views, then I take that as "good enough" evidence of the authenticity of the video. This is distinct from the related question of whether the videos, for example, are authentic (as in recording spontaneous actions) or staged (where the people in the video are essentially acting). Here too, I have no way of knowing which is which, aside from commonsense. I discuss in more detail a couple of examples in chapter 20.

## Amplification

There is a concern, especially when discussing controversial or offensive humor, that the very act of quoting the humor in fact perpetuates the negative stereotypes on which it is based and thus in fact ends up reinforcing the ideology that made possible the offensive or controversial humor. However, when we are talking about memes that have been seen and reported by literally millions of people, the causality is simply backward. I will be discussing memes, images and videos that have gone viral and so have been widely disseminated, often for years. So, I am not going to worry about the possibility that someone otherwise naive about sexist or racist humor, who happens to have picked this book up, will decide that it is OK to use sexist or racist humor because they saw it in a book by a humor scholar.

## My Sources

If any of the students to whom I have taught the rudiments of writing up research over the 30 plus years of my career in academe happens to read this book they may be shocked by the fact that I do quote as secondary sources Know Your Meme and Wikipedia entries and even (gasp!) blogs. "What happened to 'Wikipedia is not an academic source!'?" they might cry out. They have a point: I would not quote Wikipedia in a discussion of structuralism, so why quote it on discussions of memes and internet humor? There are two (related) reasons: first, Wikipedia has improved a lot. Time turns out to have been on its side: the really bad entries have been rewritten, edited and corrected so that biased and partial coverage that used to make it unsuitable to beginners has been eliminated or remediated. Second, Wikipedia always shone at covering popular culture, where academe is not at its best, if for no other reason that the time it takes for an academic paper or book to be published almost certainly ensures that any academic treatment of a subject will be hopelessly out of date. Wikipedia, Know Your Meme and other websites can be updated virtually immediately. Moreover, these online sources are not constrained by page lengths and word counts and can simply list all episodes of a show and catalog minutiae about its production: for example, a Wikipedia page exists that lists all Simpsons episodes for the 34 series that have been aired (https://en.wikipedia.org/wiki/List_of_The_Simpsons_episodes). Good luck publishing that in a journal! Obviously, this does not make Wikipedia, let alone Know Your Meme, scholarly resources, in the sense that unlike scholarly paper or books, they have not been reviewed by at least two scholars who independently were willing to vouch to an editor that the article/book was scholarly, worthy of publication and original. They remain sources. Generally speaking, I used them to validate the analyses, to look for examples or document facts, not for interpretation, but as we all know the two things can never be completely isolated.

I also use, of course, regular scholarly sources, which are quoted and documented in a bibliography at the end of the book, as is customary in academe. Since this book may end up in the hands of non-academics (Welcome! Do not be alarmed! The animals are friendly, just don't make direct eye contact...) let me explain that a reference in the text (by last name and year of publication) directs the reader to an entry in the bibliography at the end of the book in which the full bibliographic citation of the source can be found. The page number, when present, is to help you locate the exact spot in which the author says what I say they say. This is so that the reader can check for themselves that I am not distorting their words—one of the basic practices of scholarly writing. If you trust me, you can just take my word for it and ignore the references entirely, unless you interest is piqued and then those sources are a good starting point for further research.

I also used extensively two Google tools: Google Ngram Viewer (https://books.google.com/ngrams/) and Google Trends (https://trends.google.com/home). They allow a unique diachronic (chronological) perspective which I found very useful. I cannot discuss the methodology and reliability of these tools, in this context, but there is useful information to this effect on the Google websites.

## Acknowledgments

I owe a great debt to my daughter Gaia, Nikita Lobanov, Anthony Dion Mitzel, Hilal Ergül, Madeline Norris and Andrew Donahue. Musarrat Azher helped with the translation of Pakistani languages in one video. Luca Bischetti, Stephen Skalicky, Joshua Loomis and Shelby Miller co-authored papers with me upon which I drew for the writing of some parts of the book. I also owe a debt of gratitude to all the readers of my Substack who provided comments and suggestions. I am also grateful to the editorial team at Anthem and particularly to the five anonymous referees who provided me with plenty of useful suggestions. My biggest debt is of course to my wife, Lucy Pickering, who read the first drafts of all the chapters and edited them. That she still is my wife is truly a sign of love. Heart emoji, heart emoji, heart emoji.

## Further Research

This is not a book that will ever be finished. I fully expect to be corrected where I may have misinterpreted or misunderstood materials. I fully expect that some readers from other geographical areas outside the US peculiar politics will have significantly different experiences. I encourage anyone willing to contribute ideas and data to contact me via my Substack, where I plan to publish errata, corrections and updates, as available.

https://salvatoreattardo.substack.com/

# Chapter 1
# HUMOR AND THE INTERNET

**The Internet (Web 1.0)**

This is not a historical study, but it is important to start by noting that our world has changed significantly in an astonishingly short time span. Thirty years ago, this book would have been inconceivable simply because none of its subject matter existed. It is easy to forget that the changes we will consider all happened in under 30 years, and often much less.

The Internet was invented in 1989 by Tim Berners-Lee at CERN (Conseil Européen pour la Recherche Nucléaire) in Geneva, Switzerland. What Berners-Lee came up with was a transfer protocol (set of instructions) called HTTP (Hypertext Transfer Protocol) which was itself based on the older FTP (File Transfer Protocol) dating back to 1971. Berners-Lee also wrote the first browser, called WWW (World Wide Web [1990]) which allowed people to interact easily with files. Part of the development of HTTP and WWW involved laying the foundations of HTML, the code that tells browsers what to display on screen. WWW was followed by Mosaic (1993), Netscape (1994) and Internet Explorer (1995). Later, Netscape launched Mozilla (1998) as open source.

While originally meant as a decentralized network for military operations and after its adoption by academe as a way to transfer files and information about research, almost immediately the internet started being used as a way to socialize, much along the line of the first 1980s Bulletin board systems (BBSs: Fidonet, The WELL, etc.). BBSs were essentially a precursor of the internet, with the difference that they worked over phone lines and had a dial-up model (where a user would connect to the BBS, get their email or download news and log off to read them offline). Importantly the idea was to use a local BBS so that one would not have to make a long distance call, which at the time were much more expensive than local calls.

## Usenet: The Big Eight and the alt. Hierarchy

BBSs "evolved" into usenet, which was decentralized; in other words, there was no need to call a central BBS. News, posts and discussions could be accessed from any computer on the network. Usenet was organized in a hierarchy of newsgroups (discussion boards) where users could post. For example the rec groups (rec stands for recreation) include rec.music, rec.film and others. One could always add a new discussion group, through a complex process in which a proposal supported by users was approved and an appropriate location in the hierarchy was found. To the original categories an alt. group was added to handle content that was too controversial for the other groups. In a momentous decision, it was left unmoderated, so that anyone could start a group on anything.

For example, joke groups such as alt.wesley.crusher.die.die.die was started by *Star Trek the Next Generation* fans who disliked the eponymous character. Note how the name is already a joke: the idea of the usenet hierarchy is that each word after a dot represents a subclass of the previous word. This makes sense for "wesley.crusher" (there are presumably many wesleys out there); it begins to show some signs of playfulness with .die, although one could possibly hypothesize the existence of alt.wesley.crusher.live for those fans who think the character should not die. However, when "die" is repeated three times, it make no sense hierarchically but it acquires a completely different connotation, that is, that of a killer stabbing or shooting multiple times their victim, screaming "Die! Die! Die!" Another common connotation for repetition in English is also intensification, with obvious iconicity.

The alt hierarchy has another, much more serious, and completely unrelated, meaning in the expression alt-right: an abbreviation of alternative right, is a loosely connected white nationalist, white supremacist, and neo-Nazi movement. "A largely online phenomenon, the alt-right originated in the United States during the late 2000s and the early 2010s" (Wikipedia, https://en.wikipedia.org/wiki/Alt-right). It is possible that the use of alt. and alt- is unrelated, but given the commonly accepted view that the alt-right was born online, I doubt it is a coincidence.

Many BBSs and later usenet groups served as repositories of information, often technical, but also related to hobbies and popular culture (e.g., fanzines, which soon migrated onto the internet). However, having the richest repository of information in the world is pointless if one cannot locate said information. This is why the rise of the internet is paralleled by the rise of online information retrieval. For example, one of the early successes of the internet was Yahoo, which was originally not a search engine but a directory, organized hierarchically. There were categories, subcategories, etc., until you hit what you were looking for: so you'd start with Entertainment and then drill down through music, dance-pop and eventually reach Rick Astley, for example. Soon search engines (Gopher, 1991; Altavista, 1995; Google, 1998; Baidu, 2000) took over, due to their inherent simplicity of use, compared to a hierarchy.

With its email systems, newsgroups and file transfer/retrieval, the World Wide Web was more or less an extension of the professional or academic world. Yes, people downloaded pornography, discussed TV shows, films and origami, and e-commerce had been allowed in 1991 (the first online book store opened in 1992, in Cleveland; Amazon followed in 1994, eBay in 1995). However, to some extent you needed to know what you were doing in order to "go online." Which is why companies such as America Online (AOL) specialized in providing a simplified, "gated," experience for those who wanted access to video games or email, but were not comfortable accessing the big scary internet. This is the moment in time captured by Nora Ephron's 1998 film *You've Got Mail*. All this was soon to change, with the advent of social media and the web 2.0.

## Web 2.0

By "web 2.0" we refer to the shift from a rather static/passive experience for the majority of users (essentially, those who could not code in HTML) to the more active production of content by the users. Think of Facebook: you probably have no idea how the code that runs the pages actually works. However, that's (almost) completely irrelevant to your experience of Facebook as a place where you post pictures of your grandchildren, graduation, food, cartoons, memes and so on. Indeed, the site is designed precisely that way: Facebook does not want you to think about what you see and/or post as being influenced and possibly prompted by its design, algorithm and ultimately code. It wants you to think about your friends, be gratified by likes and want to come back. So, the code is not irrelevant, but it is made to look irrelevant. Thus, web 2.0 is the web of social media, of sharing, and interacting online. Quintessential web 2.0 application are YouTube, TikTok, WordPress (blogs), Wikipedia or Tumblr, the hipper version of Facebook, etc. When you review a purchase on Amazon, or a restaurant on Yelp, or your hotel on TripAdvisor, you are contributing to web 2.0.

There is a web 3.0, needless to say, but we will not deal with it in this book. The basic idea being that the web pages would be aware to some extent of the content they present and thus could reason about it, using artificial intelligence. I leave discussion of these topics for the next edition, which will be written by an AI pretending to be me. However, you will know if I have been replaced by a sentient web page from the quality of the jokes…

## From Utopia to Dumpster Fire

The early years of the internet, both in its architecture and its ideology, were almost unfailingly optimistic: the internet's self-regulating, libertarian ethos fostered a culture of sharing and collaboration. A good example is Project Gutenberg, started in 1971, which is a free digital library, now including over 60,000 books, all gloriously free. Consider open access software, for another example. The GNU project, started by Richard Stallman, in 1983, is an open source replacement of the UNIX operating system (which is owned by AT&T). EMACS, a text editor used on UNIX machines, was written in 1976, and a GNU version was created in 1984. Linux, a UNIX-like operating system, was released by Linus Torvalds in 1991, as open source. Apache, the software on which a significant part of the internet runs, was a crowdsourced project and remains an open source product. As of 2022, it is the most used software to run "busy" websites (https://en.wikipedia.org/wiki/Apache_HTTP_Server). Finally, Wikipedia, although technically already in the age of web 2.0, is perhaps the most significant, culturally speaking, accomplishment of the free, collaborative, self-policing ethos of the web 1.0. What best could summarize the spirit of the web 1.0? The largest most read reference work in history (Economist, 2021) is an open access, crowdsourced, project. In the web 1.0, some of the best software were free. Information wanted to be free. Hackers were heroes.

By the mid-2010s, however, the tone had changed, and is now much more ambivalent: while it is unthinkable to abandon the always on connection of the internet (when's the last time you paid a bill in the mail or went to the library to look something up in the encyclopedia?) the algorithms of social media are widely seen as a dark force. Nowadays, comparing the internet to a dumpster fire is a common metaphor (e.g., Packer & Van Bavel, 2021). In part, this shift of opinion is due to the mainstreaming of phenomena like trolling and the humor of the alt-right (see Chapter 22). Another reason for the shift is due, in my opinion, to the intrinsic limits of the utopian ideas on which the internet was founded. Far from being free, information, especially about our personal private lives, is increasingly monetized. Hackers are now often the "bad guys" trying to steal your credit card data and holding up your files in ransomware attacks. Advertising is ubiquitous. False information and propaganda from nefarious agents spread wildly using precisely the channels that were supposed to decentralize information production and gathering. For example, in the five-month preceding the 2016 US presidential election one-quarter of the tweets that contained news were in fact fake news or extremely biased (Bovet & Makse, 2019). Needless to say, this is not limited to Twitter, but is true also of Facebook, Wikipedia and YouTube. Take Wikipedia. Kumar et al. (2016)

examine 20,000 known hoaxes that have been identified and deleted. That is a staggering number especially if one keeps in mind that it does not include hoaxes that have not been identified…

**The Web Is Not Flat**

In short, in less than 30 years, the internet or the web has become an important part of our lives and in those of many (but not all) people of the world. The following charts show this eloquently. Figure 1.1 clearly shows the differences in penetration of the internet.

If we consider the rate of adoption, as in Figure 1.2 below, it appears even more striking how fast the adoption of the internet has been: in the decade from 1995 to 2005 we went from single digits to almost 80 percent, in North America. Europe lagged by 5–10 years but by 2015 had largely caught up. For comparison, it took 40+ years to get to 80 percent adoption of electric power, 50 years for the automobile and 70 years for the washing machine. Obviously, we are far more interested in sharing pictures of cute cats than in having power, clean clothes and being able to drive around…

The internet has had an enormous impact on the distribution of information (newspapers and news channels), entertainment (TV and film), music, video games, shopping (Amazon), politics, sex (dating apps) and more. In

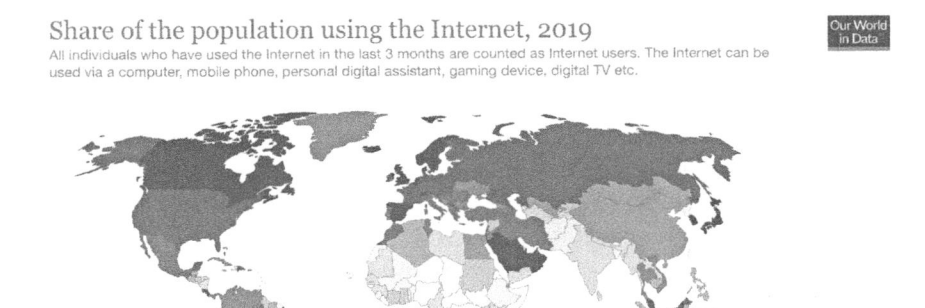

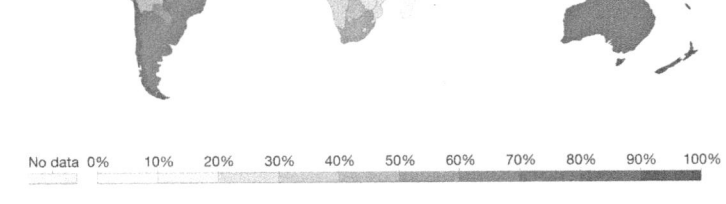

**Figure 1.1** The internet is not flat: Differences in access to the internet.

Share of US households using specific technologies, 1908 to 2016

- Electric power
- Automobile
- Internet
- Washing machine

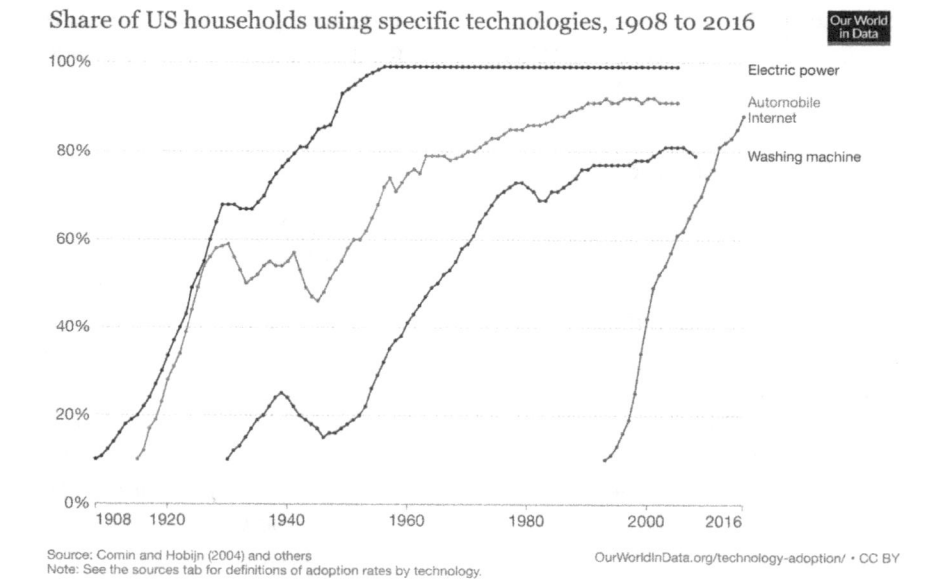

Source: Comin and Hobijn (2004) and others
Note: See the sources tab for definitions of adoption rates by technology.
OurWorldInData.org/technology-adoption/ • CC BY

**Figure 1.2** Different rates of adoption for new technologies.

fact, it would be hard to come up with examples of activities that have been completely unaffected by the advent of the internet. Let's be clear, as Figures 1.1 and 1.3 indicate, the world is definitely not flat when it comes to the spread and availability of the internet. Thomas Friedman's 2005 book *The World Is Flat* argued that the playing field among countries is being leveled by globalization, including most notably the computer and the internet revolution. My point is that there still are enormous differences in how deep the adoption of these tools goes and I am not sure that the differences aren't growing bigger, rather than smaller (Friedman's point). Even within the first world there are significant differences in accessibility between urban, affluent areas and poor, rural areas. However, clearly, the impact of the internet on Sub-Saharan Africa has been much more modest than it has been in the United States, for example, nor is there any sign of this changing anytime soon. I do not want to sweep these differences under the rug, they are very real and they may have profound macroeconomic effects on how wealth and services are distributed in the future. However, they are not my focus in this discussion.

Furthermore, even the adoption of the internet in the United States was far from uniform. McCulloch (2019) distinguishes three waves. The first wave, which corresponds to the Web 1.0 and spans the 1980s and 1990s, she dubs

Share of the population using the Internet
All individuals who have used the Internet in the last 3 months are counted as Internet users. The Internet can be used via a computer, mobile phone, personal digital assistant, gaming device, digital TV etc.

Source: International Telecommunication Union (via World Bank)    OurWorldInData.org/technology-adoption/ • CC BY

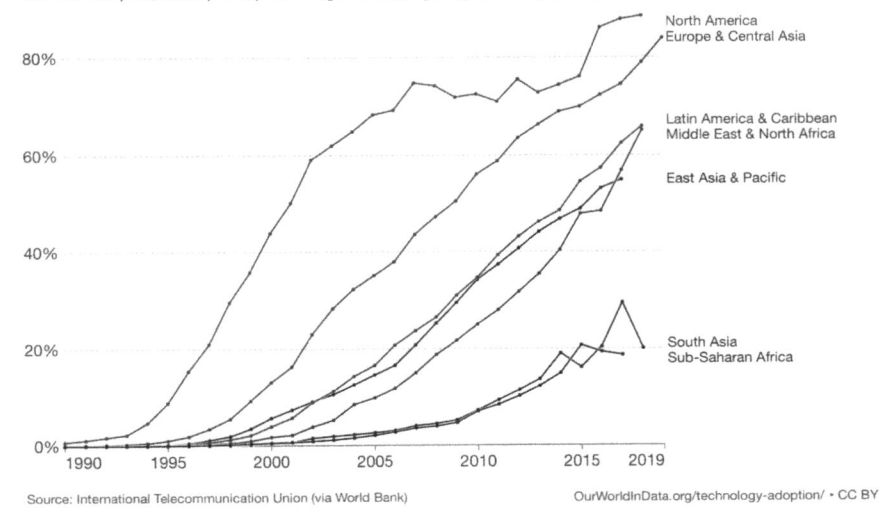

**Figure 1.3** Rate of access to the internet, by geopolitical area.

"old internet people" ("geezers with a foot in the grave" was apparently taken). Old internet people are tech-savvy, can code to some extent and accessed the internet for practical, generally professional, purposes.

The second wave corresponds to the advent of social media (Web 2.0), so roughly the decade of the 2000s (or noughties—in a felicitous British term). The second wave is divided in two groups. The first are the full internet people, who are the generation born around 1990 and so, who turned 18 around 2000 and so see social media as "natural"(Neopets launched in 1999, Myspace in 2003). Because they have always been familiar with computers, smartphones and related technology, they are computer literate, but they are not necessarily capable of more advanced uses, let alone programming. The second group are the semi-internet people: they are the late adopters, who did not see the usefulness of the internet in the 1990s. They are middle aged and more likely to have a LinkedIn account than a Reddit or Twitter account. They joined Facebook to connect with real-life friends and family. When they did so, the full internet people started leaving for other platforms (such as TikTok, Reddit, or Tumblr) because if your parents are on Facebook, the platform is no longer cool…

The third wave (from 2010 to the present) is also divided into two: the children who are using social media, such as Tumblr, to play video games and socialize (which McCulloch calls post-internet people) and the pre-internet people, seniors who use email or Skype to talk to their children and grandchildren, and may post on Facebook. The point of this subcategorization (summed up in the Table below) is that different generations and subgroups within them interact with the internet differently because they see/approach it differently. A semi-internet person who checks their LinkedIn account for professional purposes is unlikely to be familiar with the same internet that their kids experience on Tumblr.

|  | *Timeline* | *McCulloch* |  |  | *Generation* |
|---|---|---|---|---|---|
| First wave | 1980s–1990s | old internet people | Web 1 | Early adopters | Gen X, Millennials |
| Second wave | 2000s | full internet people | Web 2 | Mass adopters ("digital natives") | Gen Z, Millennials |
|  |  | semi-internet people |  | Late adopters | Gen X |
| Third wave | 2010s | pre-internet people |  | Late late adopters | Gen X, Baby boomers |
|  |  | post-internet people |  |  | Gen Alpha |

## Humor and the Internet

Much like the impact of the internet on contemporary culture has been very significant, the impact of the internet on humor has been likewise profound. There is a widespread perception that humor on the internet is different than it was before. This book is dedicated to this question, examining many cases of internet humor to see to what extent humor-on-the-internet is different from humor-before-the-internet. For ease of reference I will refer to humor-on-the-internet as "humor 2.0."

The internet has obviously brought changes, such as references to spoilers, emojis and memes, but at a deep level, the deep semantic mechanisms of humor are universal and do not change. There are no reports of any human groups that do not have humor, neither now or historically. Needless to say, not everyone finds the same things funny. We all know that British humor is very different from, say, Italian humor. You may have experienced the odd feeling of watching a foreign comedy and not finding it funny. This means that we do not all laugh at the same things. So "has humor 2.0 changed what we laugh at?" is a very good question.

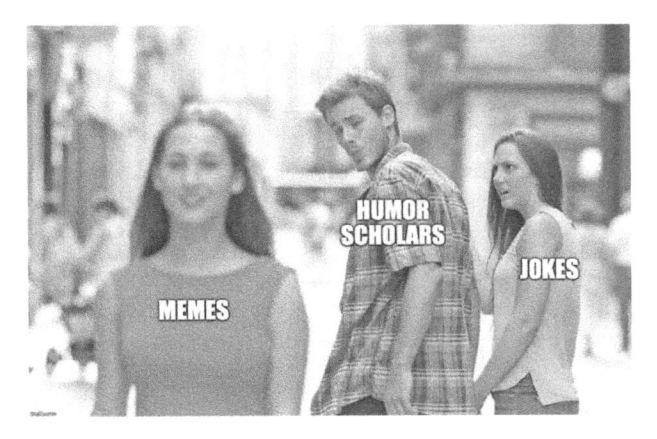

**Figure 1.4** Memes and humor scholars.

## *Memes*

Probably the most significant change is the appearance of the humorous meme, as a sort of basic unit of humorous meaning in the digital world. It has replaced what the joke used to be for humor studies: the preferred type of example, used by default when discussing a phenomenon (see Figure 1.4). Memes were not originally funny. The term "meme" was originally coined in 1976 by Dawkins as an analogy between self-replicating units in biology (genes) and the corresponding units in culture. A meme is a cultural unit, simple or complex. For example, using a fork to eat. The idea caught on (the meme was successful) and was adopted by Dennet (1991, 1995) and Blackmore (1999). The field of memetics was founded. Soon however, interest in memetics waned[1] and the original sense of meme was replaced by the current one: an image, usually with text, often humorous.[2] Some have tried

---

1 The reasons are complex and far outside the domain of this book. Let it suffice to say that the very idea of discrete "cultural units" has been questioned. I myself am agnostic as to the existence of memes (in Dawkins's sense); however, they are the perfect tool to think about the materials in this book, and so I have retained the terminology.
2 It should be stressed that memes are not necessarily images. They can be videos, animated images (GIFs), but also behaviors (e.g., planking; vocal fry) or (musical) sounds. Examples of musical memes are the opening of Beethoven's Fifth Symphony, the Beatles' pizzicato trumpets in *Penny Lane,* the "dun dun" in the TV show *Law and Order,* or the drum introduction of clips on pornography website Pornhub. The latter's semiotic force can be appreciated from the first 9 seconds of this video clip https://www.youtube.com/watch?v=frV7RQE3QvY in which a student plays the very short "sting"

to distinguish between memes and internet memes (the humorous ones). In this book, I will use "meme" in the current sense (funny pictures with text) and refer to "original memes" or "Dawkins' meme" to convey the meaning of cultural unit. It is impossible to discuss the definition of meme in this context, as this would require a separate, really technical, book, but let me mention that most scholars base their definitions on Shifman's (2014a), e.g., Wiggins (2019) and Yus (2021) and their definitions correspond to what I call a meme cycle (see Chapters 2 and 11).

Can we find a line between what has changed and what stays the same in humor? Does that line tell us anything interesting about humor and/or the internet?

### *Ch-ch-changes: Turn and face the strange*

Some things have obviously changed. The pace of humor has changed. Internet humor is faster (Chiaro, 2018; Jennings, 2018); it tends to favor shorter forms of expression (e.g., the 6-second Vine video loop, see Chapter 20). Memes are short-lived; they are ephemera. They go viral extremely fast but they also fade into oblivion just as fast. Tristram Shandy or Don Quixote are impossible over the internet. They are simply too long. The internet is where the TL;DR acronym originates. The acronym, which stands for Too Long; Didn't Read, can be seen as the GenZ manifesto of bellicosely self-satisfied ignorance. What kind of Yahoos[3] are so lazy that they refuse to read an explanation? However, if we consider blogs or other texts that accrete over a period of time, the size and complexity of the products may rival those of comic masterpieces of the age of books. For example, Randall Munroe had released, as of March 16, 2023, 2751 XKCD comics in the 2005-2022 period.

There is another way in which humor 2.0 has changed. The way humor is delivered, how it is accessed, where it is to be found and how it is socialized are now different in small and big ways. Consider how humor may be enjoyed alone, or in a group, passively (i.e., watching a video) or actively (interacting with others in a joint production of humor), privately or publicly (e.g., in a theater or comedy club). All these options are now reproduced in online environments, with obvious differences: for example, most online discussions are

---

(as these percussion phrases are called) at a school assembly and the audience explodes immediately in merriment.

3 Pun intended: Swift's *Gulliver's Travels* (1726) introduce the Houyhnhnms, a race of horse-like rational beings and the Yahoos, savage humanoids. Obviously, Swift was not part of the curriculum in the Electrical Engineering department at Stanford, in 1995, when Jerry Yang and David Filo named their web directory.

asynchronous, so if one wants to comment on someone else's comment they may do so days or months after the original comment was posted. When the users are interacting synchronously, but online, subtle differences in typing speed, choice of emojis, etc., become meaningful, much like subtle differences in prosody are meaningful in speech.

The means of delivery have changed radically. We have gone from an oral-written culture to a written-audiovisual culture. You don't tell a meme, you show it or you share it. We have gone from face-to-face communication (with conversation as the prototypical mode of interaction) to mediated communication, which is asynchronous, synchronous or mixed. This obviously affects significantly the mode of presentation and the reactions as well. Consider that many internet media allow comments (think YouTube videos) or other responses (Twitter and Reddit) which are visible to other viewers/readers and thus necessarily affect their perception. Indeed it is not uncommon for viewers to have their own comments, which may develop into veritable "side conversations" (these multiparty asynchronous interactions are sometimes referred to as "polylogues" Marcoccia, 2004; Bou-Franch et al., 2012). The fact that internet communication is mediated by the technological interface significantly affects the rules of turn taking, which is no longer primarily sequential (overlaps are rare and notable exceptions) and no longer relies on the "one speaker at a time" principle. Indeed, the comments of Twitter or YouTube posts are sometimes completely unrelated and irrelevant to the item they purport to be a comment on.

The internet as a means-of-delivery has also changed other forms of humor that we would not traditionally associate with it. Consider standup comedy, what could be considered the anti-internet format: standup comedy is generally performed live, in small clubs, for a local audience. Obviously, major stars such as Eddie Izzard and David Chappelle have performed in larger venues, recorded their acts and distributed them through traditional media (DVD, television specials, TV series, etc.). However, the bulk of standup comedy, worldwide, still happens in meatspace (i.e., in the real world): small, local, in person non-virtual performances. Yet, even that world has been changed by the internet.

Consider the case of Eleanor Morton. You have probably not heard of her. Neither should I. Eleanor Morton is a Scottish comedian, who moved to London (according to her web page). In the pre-internet world I would have never seen her perform. Yet I came across her work on YouTube, through some wrinkle of fate (also known as "the algorithm"), and I was interested, which prompted the algorithm (also known as "our benevolent ruler") to offer me more of her work. Morton is clever in that she goes beyond posting snippets of her performances (which many, perhaps most?) comedians do, in the hope of building a following on the internet that might translate into more attendance at their shows. Morton produces very short 1-2 minute skits, for the internet, with minimal props (clothing, an obviously fake painted mustache, etc.), mostly low key. She has literally hundreds of videos. Some are hilarious; some don't quite click. Esthetically it reminds me of low-fi musicians or of video podcasts. My favorites are the skits about Scottish tour guides who don't care anymore. I think she is quite funny and wish her the best for her career. Why are we talking about Eleanor? My point is that in the humor 1.0 world I would have never heard of her. Instead, due to the internet, I have had a chance to enjoy her comedy. Much like Morton, other comedians upload their performances or produce material for social media. See, for example, the material by Leggero and Notaro discussed in Chapter 19.

### *A new cast of characters*

Much like the medieval Italian commedia dell'arte had its "maschere" (masks) that is, stock characters such as Arlecchino (Harlequin), Pulcinella (Punch, in the Anglo-Saxon world) or the braggart soldier, the internet has created its set of stock characters, who exactly like the "masks" of the commedia dell'arte have a set of visuals attached to them. For example, advice dog (Figure 1.5), overly attached girlfriend, scumbag Steve, philosoraptor, socially awkward penguin (Figure 1.6), and many more.

Some characters are appropriated, such as the "most interesting man in the world" (which started out as a commercial for a beer), or Pepe the Frog (which started out as an innocent cartoon), but most appear to have

**Figure 1.5** Advice dog.

**Figure 1.6** Socially awkward penguin.

originated within the memesphere. We will examine some of the characters, such as Wojak (and its variants Soyjak and NPC Wojak) and some of the rage comics in Chapter 23.

### *Internet ugly: The esthetics of memes*

One of the first things that strikes you on the internet is how unspeakably bad looking most of the memes are. The esthetic of the imagery on 4chan, Reddit and other meme websites has been aptly named "internet ugly" (Douglas, 2014) which captures the amateurish, deliberately low-quality esthetics of a majority of memes. Take for example Rage guy (Figure 1.7), the prototype of the rage comics (see Chapter 23) which is a striking example of the internet ugly esthetics.

The other aspect about internet memes is that very often they look similar. This is not a coincidence, as often they share the same font (called Impact). There is a reason for this, which we will discuss in Chapter 12.

### *The language has changed*

It is almost a truism that the internet has affected language. Many see it as a problem, or worse as a degeneration. The only problem with that idea is that it's just plain wrong. True, language is changing, but that's a good thing. The only languages that do not change are the dead ones. We will look at these changes in Chapter 4.

**Figure 1.7** Rage guy.

## *On the internet nobody knows you're a dog*

The famous New Yorker cartoon by Peter Steiner, published in 1993, in which one dog, sitting in front of a computer tells to another dog the famous caption has become iconic of one of the most significant differences of communicating on the internet as opposed to communicating face to face or at least in "meatspace." This does not just mean that on the internet you can easily disguise your identity, but more profoundly that on the internet one communicates primarily if not exclusively what one chooses to communicate: if I create a gmail account called "HunkyLinguist" and use it to create a Facebook account where I post pictures of muscular guys working out while reading Chomsky, nothing short of a subpoena to Facebook and Google and/or serious hacking can uncover that I am in fact not hunky and I do not work out. Conversely, if we are talking face-to-face, that information would have bene evident immediately, even before I opened my mouth. In other words, there is a distance between the image of ourselves we project in real life and the images of ourselves we project in cyberspace. Because of this distance, it is much easier to disassociate our "real" meatspace identity from any pseudonymous or anonymous identity we wish to adopt online. This can be used for good or for bad purposes: a member of a persecuted minority may seek support or assistance anonymously because doing so openly would bring about retaliation; conversely, one may impersonate another user or harass them, in near certain impunity. As we will see, anonymity (e.g., Herring, 2007; Bou-Franch & Blitvich, 2014) and impunity (e.g., Phillips, 2015) are two of the most significant factors that contribute to the rise of certain strands of aggressive and pernicious internet humor.

The ultimate expression of disguised identity on the internet is "catfishing," that is, pretending to be someone, usually physically attractive, or otherwise desirable, to extort money or for (long distance) sexual gratification. When the catfisher's goals have been fulfilled, the victim is then "ghosted" (i.e., no further communication is provided). In some cases, people have faked identities in support groups or other online spaces.

## *Microgenres*

The meme is not the only new genre that originated in the digital world. Some new "genres" or perhaps "micro-genres" have appeared that would have been unthinkable before the internet. For example, the parody Amazon review or parody Twitter accounts (Vásquez, 2019) could not have existed before Twitter (2006) and Amazon reviews (1995). Amazon parody reviews are connected to collaborative pranks (Chapter 12) in the sense that a heterogeneous group (a group that lacks particularly salient common features) comes together for the accomplishment of a given task. Imagine crossing the street at a pedestrian crossing: the pedestrians wait together for the light to turn green and cross together, so they form a group, but they have little in common, besides being at that crosswalk and wanting to cross.

The parody video is also essentially a new genre (although of course parodies have existed since ancient times, see Lelièvre, 1954 for plenty of examples) made possible by the capacity to record and edit video easily and cheaply. Take what is probably one of the earliest and best-known examples: the "numa-numa" video (2004), which features a teenager (Gary Brolsma) lip synching a song by a (then) obscure Moldovan pop group. The humor in the performance consisted in Brolsma's exaggerated facial expressions and gestures and in the general sense of unbridled enjoyment he manifested. According to Wikipedia (https://en.wikipedia.org/wiki/Numa_Numa_(video)), the video has been watched 700 million times. This should be contrasted to the elaborate video parodies of Weird Al Yankovic or to the *Rutles* album, parodying the Beatles, which have elaborate production values and are professionally recorded. Brolsma's video, and countless imitators, is recorded using a web cam, and he does not move from his desk.

Moreover, one of the most significant and yet most obvious differences in digital humor is the multimodal nature of the texts. While jokes were essentially a verbal/linguistic phenomenon, the meme is essentially multimodal, that is, it involves more than one mode of communication, usually at least the linguistic and visual, but music or audio can be involved as well. Even more significantly the same meme (image, video, etc.) may be experienced on different platforms or within different apps (e.g., TikTok videos may be viewed within TikTok or in Facebook or YouTube). Thus entire genres have appeared that were quite simply impossible in the text-centric world of pre-digital humor: the photobomb, video parodies and the reaction video are new genres that are worth considering on their own terms. I argue that the affordances of the new media (e.g., easy-to-handle video editing) have enabled new forms of expression. We examine these new genres in Part 3 of the book.

What may be the most characteristic aspect of humor on the internet is its randomness. In Attardo (2021) I argued that remixing and derivative memes essentially reflect combinatorial randomness. While this may seem like a strange claim, it is in line with the often observed transient nature of posts on 4chan and similar boards. Essentially, since the posts are not archived and there is no way to retrieve a post that has been deleted, the only posts that achieve virality (i.e., spread) are those that are of sufficient high quality that other users pick up on them and repost them or disseminate them. Therefore, quite literally there is a vast number of memes that get posted only once (or a few times) and are never seen again. It is very likely that this number is much larger than the number of memes that go viral. This encourages posters to try anything and to post complete nonsense in the hope that it will get picked up and will go viral. This explains also the "ugly" nature of rage comics, for example: Why waste your time producing a good-looking image, if it may disappear within seconds?

Finally, they are other changes, equally significant, if not more, that may be harder to spot or that may be harder to fit within the established explanations of humor. Take for example the idea that humor is a benign, positive emotion. How does it square with embarrassment humor, one of the defining genres of humor in the digital age? Or how do we reconcile the nasty, racist, violent humor of the extreme right, copiously circulating on the internet with the idea that humor is a positive feeling? Is trolling a benign process? We will discuss these issues and many more in the remaining parts of the book.

# Chapter 2

# MEMETICS

As we saw in the previous chapter, memes are self-replicating[1] units of meaning, the analog of genes in biology. What we did not discuss in the previous chapter is that genes and therefore memes are the locus of evolution. Darwin's splendid insight was the evolution depends on three mechanisms: variation, selection and replication. Variation is provided by the individual producing a new meme or a variant of an old one. Selection is provided by the choices of other users to adopt or share the meme, rather than another one. For example, as we will see in Chapter 15, the Chuck Norris Facts memes were preceded by the Vin Diesel Facts and by Mr. T Facts. However, at some point, the users selected the Chuck Norris ones and the Vin Diesel and Mr. T facts more or less disappeared. In other words, memetic selection is literally choosing which memes to share/modify.

In the case of internet memes, "replication" is not a direct equivalent of what happens in the biological world. Viruses "reproduce" by infiltrating a cell of the host, using the mechanisms of the cell to produce more viruses, until the cell releases the viral particles (and usually dies). None of that happens for memes (thankfully! I'd hate it if my head exploded each time I learn something new…). Replication for memes means the reposting, sharing, forwarding, etc., of a meme. This is primarily what we refer to when we say that a meme has "gone viral": we mean that the meme spreads fast, like a virus.

**Produsage**

As we also saw in the previous chapter, internet memes are associated with the rise of social media and more generally of the web 2.0, that is, the active participation of the users in the production of content. The concept

---

1 "Self-replicating" in this context means that the units spread and generate new units without any "central planning." There is no "goal" or "objective." The diffusion of the memes is an emergent property of the individual choices of the people who forward or modify the memes. In sociology, this is called a "social fact."

of produsage (Bruns, 2008), a portmanteau word consisting of production + usage, well describes the idea of user-led production of cultural artifacts (memes). Contrast, for example, a product, like Microsoft Word, or a script of a movie. These products are meant to be used, or enjoyed, rather passively. One can marginally customize MSWord, but, by and large, the software or the movie are finished products to be used. Conversely, something that comes about as the result of produsage like Wikipedia, Know Your Meme, Urban Dictionary or a set of Reddit posts about a given topic consists of the accretion of literally thousands of users adding incrementally small bits of information, without a specific, predetermined set of goals. An artifact of produsage is never finished or complete; it is always subject to revision or addition (Bruns, 2008, p. 27). An important aspect of produsage is that it is anti-hierarchical: by definition, anyone should be able to make modifications to Wikipedia or post on Reddit, etc. Being an expert is simply irrelevant (pp. 25–26). Another crucial aspect is that artifacts of produsage are not "owned" by anyone in particular. Ownership is communal (p. 28).

Memes are clearly the result of produsage. Obviously, produsage manifests itself in many ways. Here we will be concerned primarily with three ways: (1) production and reproduction/dissemination, or in short how memes "go viral," (2) remixing, and (3) mashup.

## Meme Production (Memeiosis)

One does not simply plan to produce a meme. Or, rather, see Figure 2.1. So how is a meme born? Someone has an idea, or makes an observation. This can be serious or funny, since as you will recall memes originally were not necessarily funny. For example, one may observe that the difference between the wages paid to the workers to produce some goods and the value of the

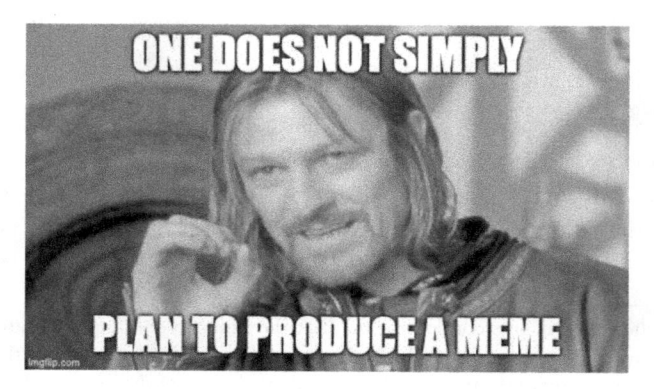

**Figure 2.1** One does not simply produce a meme: Meme produced by the author.

goods produced by the workers accrues to those who hold the capital with which the good are produced, or that a given cat looks funny. The idea is then committed to some medium of communication (a book, a picture posted in a newsgroup or just turning to the person next to you and relaying that idea to them, for example, by saying "Hey Bob, ever notice how that cat looks funny?"). There are now three possibilities: (1) the person to whom that idea was communicated finds it interesting enough to share it with someone else, forwarding it; (2) on the contrary, they find the idea not interesting and thus they do not share it; or (3) they find the idea interesting and they share it, but in modified form.

In the first case, if enough people find the idea (meme) interesting enough to share/forward it, soon the meme will "go viral" that is, it will spread through the community. However, "interest" is by no means the sole factor of memetic spread. An important aspect of forwarding/sharing a meme in an unchanged form, that is often ignored in the discussion of humorous memes, is that forwarding implies an "implicit endorsement of the content and the credibility of the message" (Harvey et al., 2011) or even an attempt at associating one's self with the author of the meme forwarded, presumably for aggrandizing purposes (Chapter 16). In other words, what Heylighen has called the "intersubjective" factors of memetic diffusion (1997 1998) matter possibly as much as more "objective" factors (interest in the subject, length, degree of arousal caused by the content, etc.).

In the second case, the meme dies out and no one is exposed to it again, unless someone else stumbles upon the same idea independently. The first case is called "memeiosis" that is, meme production. The second case is not relevant to us, since by definition these unfortunate memes are not shared enough to become part of mainstream culture. The third case, reproduction with modification, breaks down in remixing and mashup. We will start by focusing on memeiosis and cover remixing and mashups later.

## *Founder or anchor memes*

The founder meme (Shifman, 2014) or anchor meme, as I prefer to call them, is the original joke/meme that starts the process of meme production (memeiosis). For example, in the Bernie memes, we can identify very accurately the anchor meme in the image of Senator Sanders sitting at the inauguration wearing mittens captured by Brendan Smialowski, a photographer for Agence France-Presse (the image is distributed by Getty Images). According to Miao (2021), "Ashley Smalls, a Ph.D. student at Penn State, shared the photo on Twitter, writing, 'This could've been an email.' Her tweet has more than 1.1 million likes and 139,700 retweets" within a few days.

Memes are fads (Burgess, 2008; McCulloch 2019, p. 259) in the sense that their growth on popularity is very fast but it is also not lasting. We saw in Chapter 1 how the use of electricity, automobiles and washing machines spread to over 50 percent of households after a given date (the mid-1920s for electricity and automobiles, the 1960s for washing machines) but after that has grown to levels above 80 percent and stayed there until present times. In short, these technologies are not fads.

### *Virality vs. memeiosis*

It is crucial that we keep three, clearly related, aspects of memes distinct. As we saw, virality is the degree to which a meme spreads within the population. Memeiosis is the process whereby new memes are produced. We distinguish two basic cases: invention and remixing. Remixing can be simple reproduction with variation, but can also involve intertextual and meta-textual reference. We have discussed the case of invention, when a new meme is original, created ex nihilo, from scratch, as in the creation of the "Rage guy" meme. However, most of the memes that circulate on the internet are memes that reproduce a previous meme with variations (i.e., reproducing a meme while introducing some changes) or with intertextual remixing (taking elements from one meme and combining them with elements of another meme, so that understanding the new meme requires knowledge of the previous memes). Meta textual reference (i.e., commenting on the nature of the memes themselves) also serves to create new memes, but they are much rarer.

### *Affordances*

How are these variations on a theme produced? They are based on the affordances of the meme. We can use the Bernie memes to explore these affordances. But first we should define exactly what affordances are. The concept of affordance comes from Gibson (1979, p. 119) who defined it as "The affordance of the environment are what it offers the animal." In other words, they are external to the animal but they are "relative" to it. The affordances of a stick to an animal with opposable thumbs are different than those to an animal that lacks the capacity to grasp with their hand. Today, the term "affordance" is quite popular, but this is a fairly recent development. When I started using the concept (Attardo, 2005) it was very much a solitary endeavor. Particularly so in that I argued for a theory of *linguistic* affordances, whereas Gibson and many psychologists saw affordances as features of reality. Here, we will raise the stakes with a *semiotic* conception of affordances. Before you panic, it's actually quite straightforward. Much like a stone affords throwing

# MEMETICS 27

to an animal with opposable thumbs and reasonable upper body strength, but no such thing to a fish, a semiotic affordance is a sign whose features afford a speaker access to some aspect of the sign. For example, the word "dog" (a sign) affords access to the chain of sounds [d], [o], [g], to the meanings associated with dogs (the script for dog, roughly speaking) and to the syntactic environments in which the word can occur (as a noun, as a verb, etc.).

This will become a lot easier to process if we look at some examples from the Bernie meme cycle. As you will recall, the original photo (anchor meme) showed Senator Sanders sitting on a metal folding chair, wearing a heavy parka and mittens. The image contains a chair, so it affords "chair." In 1985, Bobby Knight, the Indiana University basketball coach threw a chair on the court during an Indiana University-Purdue game. Hence the meme in Figure 2.2.

Another affordance is that Sanders is sitting on the chair, so the image affords "sitting" and therefore we get the memes in Figure 2.3, which all contain sitting.

On the surface, these memes are simply a combinatorial free for all: they place Sanders anywhere sitting is plausible. However, there is a little more ingenuity: for example, the muppet in the image is masked for Covid. On the moon, Sanders wears a helmet (but no space suit!), In short, it's not just a simple photoshop trick and a basic incongruity marginally resolved by the "sitting" shared feature. There is a little bit of elaboration. And then of course, it gets just silly, as in the Sanders on Saturn's ring image.

To be clear, affordances are not limited to the Bernie Sanders memes. Consider the famous Success kid meme, (Figure 2.4).

**Figure 2.2** Bobby Knight throwing Bernie Sanders and chair.

**Figure 2.3** Composite of Bernie memes.

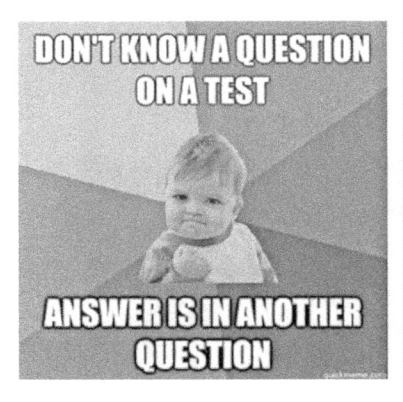

**Figure 2.4** Success Kid memes.

We see an example of threat of punching (as in the first example above) and expression of jubilance (We did it! or Yeah!). But we do not see "waving" or "thanking" (both gestures done with the hands). This is due to the different affordances of the gesture of the bunched fist. A bunched fist affords punching and symbolically "jubilance" or "success" while it does not afford waving or thanking. So, in this sense, the affordances of the meme constrain or guide memeiosis.

## *Intertextuality*

By intertextuality we mean any text that includes a reference to another text without which it cannot be fully understood/appreciated. We can use the meme known as "Woman yelling at cat" to illustrate the point. In its basic form, the Woman Yelling at Cat meme is already a remix of two previous memes: an image of Taylor Armstrong from the show *The Real Housewives of Beverly Hills* and an image of Smudge the cat. The two images were presented side by side, without further explanation by a Twitter user who remarked that the combination of the two pictures was "making me lose it" (i.e., laugh). See Figure 2.5

So far, so good. Aside from their provenance, the combination of the two pictures creates a new meme. When intertextuality comes to play significantly is when we get remixes such as those in Figure 2.6.

Replacing the woman with Trump and the cat with Greta Thunberg creates a thicket of incongruities that reinforce each other, but the point here is that if one does not know (a) who Trump is, (b) who Greta Thunberg is or (c) the meme Woman Yelling at Cat, none of this makes any sense at all, whereas the meme's affordances: the accusatory pointed finger, the smug or indifferent attitude of the cat, resonate eerily well with what we know about

**Figure 2.5** Woman yelling at cat meme.

**Figure 2.6** Remixes of Woman Yelling at Cat.

Trump and Greta Thunberg. The other example with Baby Yoda and Sonic the Hedgehog is even more surreal, as there is no explanation for the hostility between the two characters. Finally, even more intertextual baggage is brought into play by the sort of variant exemplified in Figure 2.7 in which Leonardo's Lady with an Ermine serves as a new background on which the Woman and the Cat are arranged, no longer in the anchor meme configuration (side by side) but in the organization of the Leonardo painting.

A further case of intertextuality is when the text referenced in the text is the text itself. This is known as metalinguistic reference in linguistics and philosophy ("This sentence consists of six words") but of course it can be easily extrapolated to other media (e.g., in Mel Brooks's parody of *Star Wars*, Spaceballs, one of the characters buys a copy of the video tape of *Spaceballs* and fast-forwards it to find out where the rebels took the princess; see Attardo, 2001,

**Figure 2.7** Leonardo and Woman Yelling at Cat mashup.

**Figure 2.8** Metatextual remix of Woman Yelling at Cat.

pp. 94–95, for an analysis). So metatextuality can be defined as a reference to the text itself. Metatextual references can be to the genre of the text as in Figure 2.8 above but also to the specific text, as in the Spaceballs example.

### *Remix*

We will be using the concept of mashup and remix quite a bit, so it's worth defining them. The idea of remixing has been considered central to the definition of memetic practice. Yet, it is hardly a recent invention. The genre of the "cento" is documented from the third century of the Christian Era. The centos (or centones) consisted of poetry written by borrowing lines from other poets, most famously Virgil and Homer. See for discussion, McGill (2005). Nonetheless, as Voigts (2018) puts it, "The techniques of remix and mashup may not be new, but they have become a decisive, distinguishing trait of digital network culture" (p. 392). A classical discussion of remixing is Lessig (2008). Lessig too acknowledges that remixing itself is not a new phenomenon: "There's nothing essentially new in remix. (...) All that's new is the technique and ease with which the product of that technique can be shared" (p. 82).

Voigts (2018, p. 390) stresses the preexisting nature of the materials to be remixed, "Remixes and montages are rearrangements of existing cultural particles." Cultural particles are, of course, memes. However, remixing is more than just taking a cultural item (a meme in the original sense) and recontextualizing it (as, for example, Warhol did with the Campbell soup can, or Roy Lichtenstein reuse of comics). A new genre of remixes are "communicative remixes" (Waysdorf, 2021, p. 1133) such as vidding (or fanvidding) in which clips from a TV show, movie or music video are assembled, with a new soundtrack, to produce a different story. For example, the "slash" genre of fan fiction originated from the original Star Trek TV series and features a romantic relationship between Kirk and Spock (Coppa, 2008).[2] Another example is the Honest Trailers from the YouTube channel Screen Junkies, which are essentially parodies of the movies or shows they reference. Waysdorf's point is that these forms of remixing have a point, be it satirical or to create an alternative narrative.

Another aspect that needs to be stressed is that the original context in which the meme or cultural particle (a line of text, a few notes of music, (part of) an image, etc.) retains a "shadow of meaning (a connotation) in the new context." In plain English, if I say "To be or not to be" the fact that this is a Shakespearian quote, from Hamlet, remains attached, to some extent, to the new use. Of course the non-quoted meaning of the words also is present in the new context. Needless to say, the new context may affirm, or negate, or ridicule the old meanings. That's fine. The point is that there is a dialog, so to speak, between the old and new context. Because there are two sets of meanings (the original one and the new one) we have a potential built-in script opposition. If I say "Get thee behind me, Satan" to the waiter pushing

---

[2] The following video (https://www.youtube.com/watch?v=aYdllH7jZxg) contains a history and numerous examples, introduced by Coppa herself, in 2009.

the dessert cart to our table, I am juxtaposing the religious King James bible quote (spoken by none other but Jesus) to a decidedly non-religious, vastly less important subject matter (food). The humor, what little there is of it, comes from the opposition of the scripts, from the fact that I am associating a high status text to a low status activity (eating), and possibly by a modicum of resolution given the dessert is often associated with sin (try googling "sinfully delicious" if you don't believe me) and hence like Jesus rejected the devil's temptations, I am rejecting the waiter's temptation.

## *Mashup*

Mashup is a kind of remix, originally in the music field. The mashup was invented in popular music by Harry Nilsson: "Nilsson created the first remix album (Aerial Pandemonium Ballet, 1971) and recorded the first mashup song ('You Can't Do That,' 1967)." (Wikipedia) The idea was then popularized by rap artists. *The Grey Album*, by Danger Mouse, a mashup of Jay Z and samples of the Beatles' *White Album*, in 2004, and the copyright controversy that followed arguably brought this technique to mainstream audiences. Let us note in passing the magnificent title that metonymically describes the content of the album. Mashup has been expanded to many other media. For example, the novel *Pride and Prejudice and Zombies*, as the title indicates, mixes the *Pride and Prejudice* plot with zombies. An example of mashup memes are the insertion of Trump or Sonic the Hedgehog in the Woman Yelling at Cat meme, which we saw above. An example of video mashup is the Lego Rammstein music video, examined in Chapter 19.

## *Invention*

There is a further case, that is, invention. In this case a new meme is created from scratch. Now, obviously, no memes can exist without a cultural substrate, which consists of other memes (otherwise they would be incomprehensible). Think of a song writer who decides to write a song. Obviously, the very idea of "original song" means that the song writer has a set of expectations of what a song should be like, expectations that are shared with the culture at large. If a song writer wanted to write a song lasting two seconds[3] or consisting of the same note repeated 100 times, they would have a hard time getting that accepted as a "real" song. The comments to the videos in footnote 3

---

3 It's been done: https://www.youtube.com/watch?v=vMDH2meQQHs and an even shorter example is https://www.youtube.com/watch?v=2OE8IyK3dkA&t=0s

make it clear that the hearers interpret them as jokes, not as real songs. So, memes are based on previous memes also indirectly, not just because they directly quote or reference a previous meme. So what we mean here by "creating a new meme" is the production of a new text that is recognizable as a meme, but that has not been produced before and bears no direct intertextual or meta textual references to previous memes. Here too the "Bernie" meme is the perfect example. Obviously, prior to Smialowski snapping the picture of Senator Sanders, on January 20, 2021, sitting on the chair wearing his mittens and coat, there was no prior image and when the image was combined with a text by Smalls this effectively created a new meme, which immediately went viral (interest in the meme peaked in 48 hours; see Figure 2.9) and entered the memeiotic process, spawning hundreds of variations.

The semiotic process, that is, the process whereby the meme signifies something (conveys a message) is the third, separate process. Obviously, the components of the meme (words, images, etc.) are themselves meaningful. The mittens, parka, chair, etc., are recognized as such in the image and therefore convey the meaning "mitten," "parka," "chair," etc. Senator Sanders is also recognizable as himself. They are images, not the real thing, but they refer to the real thing (Senator Sanders, his mittens, etc.). This is one basic semiotic level: the image stands for (signifies) another thing (the mittens, etc.). The images (but also any words) are signs that stand for/convey a given meaning.

There is another way that memes convey meanings: by cultural and social associations. For example, Bernie Sanders, a Vermont Senator, is widely known as a "socialist" (only in the United States, in the rest of the world his politics are seen as liberal or social-democratic at most). Other associations are that he is a man of the people, genuine and speaks truth to power. His

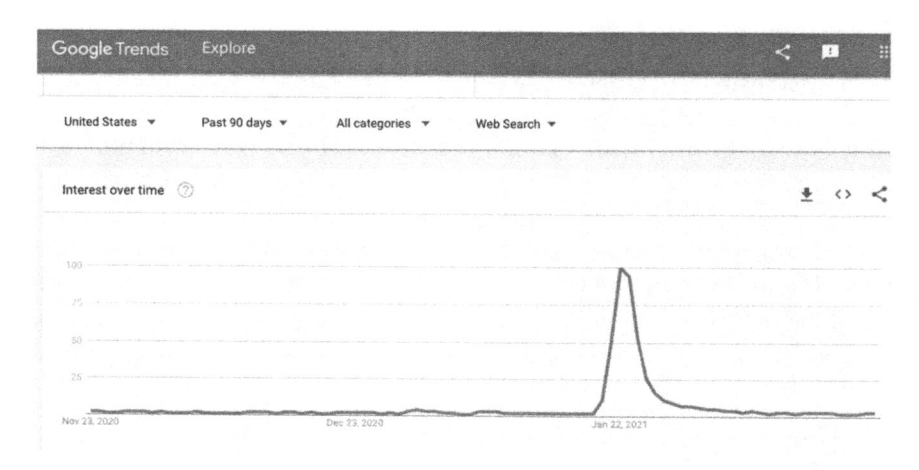

**Figure 2.9** Level of interest for Bernie Sanders around the inauguration.

informal clothing (mittens and parka at the presidential inauguration!) contrasting with the fashionable and expensive clothes of many other attendees (but not all) also sends a message of down-to-earth, man of the people. We generally refer to this sort of meaning as connotations. Connotations differ from regular meanings in that they are not required: for example, a staunch Republican may well object that they do not like Sanders or that he is not "genuine" (connotation), but they would agree it was Sanders sitting on the chair (in other words, the referent part of the meaning of the sign is usually not under discussion). This is the main difference between signs and connotations: signs are rather fixed and are conventional, whereas connotations are much looser and may differ to some extent across the population.

There is a final way in which memes convey meaning, called enregisterment. Essentially, any communicative process (language, gesture, clothing, meme, etc.) becomes associated, through repetition, with the people who use them and with the circumstances in which they use them. Think of the pronoun "y'all": what do you know immediately upon hearing someone use it? For example, you may say that they are from Texas, or from the South of the United States. Those associations are "enregistered" because those who use the pronoun tend to be from the South of the United States or Texas. Now, when we say that a meme is dank, what we mean is that it has become associated with the wrong kind of users. It is no longer cool (i.e., associated with users that are cool) and therefore projects an "uncool" image.

Therefore, when we say that a meme "signifies" something, we need to be careful to specify at which level the meaning is generated.

## Technological Affordances

One of the central themes of this book, one that will recur repeatedly in the chapters to come, is that one of the most basic aspects of digital culture facilitates enormously the possibility of remixing media. At the hardware level, what digital artifacts share is that they are digitally encoded. Be it sound, images or text they are all just bytes in a file, which can be copied with minimal effort and modified according to one's intentions. A video montage used to require relatively complex machinery, as did image manipulation and audio production. Often the equipment was extremely expensive. As Lessig (2008, p. 83) put it, "If in 1968 you wanted to capture the latest Walter Cronkite news program and remix it with the Beatles, and then share it with your 10,000 best friends, what blocked you was not the law. What blocked you was that the productions costs alone would have been in the tens of thousands of dollars." Digital media and the internet changed all that. When all you are doing is pushing bytes around, the costs and accessibility issues drop significantly. With the advent of easy-to-use drawing (e.g., Paint) and image manipulation software (Photoshop or the free equivalent GIMP), audio mixing software (Audacity, Garageband) and video editing (iMovie) all that's stopping anyone from producing new media or remixing old ones is the willingness to learn how to use the software and the talent to achieve passable results.

One place where technological affordances are clearly on display is when the technology is retrofitted to make it easier to perform a specific action. For example, retweeting on Twitter required a series of keystrokes (typing "RT @" or "via @"). Introduced in 2009, the retweet button, two curved arrows arranged in a sort of square, literally allows you to do it with a single click.

The affordances of new technologies have also enabled the creation of new memes and genres. The point is not that it was impossible to create, say, a compilation video, before video editing software available on a smartphone came about. Obviously, since as we will see, compilation shows pre-exist the internet, let alone smartphones, the technology was there. The significant change is when tools are introduced that no longer require expensive equipment and/or expertise. This is chronicled in Phillips (2015, pp. 143–144) for meme creation: prior to 2009–2010 meme creation required a modicum of image manipulation skill: one had to be able to use Photoshop or GIMP, at least to some extent in order to import an image, crop it, select the correct font, etc. In 2009, Meme generator was launched and in 2010, Quickmeme, which made the creation of memes a point-and-click process, available to all but the least skilled internet users. Today, there are dozens of meme generators online, witness pages such as https://filmora.wondershare.com/meme/best-free-meme-maker-online.html which list the 12 *best* meme generators. The effect of this lowering, or effectively removing, the technology barrier, resulted in an "explosion" of meme creation. The same is true of video editing. Today, one can edit, apply filters, do a slow-mo, etc., on one's iPhone. By downloading iMovie, a free video editing software, one has essentially complete creative control—again on one's phone! In short, you would not have YouTube or TikTok without cheap (free), easy to use video recording and editing capabilities, that one carries in one's pocket. There are obviously much more significant consequences of ubiquitous video-recording capabilities (think of the videos documenting police brutality) than the creation of funny TikTok video clips, but it is the same easily available technology that makes possible Karen videos. A "Karen" is the quintessential annoying, entitled person, often harassing people of color (https://knowyourmeme.com/memes/karen).

The technological affordances should not be confused with the visual and semantic affordances of the text and/or images in, say, a meme or video, which have been discussed previously in this chapter. While they are both called "affordances" the technological ones are praxeological, which is a fancy way of saying they relate to how to do things, whereas the visual and semantic ones are semiotic, which is a fancy way of saying that they are related to the process of communicating meaning.

# Chapter 3

# HUMOR THEORY

When reading a title like "humor theory" most readers' eyes glaze over. In fact, a common joke is that analyzing humor is like dissecting a frog: it kills it. Indeed comedians have long known that if you have to explain a joke, it failed. However, we are not here just for fun; we want to get an understanding of what the evolution of humor in the age of the internet means. This goal requires some understanding of how humor works, in general, so that we can then compare how digital or internet humor works. This requires a little knowledge about humor theory. First, we need to distinguish between humor, which is a cognitive (mental) process which causes an emotion (mirth or exhilaration) which may manifest itself in various ways, including laughter, smiling and other bodily or verbal reactions (e.g., the hearer may slap their thighs or may say "that's funny"). Often the reactions are a mix of all the above. Sometimes the hearer may not react positively, either because they fail to identify the humor or because, while they are aware that the speaker intended what they said as funny, they think the intention is inappropriate. The reactions then may be frowning, staring at the speaker, saying "that's not funny," etc. If both the speaker and the hearer agree that what was said (the text) is funny, then the humor succeeded and the hearer (and the speaker) experience mirth. If they do not agree, the humor failed and one or both of the people in the exchange will not experience mirth and will instead be annoyed, offended or hurt.[1]

Surprisingly, people have pondered the question of why humor is, or may be, funny for millennia. Perhaps we should say "unsurprisingly" if we realize that humans have probably been laughing since they were human given that

---

[1] Incidentally, in the above we have used "speaker" and "hearer" but obviously this applies to texts produced in any modality: visually (images), auditorily (sound, music), kinetically (gestures, bodily positions), etc. The verbal modality (i.e., humor that is expressed through language) has a special status, due to the prominence of language among the systems of communication (aka, semiotic systems) and also because I am a linguist and so I tend to be interested in languagey-things.

humor is universal: there are no reports of human groups lacking humor, in one form or another, as we said before. Be that as it may, some of the earliest documented reflections on humor go back to Plato and Aristotle (so as far back as the fourth century BC). Plato claims that humor is a "mixed" feeling because it mixes pain ("envy") and pleasure. For Plato laughter comes from ridicule and as such it is a negative emotion, which is mixed with the pleasure of amusement. Aristotle, Plato's student, follows his master in defining humor as something wrong but that does not produce pain or harm. This has become known in modern times as the "benign violation" theory (McGraw & Warren, 2010).

## Release Theories

The kind of psychological explanation we just saw in Plato and Aristotle is the source of other more recent theories known generally as "release" theories. Freud famously speculated that humor released psychic "energy" blocked by repression. That's no longer taken seriously, but the idea that humor allows us a release from social constraints is nonetheless still valid. This ties in with the idea of humor as play, which we take up below.

## Superiority Theories

Plato and Aristotle are also considered the founding fathers of the superiority theories of humor, because they see humor as a form of ridicule, albeit a mixed, non-harmful one. Another well-known proponent of a superiority theory of humor is Thomas Hobbes (1588–1679), the author of the *Leviathan*, who speaks of a "sudden glory" experienced by one who one-ups their target, that is, the butt of the joke. Let's consider an example: the Babylon Bee, a right-wing evangelical website that parodies the news, titles one article as "Joel Osteen Tests Negative for Christianity" (March 26th, https://babylonbee.com/news/joel-osteen-tests-positive-for-heresy). Joel Osteen is a televangelist and a proponent of "prosperity theology," the repugnant ideology that financial prosperity is a sign of God's favor. Prosperity theology has been widely criticized, both within and outside the religious community (see https://en.wikipedia.org/wiki/Prosperity_theology#Criticism). The Babylon Bee is thus entirely in line with the evangelical view that Osteen's creed is flat out unchristian. What makes the headline humorous? Clearly, it is an attack on Osteen and ridicules him for not having any Christian values. So, Osteen is the target of the humor and the readers feel superior toward him, since they presumably have more Christian values than he does. However, this is not all: the headline uses a metaphor which compares Christianity to an infectious disease (note that this was published in the middle of the Covid pandemic). So there is an unusual comparison between the Christian faith and an infectious disease. Moreover, as a Christian pastor, Osteen should want to test positive for Christianity. Therefore, by inference the Babylon Bee is implying that Osteen is not a true Christian. This has taken us outside superiority theory and squarely in the camp of incongruity theory. However, before we move on, we should mention that a more nuanced version of the superiority theories has emerged, called "disposition theory."

## *Disposition theory*

The superiority theory is all too open to the devastating counter-argument that there is non-aggressive humor, in which no one is targeted, in which the teller does not feel "superior" to anyone. Think of a parent roughhousing with their child, singing a funny song or telling a silly joke. For example, my favorite joke for kids and always a hit with children between the ages of 6 and 10: "Knock, knock. Who is it? Interrupting cow. Interrupt… Moo!" Am I seriously ridiculing the child and enjoying my superiority over them? Obviously not. We are playing, having fun, together. Disposition theory (e.g., Becker, 2014; McGhee & Lloyd, 1981; Zillman, 1983) is far more sophisticated than plain aggression theory: it states that the disposition (attitude) of the speaker/hearer of a joke toward the target of the joke lies on a continuum, that is, you can either feel that you are very similar, somewhat similar or dissimilar from the target. Disposition is mediated through empathy: empathy leads us to feel better disposed toward those that are closer to us in terms of experiences (i.e., those that resemble us). So, if the hearer of a joke strongly identifies with the target they are less likely to find a joke funny, and if they do not identify with the target they are more likely to find the joke funny. This has been shown on gender, ethnic and political lines.

Take the meme in Figure 3.1, which is an instance of the "Success kid" meme we already encountered.

Our reactions are to empathize and thus identify with the anonymous poster who uses the "success kid" as a proxy, because we all have been late for work, and we all have or have had a boss, and so we counter-empathize with the boss, who becomes the target of the ridicule. Our positive disposition toward the employee and the negative disposition toward the boss explain our emotional reactions.

## *Punching up or down*

Aggression can be directed up or down, within a social hierarchy. This is often referred to as punching up or down. For example, if I make a joke about one of my students, I am punching down, since I exert a modicum of power over

**Figure 3.1** Success kid meme.

the student. Conversely, when one of my students started producing (hilarious) memes about me in one of my classes, he was punching up. Obviously, this holds in more general settings: punching down can be defined as mocking "socially marginalized or vulnerable" groups (Julin, 2021, p. 143) whereas punching up is attacking or satirizing members of powerful groups. The idea then is that punching down is morally reprehensible, whereas punching up is good, as is presumably punching sideways (i.e., targeting one's peers). While somewhat simplistic, we will see that the distinction offers some explanatory power, for example when considering why trolling is viewed as obnoxious (see chapter 22).

## Incongruity Theories

Incongruity theories are the cognitive-side of humor. They are focused on the cognitive (mental) processes that cause the feeling of mirth or exhilaration. Modern versions of the incongruity theory consist generally of two phases: incongruity and resolution.

### *Incongruity*

An incongruity is a violation of expectations. The famous "weights experiment" conducted by Nerhardt (1970) consisted in participants being asked,

**Figure 3.2** An old-fashioned penny-farthing bicycle.

under the pretense of comparing them to a standard, to lift a series of suitcases of increasing heaviness. When the participants encountered a suitcase that was lighter than the previous ones, they smiled or laughed (i.e., they were amused; they experienced mirth). Expectations are encoded in people's minds in the form of cognitive structures of information, variously called scripts, frames or schemata (and a bunch of other names). We will use, as is common in humor studies, the term "script" but as I said above, the terms are interchangeable. Suppose you come across the word "bicycle." You immediately conjure a two wheeled machine, with pedals and a chain, handle bars, a seat and probably a bell. This is the typical information for a bicycle. You share this information with all (or at least the vast majority) of the speakers of English. Sure, there are atypical bicycles (unicycle, tricycle, "penny-farthing" or high wheeler; see Figure 3.2) but the wheel(s), the pedals, the seat, and the handle bars, except for the unicycle) are there.

Suppose now that I tell you that Johnny grew up poor and so he was very happy when his parents told him he'd get a bicycle for his seventh birthday and the wheels for his eighth one, you should experience a certain degree of surprise at the perception of the incongruity of saying "You are getting a bicycle for your birthday but it comes without wheels." The surprise comes from the sudden perception of the incongruity: in my little story, all is going well for Johnny until the explicit mention of the wheels alerts us to the fact that something anomalous in regard to the script of bicycle is coming (why mention the wheels unless something is the matter with them?) and then finding out that Johnny will have to wait a year to receive the wheels (which renders the previous gift useless, until the next year) happens literally in the very short span of time that it takes a reader to scan and process the prepositional phrase "for his eighth one." Some incongruities are not sudden and hence they are not humorous: for example, if you are familiar with the double-slit experiment in physics which shows that light is both a wave *and* a particle, that's incongruous and painfully unfunny.

Within linguistics the incongruity that psychologists have found to be the basic cognitive mechanism of humor is described as the activation of a script followed by the sudden switch to another script. The relationship between the two scripts is called a "script opposition." Let's look at a simple example: you receive a text message from a friend, with a link promising to be an interesting video of, say, a new recipe. When you click on the link, a video of Rick Astley singing *Never Gonna Give You Up* plays. You have been "rickrolled." Your expectations were a recipe, so you activated the script for "recipe" (ingredients, procedure for preparation, cooking time, possibly a wine pairing or some historical background about the recipe), instead you see a 1980s video, so the scripts for 1980s videos are activated (hair, synthesizers, etc.) and specifically for Mr. Astley's song. The switch from one script to another is the incongruity (you expected a recipe, you got *Never Gonna Give You Up*). If you were unaware of the practice of rickrolling you may be surprised and possibly puzzled, but if you were aware of it, you then inscribe it into a playful frame of trickery. More on that later.

Crucially, the two scripts are opposed, that is, they cannot both be compatible with the situation. If your friend had promised you Astley's song *Together Forever* and *Never Gonna Give You Up* played, you'd think about a mistake, not a prank. Linguistically, beyond the script opposition, it is generally accepted that you need more information to be able to fully understand a joke (or meme, etc.). For example, you need to know who, if anyone is being targeted, what kind of situation the joke or meme depicts (in our case, it would be forwarding a recipe), how the text or image is organized (for example, in our case, it would be a suggestion: "Click here") and the specific linguistic or visual choices of the joke, meme, etc. Again, in our example the choice of "click" and "here" could have been replaced just by a link, in its http://www. etc format, or by a blinking icon saying "click me." The last component is the resolution, which we address in the section below.

Summing up, this gives us, for any humorous text (joke, meme, funny song, etc.), the following schema, which sums up the General Theory of Verbal Humor[2] (or GTVH, for short)

---

2 Victor Raskin and I developed the GTVH back in 1991 (Attardo & Raskin, 1991). We've kept the original language-centric terminology mostly for nostalgic reasons. For a more recent and more accessible presentation of the GTVH, see Attardo (2020a).

*SO:* the script opposition, the basic mechanism of the incongruity;
*LM:* the logical mechanism (aka, resolution; see below);
*SI:* the situation, what the joke is "about";
*TA:* the target, who or what is being made fun of;
*NS:* the narrative strategy, that is, the organization of the text;
*LA:* the language, or more generally the linguistic, visual, auditory, etc., choices made in the text.

We will have several opportunities to provide full analyses of memes or other examples of internet humor in the chapters that follow. However, before we do so, we need to address the last cognitive component of humor, that is, the resolution of the incongruity.

### Resolution

Psychologists who study humor maintain that in many (but not all) cases of humor the incongruity is "resolved" by a second cognitive mechanism, distinct from the perception of the incongruity. We need to be very clear that the "resolution" is not necessarily a full resolution of the incongruity (i.e., its elimination) or even a real resolution (i.e., one that would withstand scrutiny). The resolution is partial and playful. Recall the Bernie meme cycle, of which Figure 3.3 is an example

**Figure 3.3** Bernie meme.

The image is a mashup of the "sad Keanu" meme and of the Bernie meme. That's incongruous (the two memes are unrelated). The resolution, minimal as it is, is provided by the fact that both Keanu Reeves and Bernie Sanders are sitting, and thus we can establish a parallelism of sorts between the two. This is the logical mechanism of the resolution. Needless to say, this parallelism is marginal (after all, we all sit at some point or another), but playfully we accept that there is a similarity between the two images which justifies putting them in parallel and hence "resolves" the incongruity (they are together because they are doing the same thing). Note that the caption helps push along this parallelism, by stressing that the Sanders ("Mitten Bernie") meme has united us all. Another logical mechanism is the "figure/ground reversal" which we will examine in some detail in Chapter 18, in the context of photobombing.

## *Humorous stereotypes*

Before we move on to the playful key of humor, we need to address the issue of humorous stereotypes. Every culture has a list of scripts that are reserved or, if not restricted to humor, at least particularly evident within it. For example, in the United States, the targets of dumb jokes are blondes and Poles, who are supposed to be "dumb." This news was puzzling to my Polish friends, who of course had never heard of it, and to me as well, because the target of dumb jokes in Italy were neither blondes or Poles but in fact the members of the Carabinieri (a part of the Italian army with police functions). Christie Davies (1990) provides an impressive catalog of the various groups that are considered dumb, or canny, or stingy, or dirty, etc. Needless to say, these are stereotypes and they are largely mythical. Recall the "Karen" example: obviously, not all people named "Karen" are Karens. The stereotypical nature of these scripts should not be a distraction: the knowledge encoded into scripts is largely (stereo)typical: as we saw, some bicycles are atypical, but they are still considered bicycles. In other words, the information in scripts is, at least to some extent, a matter of prototypicality, which is fancy way of saying that some bicycles are "better" examples of the category of bicycle: a two-wheeled bicycle is a better (as in more typical) example of bicycle than a unicycle or than a bicycle with a motor.

Not only do speakers (and their cultures) have lists of scripts stereotypically linked to humor, but they have a related list of scripts that are not available for humor. In current Western culture, topics such as incest, pedophilia, necrofilia, people suffering physical handicaps, etc., are generally considered to be "out of bounds" for humor. Of course, one can be "hedgy"[3] and deliberately

---

3 Note the metaphor of a bounded area within which humor is permitted, an outside where it is forbidden, and the hedge between the two as a "risky" area, because one may end up in the forbidden area.

joke about an out of bounds subject. Jokes about these "risky" subjects are inherently dangerous, because they test the boundaries of what is acceptable, but more importantly of what the members of the community consider appropriate. For example, mocking people with physical handicaps, which was a practice common in the Middle Ages, where, for example, people suffering from dwarfism were often jesters, is nowadays considered unacceptable. So when Donald Trump mocked a reporter with a disability (see the video https://www.bbc.com/news/av/world-us-canada-34931215) he was widely critiqued. When, about two weeks after the September 11 attacks, comedian Gilbert Gottfried made a joke about it, someone in the audience shouted "too soon." (https://www.youtube.com/watch?v=6tmI-Rh2atM).

## Playfulness

In order to be appreciated as humorous, and therefore trigger the experience of mirth, an incongruity needs to occur in a play frame or key. The terminology does not really matter in this context, but if you want to be picky in Goffman's terms it is a key. The more general point is that the frame or key must be playful. The connection between humor and play is rather obvious, but what is less obvious is what constitutes the nature of the playfulness: essentially (Bateson, 1972) it is the assurance that the incongruity is not dangerous, that there is no real threat. When monkeys or dogs play, they do not really bite each other, they play-bite. What differentiates a play-bite from a serious bite is simply that the play bite does not hurt/draw blood. Of course, a playful key can easily shift into a serious one, if someone gets hurt accidentally, for example. Suppose one of the players exerts too much pressure in the bite, or a person joking says something that offends one of the hearers, suddenly we are out of the play keying and into the "real" key (a.k.a., reality).

A non-playful incongruity is perceived as a cognitive dissonance and it is not a pleasurable experience. Cognitive dissonance is experienced as stressful and uncomfortable and therefore people try to eliminate it, by either adjusting their beliefs or simply by refusing to hear/listen to information that contradicts their beliefs.

So we have seen that humor, cognitively speaking, comes from an incongruity and its resolution, in a playful key. However, there is yet another level at which humor is incongruous. Humor is also communicatively "anomalous" in that it behaves differently than serious, on task talk.

### *The non-cooperative status of joking*

Grice (1989) introduced the idea that speakers, if they want to communicate efficiently and so be understood with the least amount of effort necessary, need to follow a set of maxims, which embody the "Principle of cooperation." These maxims are quite commonsensical, such as the maxim of relevance: "speak to the point" or "be relevant"; the maxim of quality: "tell what you know to be true"; the maxim of manner: "speak clearly"; and the maxim of quantity: "say enough, not too little and not too much." Very early on, Grice himself and others realized that violations of some of the maxims lead to humorous effects, such as in puns and irony. More general treatments found that humor in general is characterized by a violation of the principle of cooperation. The subject is fairly technical, so we will only mention that often the maxim of quality (tell the truth) and the maxim of relevance are involved, but all the maxims can be violated, singly or in combination with others (Attardo, 2017).

This becomes all too relevant when we consider satirical news, as we will do in Chapter 10 Consider the story "NASA Finds Message from God on Mars" which was published on *The Daily Currant*, a now-defunct satirical news website. We have a thorough analysis of the story in Vookoti (2013) which details the source and the reasons why it is in fact a hoax (simply put, none of it is true: the speaker is flat out being deceitful). In other words, it violates the maxim of quality. Why would one do that? Well, the story is funny, because it mocks a certain kind of religious person, of course, but that's hardly the only motivation of hoaxers. Deceit is crucial for pranks and hoaxes, which consist largely of fooling the hearer. The reasons are discussed in more detail in Chapter 10 on pranks and hoaxes and satirical news.

### *The Social Aspects of Humor*

Humor has of course a social component, blending incongruity and superiority theories. On the one hand humor can be seen as a social corrective, as a way that society has to discipline those who violate the norms of socially acceptable behavior. The French philosopher Bergson (1901) is generally associated with this idea. Bergson is also associated with the idea of humor as a mechanical repetition contrasting (incongruous) with the natural flow of life. On the other hand, humor is used to establish a social bond with those who share the production and appreciation of the humor, at the expense of those who are laughed at. This process is known as the in-group vs. outgroup, a.k.a., inclusion vs. exclusion, social dynamics of humor. For a more detailed discussion of the sociological aspects of humor, see Kuipers (2015).

This ends our short discussion of humor theory. Should you want more, Attardo (2020) is a good place to start. Martin and Ford (2018) is more psychologically oriented. For an encyclopedic perspective, see Attardo (2014).

# Part 1
# NEW GENRES

In Part 1, we will consider a number of innovations, which I loosely classify as new "genres" or types of texts. Chapter 4 is a sort of bridge with the introductory chapters. It deals with more traditionally "linguistic" topics, such as internet slang and the ways in which humor and laughter are marked. The other chapters are more properly innovative genres: the compilation, the spoiler alert, new cartoon genres, satirical news and perhaps the most innovative new genre, the humorous currencies.

# Chapter 4

# THE NEW LANGUAGE OF HUMOR

In this chapter we will consider some "properly linguistic" topics. How much has the English language changed in the 20 years of the era of the internet? Spoiler alert: not much.

**Does OMG Spell Trouble for the English Language?**

McWorther (2013) notes, "We always hear that texting is a scourge. The idea is that texting spells the decline and fall of any kind of serious literacy, or at least writing ability, among young people in the United States and now the whole world today." McWorther goes on to debunk this, as does McCulloch (2019). Indeed, Baron (2004) and Tagliamonte and Denis (2008) show that an extremely small percentage of text in IM actually consists of internet slang, such as OMG, TTYL, or LOL. Baron (2004, p. 416) concludes that "the use of CMC abbreviations and CMC acronyms was minimal" in fact in some cases less than 1 percent of the data. Tagliamonte and Denis (2008), using a much larger corpus, report a comparable figure of 2.4 percent. In short, the reports of a "breakdown in the English Language," "bastardization" and "linguistic ruin" (quoted in Tagliamonte & Denis, 2008, p. 4) are merely the current expression of the old alarmism used to stigmatize language change since the birth of prescriptivism, in the 18th century. Swift writes in 1710 about "the corruption of the English tongue." Lowth's grammar is published in 1762; Murray's in 1795. Of course there was nothing wrong with the English language in 1710, much like there's nothing wrong with it in 2020. The fundamental problem with prescriptivism is that it's not a scientific approach. It is based on prejudice and misconceptions. Linguistic change, the invention of new expressions and the progressive adjustment of forms and meanings to reflect new realities that the speakers of the language want to talk about, is not only normal, but what makes a language a live one. The only languages that do not change are the dead ones. So, the fact that a negligible percentage of IM speech consist of new acronyms or other expressions is not a problem; it is a sign that the language is lively. We will return to some of these expressions, most notably LOL.

## Internet Slang

Let's start by defining the much misused term "slang." Slang is a term for a variety used by a restricted part of the population, often with a low status (students, criminals). It is characterized by very informal and innovative lexicon (meaning, it creates a lot of new words) that often disappears very fast (it becomes "uncool"). The main function of slang is to set apart its users as being the in-group (they are literally in the know). One of the clearest novelties of the internet is the development of a new set of slang terms (see Table 4.1 for a few examples, but many more are available, for example see https://www.noslang.com/dictionary/)

The use of slang to establish ingroup/outgroup boundaries is of course well known and documented, as far back as the Middle Ages (some of the poetry of Villon, France's best-known medieval poet, is written in the argot of the "Coquille" a group of 15 century thieves). Nothing new under the sun, here. What is more interesting however is that unlike other argotic forms, such as rhyming slang in Cockney London, here a deliberate attempt has been made to render these forms offensive (e.g., newfag, which the use of "fag" as in "faggot," a derogatory term for male homosexuals) so that they cannot easily be adopted by mainstream users (Phillips, 2015, p. 55). An even more blatant use of slang for othering (i.e., relegating someone to outsider status) is the expression "Tits or gtfo" with which users that identify as female were, and possibly still are, confronted. The expression stands for "Show us your tits (breasts) or get the fuck out" and both assumes that the default user is male (Phillips, 2015, p. 55) and that the only interesting contribution that a female user may have is to show her breasts to the male users. Tagliamonte (2016) gives a general overview of the slang.

Some internet slang consists of puns and inside jokes, often mocking non-computer literate people. Let's consider the expression "ID-10-T error" which means "user error," that is, a problem caused by the user. If one spells out the word "ID10T" it is easy to see an alternative spelling of the word "idiot" that is, the user (https://en.wikipedia.org/wiki/User_error#ID-10-T_error).

**Table 4.1** Examples of internet slang.

| | | | |
|---|---|---|---|
| normie | non-internet aware person | no cap | truthfully |
| normalfag | non-internet aware person | rizz | charisma |
| dank | cool or past its prime | irl | in real life |
| troll | someone who deliberately disrupts a discussion | aita | am i the asshole? |
| lulz | enjoyment from trolling | fap | masturbation |
| newfag | novice poster in 4chan | doomer | pessimist/fatalist |

A similar sentiment is expressed by referring to the user as a "luser" (L-user) which sounds like "loser."

However, while there is a degree of playfulness in internet slang, of course most of it is not particularly funny and so we will not pursue this any further. We turn instead to the central problem, from this book's perspective, of how humor is marked in interactions on the internet.

## Markers of Humor

Another area where change is most evident are the markers of humor. In the beginning was the smiley face. The first instance of a smiley face goes back to the Hittite culture (1700 BC: https://www.hurriyetdailynews.com/worlds-oldest-smiley-emoji-found-in-turkey-115642). There are numerous instances of "smiley faces" in history (https://en.wikipedia.org/wiki/Smiley). The yellow face in a circle that we are now familiar with originated as a design in the early 1960s, by Harvey Ball, seated in Figure 4.1.

Ball's smiley faces lived on buttons, t-shirts and other artifacts. How did they end up on our computer and phone screens? Here we need to take a little step backward. The first computers had no screen at all. They used lights to display the status of registers (for example, eight individual bits, i.e., yes/no, on/off binary decisions). Output was printed on fanfold paper. The early cathode-ray tube (CRT) computer displays were monochrome and

**Figure 4.1** Harvey Ball, surrounded by smiley paraphernalia.

had limited resolution, thus only allowing the display of the 128 symbols of ASCII, that is, the American Standard Code for Information Interchange: letters, numbers and a few mathematical symbols.

In 1982, Scott Fahlman, a computer scientist at Carnegie Mellon, proposed the infamous sequence :-) as a "joke marker." This may be one of the most successful memes (in the original meaning) in history. In 1993, it was given its own Unicode character. Soon people started producing other smileys, now dubbed "emoticons," such as the winking emoticon ;-), the surprised emoticon :-o, and, my personal favorite, the drooling emoticon :-)~ . By 1997, Sanderson (1997) collected over 650 smileys. According to Wikipedia, by the early 2000s, a list of emoticons included over 3,000 items (https://en.wikipedia.org/wiki/Emoticon).

Computer screens later became more capable of displaying color and sophisticated graphics. In the late 1990s, first in Japan and then worldwide, phones began being able to display little pictograms, called emojis. They included the smiley face, the infamous pile of poo (poop emoji) and many others. Emojis were given Unicode characters and thus became available on any device that displays Unicode. Of particular interest to us is the smiling face with tears of joy emoji, which is very commonly used to mark humor. Emojis display slightly differently on various devices, as seen from the part of a Unicode table in Figure 4.2.

Finally, some streaming platforms, such as Twitch, a subsidiary of Amazon, have recently introduced emotes in their chat. Emotes are not character-based

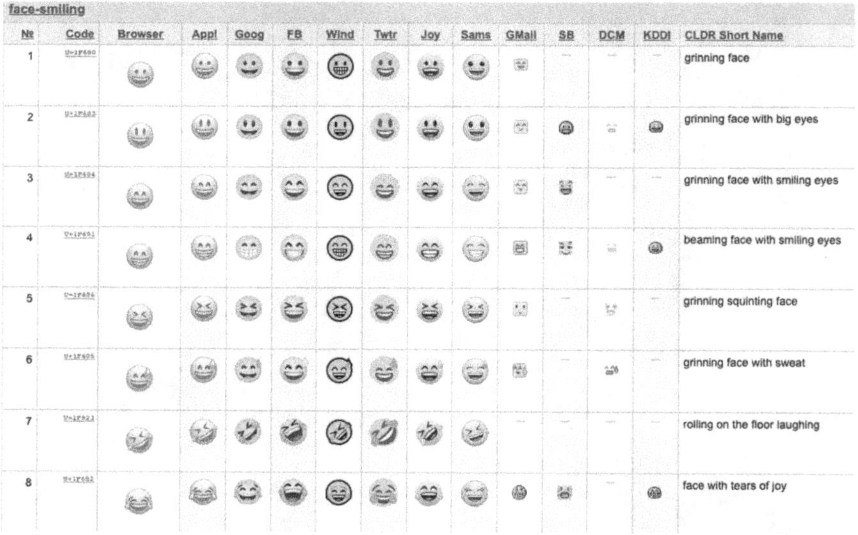

**Figure 4.2** Unicode table for emojis.

(i.e., they cannot be generated with an ASCII keyboard) unlike emoticons and are closer to emojis, but may consist of any image and its modifications. A good example is "kappa" the emote used to signify irony or humor; see Figure 4.3.

Other emotes include variations on Pepe (see Chapter 22), cartoons and more. An important feature is that anyone can create and upload one's emote, provided one is a subscriber (https://help.twitch.tv/s/article/subscriber-emote-guide?language=en_US). This can be a status marker on Twitch. Figure 4.4 displays a screen capture of a Twitch.tv streamer, with the chat displaying some emotes. On the use of emotes to mark humor, see Donahue (2022).

So, what is the function of emoticons, emojis and emotes? There is a vast literature on emojis and smileys, see Danesi (2017), Evans (2017) and McCulloch (2019) for good syntheses. Adams (2012) showed that humor online was recognized more easily when accompanied by markers such as emoticons or "lol," and there is general consensus that to some extent these do work as markers of humor. Further results include the following. First, emojis (and their variants, emoticons and emotes) exactly like laughter graphic visualizations (lol, haha, etc.) have a phatic function: they can precede or follow an utterance (i.e., saying something, it makes no difference if it's in writing), and they can function as gap fillers, the ultimate phatic expression, essentially just signaling that we are paying attention. In this respect, they are exactly like laughter and smiling in speech. Second, they have the expressive function of displaying clues to the stance, emotional or epistemic, of the speaker: for example, "lol" may indicate that the speaker is amused, a :-) may indicate that the speaker is smiling and 🙄 (the "face with rolling eyes" emoji) may indicate that the speaker is being ironical and hence does not believe what they

**Figure 4.3** The "kappa" emote; actually, a photo of Josh DeSeno, a Twitch early employee. The emote is rigorously greyscale.

**Figure 4.4** Screen capture of a Twitch streamer.

are literally stating (i.e., their epistemic stance is "disbelief.") Another marker of irony that has emerged online is "/s" short for "</sarcasm>". This is pseudo HTML code. Another recent approach is the alternation of lower and uppercase, as in the example in Figure 4.5 (https://knowyourmeme.com/photos/1252994-mocking-spongebob)

Danesi (2017, p. 56) sees emojis as having phatic functions: opening and closing utterances and avoiding silence; in other words, rather than having an awkward "silence" after a text, one responds with an emoji, which carries little to no semantic meaning, but does carry an important social-pragmatic meaning of "I heard you." More generally, he sees emojis as having the function to cue the receiver as to the "frame of mind" (p. 56) of the sender and in particular their emotional status. Evans (2017) also sees emojis as having primarily the function to convey emotions. McCulloch sees emojis as gestures, keeping in mind that facial expressions are also gestures. As such they are not strictly linguistic: indeed emojis do not have syntax, a point already made by Evans (2017, p. 17), although they do have repetition (p. 170) and they have no metalinguistic function. McCulloch (2019) lists three categories: (1) emblems are gestures with stable meanings, are arbitrary, can be "named" (e.g., wink, smile), (pp. 162-163), (2) co-speech (illustrative) gestures, for example, birthday cake or cat (p. 167). These are not arbitrary, unlike language. Finally, (3) beats are similar to batonic gestures; they keep a rhythm: for example, kiss, kiss, kiss (Figure 4.6). Obviously, there is much more to be said about emojis and related concepts but since not all of them are humor-related we will leave it at that. However, it is worth mentioning that they are particularly important in mobile-messaging (see Yus, 2022).

THE NEW LANGUAGE OF HUMOR 57

> **Danyelíta**
> @DaniLevyyy
>
> Americans: I need healthcare because I have cancer and I'm dying
>
> Republicans: I NeEd hEaLtHcArE bEcAuSe I hAvE caNcEr aNd iM dYinG

**Figure 4.5** Sponge Bob example of irony marking using mixed upper and lower case.

**Figure 4.6** Kiss, kiss, kiss batonic emoji.

## LOL

Probably the best-known marker of humor created on Usenet, the precursor of the internet, is the acronym LOL, which stands for Laughing Out Loud. It is often spelled in lowercase. There are also variants such as lolol, lollll or loool. I have kept the uppercase spelling for ease of reading. The acronym was apparently created in 1980 (https://en.wikipedia.org/wiki/LOL) along with the less popular lmao ("laughing my ass off"), lmfao ("laughing my fucking ass off") and rofl/rotfl ("rolling on (the) floor laughing"). The *Oxford English Dictionary* listed LOL as a word in 2011. Originally it was just used as a replacement of laughter. However, it has spread much more broadly, and there is now a consensus that it does not just indicate laughter.

What LOL means or indicates is open for debate. Baron (2004, 2008) noted that LOL was the most frequent acronym in her IM (instant messaging) data, but that its meaning was more of a phatic device (i.e., something said to keep the channel of communication open, akin to "yeah" or "OK"; see also Tagliamonte & Denis, 2008). Garley et al. (2009) and Markman (2013) see it as a discourse marker, along the lines of "well" or "right." McWorther (2013) thinks of it as a discourse marker of empathy. Varnhagen, et al. (2010) consider LOL as an emotion marker. Schneebeli (2019) considers LOL in YouTube comments. She argues that LOL expresses amusement but also approval of and alignment with the video and/or who posted it. McSweeney (2016, 2018) argues that it marks indirectness, that is, that the speaker does not mean literally what they are saying. In an interesting twist, recent mostly non-academic observations (e.g., Gallucci, 2019; Heaney, 2014) note that the use of LOL may no longer be connected with the expression of laughter or even playfulness. This may be semantic bleaching, that is, loss of meaning on the way to grammaticalization (see Chapter 11), and even possibly use as punctuation (to indicate the end of a clause; Michot, 2007).

Tagliamonte and Denis (2008) also show that there is age grading in relation to the use of LOL. Specifically, younger speakers (age 15–16) use more LOL than 19–20-year-olds. Since they collected their corpus of IMs in 2004–2006, this almost perfectly matches the "generations" described by McCulloch (2019), since they would have been born around 1990 and entered their teenage years right when web 2.0 was building steam.

Are speakers justified in their desire to disambiguate their humorous, playful or simply emotional communication compute mediated contexts? Indeed they are: Laubert and Parlamis (2019) found that a shockingly high number of interlocutors completely misinterpreted the emotional valence of the messages intended by the writers. So, it appears as if the communicators who use emojis, lol and assorted emotional signaling paraphernalia are on to something.

## Affordances

Both in the case of lol and haha, as well as emojis, emoticons, and emotes, we see that meaning is the outcome of a soft assembly, an unplanned process, which takes advantage of whatever the environment is (the users, the affordances of the technology, etc.) to convey the social, interactional aspects of meaning. McKay (2020, p. 98) notes very interestingly that telegraph operators in the late nineteenth century used expressions such as "haha" to "laugh" over the telegraph. McKay notes that the quasi-synchronous nature of the transmission and the lack of a visual channel impose "restrictions" that the telegraph operators, much like internet users on Twitter or WhatsApp have

THE NEW LANGUAGE OF HUMOR                59

to "accommodate." I prefer to think of this in terms of affordances: an audiovisual channel affords intonation and facial expressions, but a quasi-synchronous text-only (or text + emoji) affords other things, for example, modulating the speed with which one responds, since there are "time gaps" (Baron, 2004) between most turns. In short, speakers take advantage of any aspect of the medium to squeeze meaning out of it.

## Of Covfefe and Men

An aspect that, to the best of my knowledge, has not been investigated is that the peculiar dynamics of stardom in the age of the internet and virality have affected the mechanisms of linguistic diffusion. Generally a new word has to take decades to insert itself in language.

Consider the graph for "syntax" (Figure 4.7) which goes up from a baseline of technical uses in linguistics to some serious action growing steadily from the 1960s to 2000, and then starts to decline, mirroring the fate of Chomskyan linguistics. Similarly, the graph for postmodern (Figure 4.8) again reflects a sudden rise in from the mid-1980s to roughly 200 and a precipitous fall. Now contrast this with the graph for "covfefe" (Figure 4.9) a typo in a tweet sent by then-president Trump on May 31, 2017.

Granted that the time scales are vastly different (the figures above span over two centuries, whereas the covfefe graph spans six months) and that the latter is a Google trend graph and not an N-gram graph; nonetheless there is a stark difference between these graphs. The diffusion of words generally takes

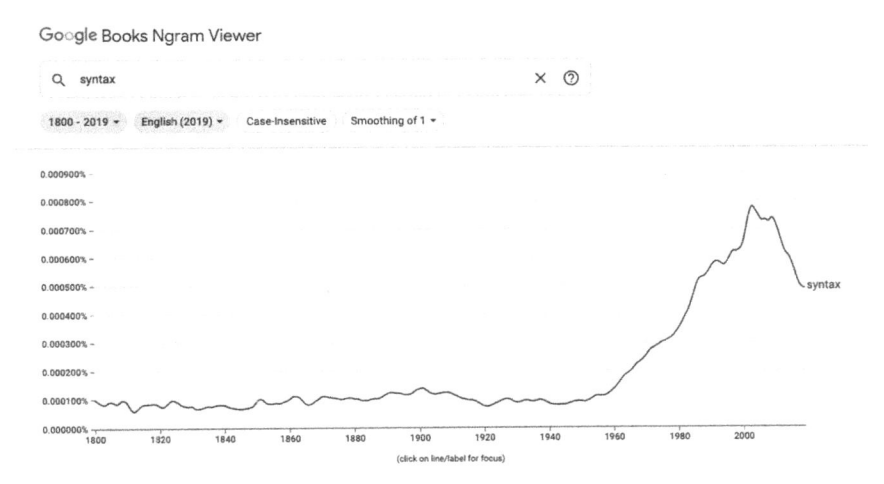

**Figure 4.7** The "syntax" usage graph.

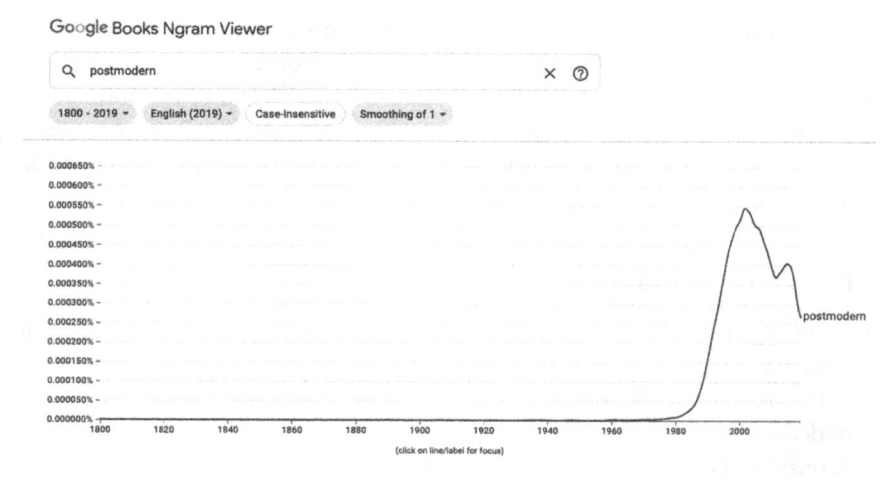

**Figure 4.8** The "postmodern" usage graph.

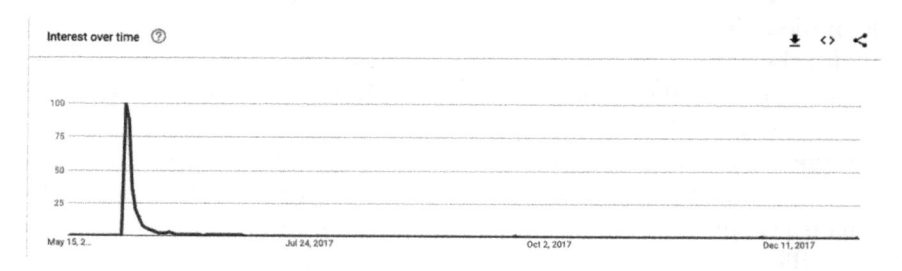

**Figure 4.9** The Covfefe usage graph.

decades. In the "covfefe" example, a combination of celebrity politics and the perverse logic of social media, where any reaction, positive or negative generates a spike in attention, produced the viral exponential spike growth and correspondingly fast decay of memes (see Chapters 2 and 15).

The covfefe fiasco generated a "deluge of jokes" (https://knowyourmeme.com/memes/covfefe) including many that merely introduce the new word into previous image macros, such as the following (Figure 4.10), which uses a still from the 2016 sci-fi film *Arrival*, one of two major Hollywood movies to feature a linguist as a main character (the other was *Stargate*). The incongruity of teaching aliens the pseudo-word should be obvious (at least to a linguist).

In conclusion, the impact of the internet on language, as it pertains to humor, is less significant that most would think. Aside from emojis and emoticons, which have been the object of significant research, and which we

**Figure 4.10** Altered still from the film *Arrival*.

have barely touched upon, as they are not central to our concerns, the only significant difference is the speed at which new terms, slang or not, spread. Of course, we have not yet considered the social and interactional aspects of "doing humor" online, for example, the community building aspects discussed in the literature, for example, Yus (2011), Tsakona (2020). Those will be examined in Parts 2–4 of the book.

# Chapter 5

# THE COMPILATION

The compilation of gags preexists the internet. America's Funniest Home Videos debuted in 1989. It has been running uninterrupted since 1990. It was directly inspired by Kato-chan Ken-chan Gokigen TV (加トちゃんケンちゃんごきげんテレビ, Kato-chan Ken-chan Gokigen Terebi), a Japanese TV show that featured a segment of home videos sent in by viewers. Indeed, it pays a royalty fee to the Tokyo Broadcasting System.

Conceptually, the compilation is not a new idea at all: collections of sayings or of notable passages have been popular since ancient time. What is different is that the medium of video made it impossible for the average person (i.e., someone without a video editing suite) to create collections of highlights until the advent of cheap or free video editing software. Today, any smartphone contains video editing software that would have been found in a well-equipped TV studio or in a film production company. So, here too we see that the affordances of the technology have facilitated the emergence of a new genre by allowing the general user to extend a practice that was common in other media (e.g., writing).

However, the convergence of video editing software and the existence of platforms to share publicly these video clips were necessary for the form to become as popular as it has become. The America's Funniest Home Videos phenomenon is still a centralized broadcast model, in which individuals send their video clips to a central repository which packages them and re-broadcasts them. With the advent of YouTube, Vine, TikTok and many other platforms dedicated to video clips and eventually the widespread distribution of videos in platforms such as Facebook and Twitter which were not necessarily video-centric, the video clip distribution becomes decentralized.

The sheer number of videos and the indexing capacities of platforms such as YouTube and Google make it possible to search for videos that share some feature and therefore allow the creation of thematic compilations (fails, lucky breaks, funny animals, people behaving badly, etc.).

The most salient feature of a compilation (be it thematic or not) is its lack of narrative structure. The syntax of the compilation is mere juxtaposition: one video follows the other, at most motivated by thematic similarity. However this characterization may be too restrictive, as some organization, albeit non-narrative does appear: for example, the "most appealing" clip is often featured on the still that illustrates the video compilation. Often, this includes scantily clad women, giving us a hint as to the targeted audience. Celebrities are also prominently featured in these stills.

A significant sub-genre of the video compilation are the collections of "fails." A fail is simply a failure at doing something. Fails can be epic, or when they are really massive the person "fails at failing." The humorous nature of fails is most obviously explained by the superiority theories of humor: watching countless people fall into bodies of water, waiters dropping plates, people tripping, breaking objects or falling over while practicing some exercise unquestionably proves that we find other people's humiliation and embarrassment humorous (provided no serious harm ensues, as per the Aristotelian "benign violation" theory). Along the same lines, the compilation of "fails" adds a Bergsonian "mechanicity" (essentially a repetition element).

## Fails Compilations

Compilations of fails became quite popular on YouTube. Know Your Meme reports that "On July 5th, 2011, the YouTube channel FailArmy launched (…). Within seven years, the channel has more than 14 million subscribers and more than 5 billion views." We will analyze on of their compilations below. Subtopics have also emerged, in which thematic compilations of fails are produced. For example, tattoo fails collect images of poorly executed or thought out tattoos. A particularly famous example is the "No regerts" tattoo, sported by a character in the movie *We're the Millers*. Spelling mistakes are also quite popular as sources of tattoo fails. The "You had one job" meme has generated quite a few popular fail collections. The meme originates from the 2001 remake of *Ocean 11*, the 1960 "rat pack" movie. At some point, one of the characters utters the line: "You had one job to do!" There exists even a Reddit page dedicated to "You had one job" (Figure 5.1)

We will now analyze a compilation of fails (Figure 5.2). https://www.youtube.com/watch?v=hAKcWzjJKwk

The video Down Bad - Fails of the Week | FailArmy (March 11, 2022) had had 1.3 million views by March 14. In other words, the video received about 0.45 million views per day. Only 15 seconds of the video are used to advertise and introduce the brand. Excluding the two commercial clips, there are 44 clips in the FailArmy compilation. They are listed below.

THE COMPILATION 65

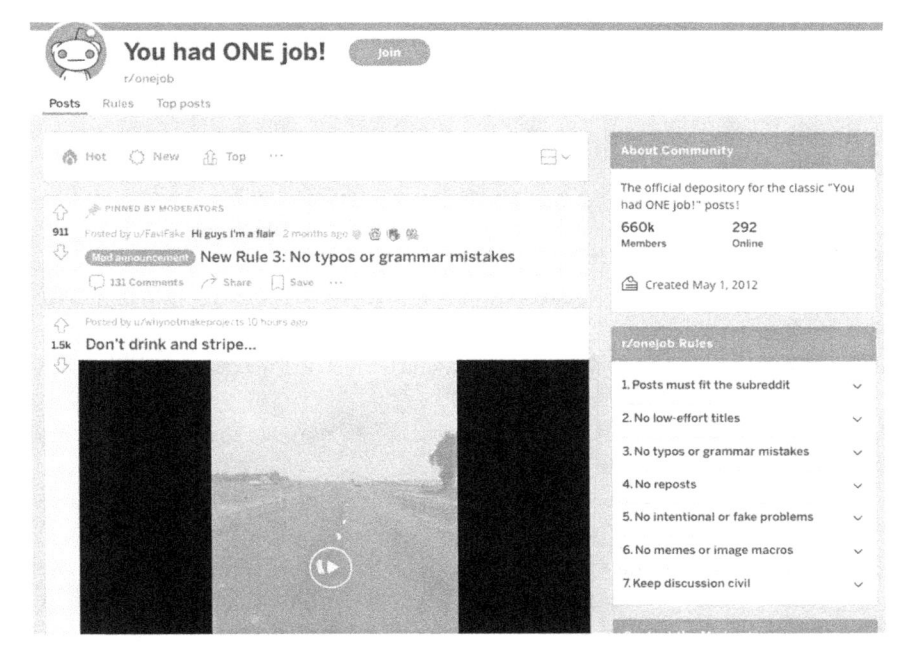

**Figure 5.1** The "You had one job" Reddit page.

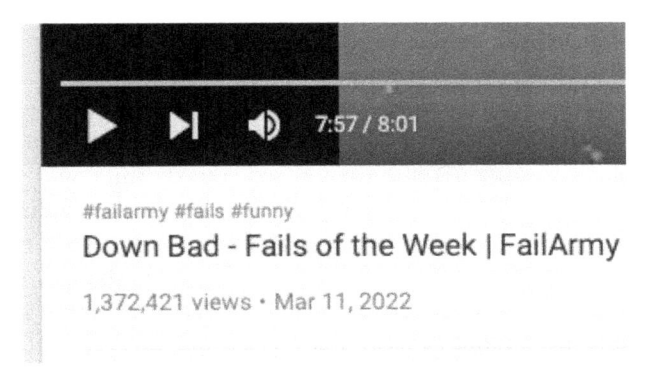

**Figure 5.2** Title of the fails compilation.

0:01–0:06 Young male falling down during a skateboarding trick
0:07–0:12 Logo and intro music
0:12–0:23 Male fishing on boat falls into the water. Laughter is heard.
0:24–0:32 Prank with fake ketchup bottle which an unseen person pretends to squirt into a cook's pot
0:33–0:44 Man falls on frozen ground while carrying drinks and curses extensively.

0:45–0:51 Car hits another car that turned into its way at intersection.

0:52–9:00 Young woman trying to do a trick with a pan accidentally hits friend in her face when pan breaks

1:01–1:06 Young woman surfing down a hillside falls and flips in the air repeatedly

1:06–1:27 Man moving a phone booth drops it on a mowing tractor and damages the tractor

1:27–1:35 Man jumps in a puddle and falls in it.

1:36–1:41 Young man handles a hose and a fire breaks out [unclear what happens].

1:42–1:47 Man snowboarding uses an avalanche and snowboards in it [comments off camera are concerned].

1:47–1:57 Woman falls off bicycle [comments off camera are concerned and identify her as "Mom"].

1:58–2:12 Man flies drone which crashes immediately. He comments "awesome" and picks up the pieces.

2:13–2:22 Baby falls asleep at the table and goes face first in cake. He says "Oh."

2:22–2:36 Man in orange shirt drinks beer with a live crawfish in his hand and is scared by it. Raucous laughter follows.

2:37–2:43 Woman on small motorcycle loses control, falls and crashes against a wall. She laughs.

2:44–2:51 Skiers perform a stunt in which one of them passes under their legs but he hits the last person in the crotch. Laughter & cries are heard.

2:52–3:06 Man drives van in a ditch. After the van comes to a stop, the GPS voice is heard saying, "You have reached your destination."

3:07–3:11 Slow motion clip of a person on a mountain bike falling over and flipping head first. Laughter can be heard and is indicated in the subtitles.

3:11–3:18 Man is hit on the head by a falling ladder. He shouts "Ah!"

3:19–3:27 A car or truck tire rolls down the street and hits a stopped car. Ambient sounds but no reaction sounds.

3:28–3:50 Man tries to flip omelet but the handle of the pan breaks and it falls on the floor. The woman videoing says, "Oh!" and then laughs. He laughs after her, ironically. Then they both laugh.

3:51–3:56 A woman at an upstairs window is retrieving a small parcel from a man in the street. She drops the parcel (or the rope breaks) and shouts "Oh."

3:57–4:02 A young man is standing on a board balanced on a log-like object. He tries to turn around and falls. He laughs.

4:03–4:13 Man walk outside in the snow and falls over steps. No reaction sounds.

4:14–4:22 Man looking at display slips on wet floor and falls down. Mocking laughter is heard.

4:22–4:26 Cat knocks over elaborate hydroponic garden setup.

4:26–4:36 Man spotting climber breaks her fall by being lifted from the ground by the safety rope. No sound; she seems elated.

4:36–4:46 Child snowboarding falls off board. No sound.

4:47–4:50 Woman cleaning floor around husband with a small dog in his arms and a glass of wine. He falls backward, but manages not to spill much wine.

4:51–5:11 Extremely strong wind forces cyclists and pedestrian to various antics to keep their equilibrium. No reaction sounds. [Video consists of two segments.]

5:12–5:21 Small dog falls off steps. No reaction sounds.

5:22–5:26 Skier falls over. Bystanders laugh.

5:26–5:41 Barge on flooding river destroys dam. Ambient sounds, no reaction.

5:42–5:47 Dog falls off a table. Ambient sounds, no reaction.

5:47–5:51 Skier falls. Off camera shouts of "Yes!" and "Fuck!"

5:52–6:07 Woman wearing short skirt and boots walks in windswept snow-covered street; she pulls her skirt down. She walks toward a group of similarly underdressed women and someone says "Oh my god it's so…"

6:08–6:18 Small dog is frightened by a Roomba. A female voice can be heard saying "You OK?"

6:19–6:42 Black car drives in flooded area and has to be pushed out. A female voice is heard saying "What are you doing?" and more. [Video consist of two parts.]

6:43–7:02 Woman falls from stairs, tries to catch herself and ends up falling over head first. Says "Ouch my head!" and laughs.

7:02–7:22 Man describes "secret drawer" which only opens if the oven door is open, etc. No sound beyond narration. This is a poorly installed oven, so a job fail.

7:23–7:31 Father pulling kids on sled falls down. Faint laughter from the person filming can be heard.

7:32–7:41 Dog runs in front of bicycle and causes cyclist to fall. Laughter can be heard from person filming.

7:42–7:50 Man on basketball court kicks a ball against a fence and breaks the fence. He is heard laughing and commenting: "Fail Army."

7:51–8:01 Advertisement for Fail Army.com

The first observation we can make is that the length of the clips is remarkably short. Many are under 10 seconds. The average length is 10.04 seconds (with the shortest clip lasting 3 seconds and the longest 23 seconds). It should also be noted that two of the longest videos actually consist of two connected clips.

With such short duration it is obviously impossible to establish any real characterization. At most we find out that someone is the mother of the person doing the recording ("Woman falls off bicycle") or that the prankster and the prank know each other ("fake ketchup bottle") but, generally speaking, we know as much about these people as we know about the guy walking into a bar, that is to say, nothing. The real people to whom these things happened are de-identified; they become ciphers, that is, non-specific individual who fits a functional role in the events. There has to be someone on the bicycle or on the skateboard—it does not matter who fulfills that role. The name or identity of the skateboarder, the clumsy mother cycling or the snowboarder who causes an avalanche are humorously irrelevant and thus elided from the compilation.

However, in some cases we can hypothesize an implicit negative judgment toward some of the characters in the clips: the under-dressed women in the snow covered street have clearly not planned their clothing appropriately; the man who falls over while looking at a display is clearly not paying sufficient attention to his surroundings; the driver of the black car who gets stuck in the flooded area is in fact criticized by the person doing the recording who can be heard saying, "What are you doing? Oh, my god! Dude, no. He's stuck." In these cases the corrective function of humor seems to be warranted.

The next observation is that not all the clips actually document humorous failures: some videos are not even humorous in any discernible sense—the barge destroying a dam or the tire rolling down the street may be interesting or awe-inducing, but they are not humorous. In other cases, the videos are funny but they do not document failures: the fake ketchup is a prank, not a failure; the car hitting another car is not a failure of the driver whose perspective we share (whose dash cam shot the video), but, if it is anybody's failure, it is that of the other driver, who turns into an intersection when they do not have the right of way. To be fair, most of the clips do documents failures and as such have a built in target: the person who fails to perform the skateboard trick, or to fly the drone, or to catch the fish. Presumably we laugh at them out of a sense of superiority: we know that fishermen should not fall in the water, drones should not crash immediately, heavy loads should not be dropped on one's lawn mower, etc. From this perspective, the significant number of falls in the fail videos represents the most basic loss of control on the part of an agent. The "falling on a banana peel" stereotype is famous for good reason. Bergson (1901) argued that when a man falls down we laugh because of rigidity, of a mechanistic concept superimposed on life, which is flexible and in perpetual movement. This seems to be exactly backwards: we laugh because the man who falls down does not exert enough control on their body, or fails to perform an activity in an efficient manner, or the tools fail to perform as designed (there are two instances of pans breaking, for example).

However Bergson was right, as was Pirandello (1908) who claimed that same thing, that this sort of situations must be perceived through intelligence and not through sensibility: if we start thinking about the fact that the man who fell down and spilled his drinks must be in pain, or embarrassed, that mother who falls off the bicycle may be hurt, the snowboarder may have died and so on, the situations are no longer appreciated as funny but they become pathetic. However, to claim as he does, that humor requires an anesthesia of the heart, albeit momentary, is too strong of a claim: as we will see in cringe humor it is precisely the presence of affective factors in the humorous situation that causes the "cringe factor."

In the clips there are some instances of onlookers expressing concern: the snowboarder's friends curse (in Italian), thus expressing concern; the daughter of the woman falling off the bicycle also expresses concern. However, in most cases either there is no other person to express concern, since the video is recorded by a security camera or by a phone propped up by the person trying a stunt or the onlookers are not concerned and laugh (for example, the other person on the boat with the fisherman who falls in the water laughs). Even when concern is expressed the videos de-emphasize it. In one case (the snowboarder) the expression of concern are in a foreign language and so presumably unintelligible to the non-Italian speaking audience.

There is a widely quoted saying, attributed to Mel Brooks that "Tragedy is what happens to me; comedy is what happens to you." Several of the people in these clips seems to disagree: for example the woman who falls off the stairs (6:43–7:02) is visibly in pain (she limps when she gets up and holds her side) and her first reaction is to say "Ouch," but even as she says so, her utterance is interspersed with laughter pulses and she continues to laugh until the end of the video. This clearly shows that she herself considers her misadventure funny.

So, we can safely say that the superiority theory of humor can account for most of these clips. Can we find any incongruity in these clips? Yes, because the very idea of failure presupposes that there is a correct, conventional, expected way of performing the activity (landing on one's skateboard, moving a heavy piece of furniture, riding a bicycle, etc.). Thus failing at the activity is incongruous with the way the activity *should* have been performed. That a grown adult fall into a puddle (while a child who is nearby does not) is incongruous with the standards of behavior of adults. Moreover there are some instances of sheer incongruity: for example, the young woman surfing down a hill. Surfing is not a land sport, so that certainly qualifies as an incongruity.

# Chapter 6

# INTERNET CARTOONS

The explosion of niche narrowcasting and the geek culture of the internet began a new breed of hyper-sophisticated but low-quality graphics cartoons. Inspired by *Dilbert*'s easy to produce characters, *XKCD* stick figures and *Dinosaur Comics* recycled images that do not change from strip to strip ("fixed art") read like visual self-parodies, in which the author self-consciously decides to not even try to produce visually appealing cartoons. *The Order of the Stick*, a webcomic set in the world of Dungeons and Dragons (D&D) even in the title references its stick figure art.

## Narrowcasting

The term "narrowcasting" was introduced to "emphasize the rejection or dissolution of the constraints imposed by commitment to a monolithic mass-appeal, broadcast approach" (Licklider, 1967). Licklider, in what was a truly prophetic call, envisions a television network (this was the 1960s, a good 20 years before the internet!) in which the "audience divides itself into many subsets" and thus the network can offer "a multiplicity of programs, services, and techniques, using a multiplicity of channels" (1967, p. 212). Licklider saw that this was not only more efficient but that the content can be designed to appeal to select groups "of medium and even small size" (p. 215). Naturally, Licklider who imagined a network of computers reaching individual homes to access libraries and classrooms would have been appalled by Facebook, Twitter, and Pornhub. However, his visionary intuition of the fact that "niche marketing" (as narrowcasting has been called in advertising) would mean that extremely narrow (i.e., small) "discourse communities" could be effectively reached and could sustain the production of content (art, video, cartoons, etc.) perhaps not necessarily economically, but certainly in the currency of the internet: attention (which can be monetized through platforms such as YouTube, Patreon, etc.). Through platforms such as YouTube, Facebook, Twitter, TikTok, Reddit and so on, anyone can become a narrowcaster (and if they are lucky and go viral, a broadcaster). In fact, the raison d'être of Facebook, Twitter, TikTok and so on, is to lead people to share content. Furthermore, the internet effectively abolishes the location issue. One can produce and distribute videos, cartoons or any other digital media literally in one's bedroom, wherever that might be. No need to get in a bus to Los Angeles or New York (or Paris, Moscow, Beijing, etc.) to try and become a star. Just fire up your computer or smartphone.

The effect of narrowcasting on the artistic product is very significant. Let's consider the differences between Schulz's *Peanuts* or Gary Larson's *Far Side* and such comics as *XKCD* or *The Order of the Stick*. The digital strips can rely on truly esoteric information: physics or more generally hard science, in the case of *XKCD* (see Figure 6.1), and D&D, in the case of *The Order of the Stick*), whereas the syndicated cartoons that were distributed in print media have necessarily to appeal to a generic mid- to low-brow audience. It is instructive to read Larson's recollections of the grief he had to endure when one of his cartoons was "too difficult" for his audience (Larson, 1989).

## Geek Culture

Because of the highly focused audience of narrowcasting, it is ideal to embody geek culture. One of the ways that geeks are identified/defined is by a high level of expertise in a given subject (e.g., Japanese anime, comics, etc.) or participation in cosplay, comics conventions, D&D play, participation in historical reenactments (e.g., Medieval fairs), etc. If one has a very specific interest, let's say for example in the British show *Dr. Who*, it is difficult to find other people interested in *Dr. Who* in, say, Greenville, Texas, a town of about 30,000 people, 10 minutes away from where I live. If I was willing to drive an hour or so I would probably have better luck in Dallas. However, with the internet

**Figure 6.1** An XKCD strip with a joke based on data analysis and AI. https://xkcd.com/2494/

one can find other people with similar interests from around the world with a few keystrokes. In other words, the internet makes it easier to find people with specific interests and to interact with them. So it is not surprising that we find that a lot of cultural and artistic productions revolves around niche topics, as we saw above for *XKCD* and *The Order of the Stick*, but the same can be said for *Ctrl+Alt+Del*, *Clueless Hero*, *Penny Arcade* and *Epic Gamer Comic* all webcomics with content related to gaming, with the latter distinguished by the fact that it is a parody of the others.

## Webcomics

Wikipedia gets it exactly right: "Webcomics can be compared to self-published print comics in that anyone with an Internet connection can publish their own webcomic. Readership levels vary widely; many are read only by the creator's immediate friends and family, while some of the largest claim audiences well over one million readers." (Wikipedia, https://en.wikipedia.org/wiki/Webcomic)

So, essentially, a webcomic is a comic produced for and distributed primarily or exclusively on the web. This unquestionably democratized the medium removing the filtering process of publication (in which an editor has to decide that their paper's audience will enjoy the comic) and a fortiori syndication, in which the original paper licenses publication in other paper. For example, Peanuts started in the St. Paul Pioneer Press, Schulz hometown paper, under the name *Li'l Folks*, in the 1940s. The name was then changed to *Peanuts*. It ran under that name from 1950 to 2000, and at its peak was syndicated to 2,600 papers.

There is a seemingly common distinction between webcomics and digital comics, which are regular comics distributed digitally (e.g., *Avenging Spider-Man* by Marvel comics was distributed with a free digital version of the first three issues and given the success the digital distribution was extended to the rest of the series.

While the digital medium allows potentially a much greater freedom of formatting (McCloud, 2000) many (most?) webcomics have kept the panels, or the strip format of print media comics. Otherwise the medium has changed significantly, as can be seen from some of its subgenres. One example of digital-media-only feature is present in *XKCD* in which hovering the mouse over the strip causes a text box to appear which contains a further gag, related to the topic of the strip. Bramlett (2018) analyzes two other webcomics with this feature. This is called alt text in HTML or Cascading Style Sheets (which are the markup languages used to build web pages—essentially what runs behind the scene of the web pages you see). Originally "alt text" (short

74　　　　　　　　　　　　HUMOR 2.0

for "alternative," specified in an "alt" attribute to an image) was supposed to display if one had a slow connection, or for visually impaired users using readers, to describe the image. The metalinguistic nature of the process lent itself to using it to provide a commentary on the image, rather than a description, and from there it's only a short step to using it for humorous purposes.

Types of webcomics include sprite comics, which use video games images, pixel art comics, which use exclusively pixel art, reminiscent of the early computer graphics.

*Bitmapworld* is a webcomic that has smileys as characters. Furniture and other props are minimally drawn and reused from panel to panel. http://bitmapworld.webcomic.ws

Stick art comics are comics that are deliberately drawn as stick figures. *XKCD* is the prime example, but Nathan Pyle's *Strange Planet*, distributed on Instagram, is another very good example (Figure 6.2). The humor in Pyle's *Strange Planet* comes almost entirely from what the Russian Formalists called *ostranenie*, estrangement, that is, the description of a given thing using non-familiar, non-idiomatic language.

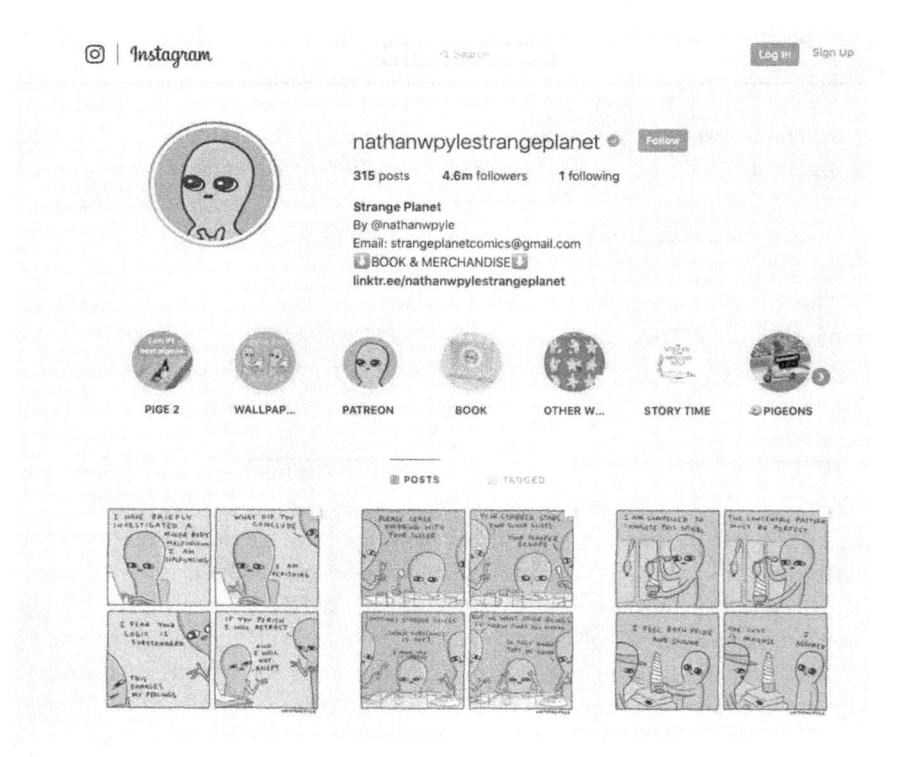

**Figure 6.2** Nathan Pyle's *Strange Planet* Instagram page.

INTERNET CARTOONS 75

## indietits

little birds who talk about obscure bands and make stupid jokes. email the indie tits at indietits [at] gmail [dot] com.

Friday, September 21, 2007

# WHODUNIT

**Figure 6.3** Indietits example.

**Figure 6.4** Indietits with alt text displayed.

Thus in one cartoon, oversleeping is described as "I was unconscious longer than planned" and an umbrella is described as a "sky shield." The stylistic choice affords a fresh take on everyday life, sometimes achieving poetic quality.

Dinosaur Comics are a successful example of fixed art: that is, the panels never change. Only the dialogue changes. An example of (defunct) fixed art comic is *indietits* (https://www.indietits.com), which ran from 2005 to 2007. *Indietits*'author was Jeph Jacques (https://en.wikipedia.org/wiki/Jeph_Jacques) better known for the webcomic *Questionable Content,* an "internet comic strip about friendship, romance, and robots" (https://www.questionablecontent.net/about.php),

The example of indietits in Figure 6.3 makes an extreme use of the alt text feature. As can be seen, without the alt text, the cartoon is not that funny, although there is some incongruity in that the bird is aware of the existence of HTML and alt text, which would imply that it is metanarratively aware of its existence as a character in a webcomic. However, if we consider the alt text, displayed below (Figure 6.4), we get a much different picture.

Now we get a conflict between the bird character and the improbable alt text "character," which may not be exactly hilarious, but it is fairly novel.

All in all, internet cartoons have exploited some of the affordances of the digital medium, but have not been revolutionized by it.

# Chapter 7

# STUFF WHITE PEOPLE LIKE

Stuff White people Like (SWPL), as it has become known, started out as a blog by Christian Lander and Myles Valentin in 2008. Lander is white; Valentin is part Filipino. The blog went viral, and a book was released that same year, single authored by Lander (Lander, 2008). A second book followed in 2010, as well as a set of cards: *Stuff White People Like (to Talk About): 50 Ways to Start Conversations with Caucasians* in 2011. Since it would be too complex to try and disentangle authorship, I refer to the author of the blog as Lander and Valentin, regardless of when the text was actually produced.

The blog is still available, but is frozen at entry #136 in 2010. It reports, as of December 2022, more than 100 million hits. Among the list of "stuff" are TED conferences, Vespa Scooters, Moleskine notebooks, hummus, The Onion, Facebook, appearing to enjoy classical music, grammar, bad memories of high school, study abroad, irony, Apple products, wine, David Sedaris and Farmer's markets. Some topics are explicitly about race: Barack Obama, being the only white person around, having black friends, black music that black people don't listen to anymore (jazz, blues and "old school" hip hop), but the majority of topics are consumerist and/or cultural. The format of the pieces is fairly uniform: they are short essays, illustrated with generic images, that make a few humorous points about the phenomenon, generally couched in the form of observations about white people; for example, in the Grammar piece, we find: "Without a doubt, the rule system that white people love the most is grammar. It is in their blood not only to use perfect grammar but also to spend significant portions of time pointing out the errors of others." (https://stuffwhitepeoplelike.com/2008/05/12/99-grammar/)

My interest in SWPL is motivated by the fact that it has been the object of a sophisticated analysis in Walton and Jaffe (2011), Grzanka and Maher (2012), and Jaffe (2016). However, despite the fact that Walton and Jaffe and Grzanka and Maher make some claims about the humorous nature of SWPL, no actual discussion of the humor is included. I intend to remedy this lacuna and at the same time engage some of the more interesting points. I think that these authors miss or deliberately choose to ignore (part of) the joke. More specifically, SWPL is not mainly about race, but about class. In short: the discussion on SWPL (1) (mostly) misses the joke and (2) mistakes the target of the satire, which is not white people but in fact the progressive, educated, upper-middle class.

Surprisingly, SWPL was taken seriously, not in the sense that people missed the satirical intention, but in the sense that people started debating racial and identity issues. The discussions of SWPL pay lip service to the humor, but turn immediately to the "serious" discussion of race. Walton and Jaffe (2011, p. 287) dismiss SWPL as a "metaphor of race" and single out the real target of SWPL: the "elite, educated class" (p. 287); they also mention that race is a proxy for "class" (p. 288) in several spots. However, their interest is squarely on race. The same goes for Grzanka and Maher (2012): "It is clearly a joke, but what actually is the Whiteness (i.e., 'stuff') of SWPL?" Grzanka & Maher (2012, p. 369). To be fair, a section of the comments reported by Walton and Jaffe (2011) shows that a completely serious reaction to the blog was not uncommon. For example, the following comment, reported in Walton and Jaffe (2011, p. 294), shows that this reader completely missed the joke and treats SWPL as a straightforward attempt at characterizing the racial essence of white people: "My point is that it's suddenly pc to stereotype white people, but god forbid anyone mentions watermelon and blacks, or Mexicans and beans in the same sentence."

The responses from the audience in the comment sections number in the thousands. They range quite widely, from missing the joke entirely, as we saw, to mode adopting (suggesting other things that white people like), agreeing and complimenting the authors, arguing seriously against the validity of the stereotypes, and "a gleeful self-identification with SWPL" (Walton & Jaffe, 2011; Grzanka & Maher, 2012, p. 370).

The blog adopts "the facetiously distanced voice of an anthropologist" (Grzanka & Maher, 2012, p. 368) or that of a "cultural outsider" (Walton and Jaffe, 2011). This is a good observation: the use of "ostranenie" (estrangement) to satirize one's society is an old trope. For example, the same joke was already applied by Umberto Eco in an essay from 1963 (Industry and Sexual Repression in a Po Valley Society) in which anthropologists from Tasmania come to Milan, Italy, to study the local indigenous population (i.e., the Italians). The essay hilariously uses the format and style of an anthropological study, for example starting by providing a geographical description of where the city of Milan can be found and thanking the sponsors of the research for a grant of 24,000 dog teeth to fund the trip. Before Eco, we find the same idea, minus the anthropological trope, in many enlightenment epistolary novels (e.g., Montesquieu's *Lettres Persanes*, 1721). That idea itself originated from an actual interaction between a French administrator and an explorer in Canada, by the name of Lahontan and Kondiarok a Wendat (Huron) chief. In 1703, Lahontan published a book recounting conversations with a fictionalized Kondiarok, who expresses critical views of Western society. This book was quite influential, and the idea of having an outsider discuss (and hence critique) the Western society was quite popular (see for example a list in Graeber & Wengrow, 2021, p. 58). Of course, what the "anthropologist" stance gives us is a built-in script opposition ("civilized vs. savage"—where the whole point of the story is "Who is the real savage?") but also "insider vs. outside" and "normal way of looking at things vs. abnormal way of looking at things."

## Ideology and Consumption

French (2010) argues that SWPL

> not only critiques a specific and recognizable socio-economic demographic, but he also lays out clearly that when these characteristics come together, they are primarily a very specific sub-set of whites who not only share tastes and interests, but an ideology. That ideology is one of being un-white, or at least less (annoyingly) white than other whites, while maintaining the privilege associated with whiteness.

While white privilege is explicitly one of the targets of SWPL, the idea that SWPL embodies an ideology is worth examining more closely. French's idea is that the ideology underlying SWPL is distancing from "whiteness" or "less-white." By this she means that Lander and Valentin's "white people" consumptive behavior is geared toward displaying status (what Veblen (1889) calls "conspicuous consumption") but the status they seek to display is not merely financial success but a more subtle financial success and social responsibility. As French (2010) puts it, "They are distancing themselves from other whites: Middle America, Wall Street Suits, the Nascar set (...)". Let's consider this example from a 2008 entry in the blog:

> Over the years, white people have gone through a number of official cars. In the 1980s it was the Saab and the Volvo. By the 1990s it was the Volkswagen Jetta or a Subaru 4WD stastion [*sic*] wagon. But these days, there is only one car for white people. One car that defines all that they love: the Toyota Prius.
>
> https://stuffwhitepeoplelike.com/2008/02/07/60-toyota-prius/

If we think in terms of cars, at least in the United States, things come into focus. The nouveau riche drive Lamborghinis or Ferraris, the epitome of crass consumption: for example, in *Wolf of Wall Street*, Leonardo di Caprio drives a Lamborghini Countach. Socially responsible progressives drove Priuses in the 2000s. Rednecks drive Mustangs and Camaros, etc. So, in conclusion, Lander and Valentin's "white people" consume to signal not their racial identity, but their social progressive values, their sophistication, as well as their affluence. As French (2010) puts it, "Their consumption patterns portray who they are not as much as they portray who they are."

We now need to cycle back on French's use of the term "ideology." There is a quote falsely attributed to either Goering, Himmler or Goebbels, that goes: "When I hear the word culture, I reach for my pistol." The quote does in fact come from a play by Hanns Johst and is slightly different. Johst's play was appreciated by the Nazis which may explain why it is attributed to well-known Nazi figures rather to the, at least to me, unknown Johst. The point remains the same: some words are so evocative of a way of thinking that they evoke an inordinate reaction. "Ideology" is one such word. I invite my reader to re-holster their gun: I am interested in only two aspects of ideology: first, an ideology is a more or less coherent set of ideas, some of which may be false, that legitimate a political power. So, if you believe that Grandma's blueberry pie is the best in the world, that's not an ideology, just your belief. However, if you believe that the United Stated is destined by God to expand its dominion across North America, you are in the thrall of an ideology. No political power, no ideology. Significantly, some and perhaps all of the ideas that constitute the ideology may be false or unprovable. It does not matter. So, under this definition, what French describes as the "ideology" of SWPL is not a full-blown ideology, but at best part of one.

The second point is subtler. The beliefs that form an ideology are considered "so commonsensical that they are no longer questioned" (Verschueren, 2000, p. 450). For example, for over a thousand years it was commonsensical that people of noble lineage were entitled to ruling those who came from a lesser lineage. It took the French revolution (and a judicious application of the guillotine) to convince people that everyone is equal. For the previous millennium, if you'd have brought up the idea that hereditary power was no grounds to choose the ruler of a state, you would have ended up in shackles (best case scenario). The point is that most people would not have even thought about the possibility, because it was self-evident that kings (and queens) were there to rule countries. This is what is meant when we say that ideology is invisible. There is a joke that sums it up perfectly:

Two fish are swimming when they come across a third fish, who greets them by saying "Hey, how's the water?" The two fish swim away and then one turns to the other and says, "What the hell is water?"

For more discussion of ideology, the interested reader may refer to Eagleton (1991).

## Metasemiotic Awareness

One of Jaffe's (2016) points is worth quoting in full, despite its length.

> Writers/performers do not just evoke but take up a reflexive position vis-à-vis the conventional indexicalities deployed as comic material (…). In other words, this kind of humor is often about the recontextualization of semiotic relations that circulate as *icons* (ethnic or racial stereotypes) as object of reflexive evaluation and resources for creative performance. To the extent that this process reveals those semiotic relations as situated, emergent, and political, we can say that it *indexicalizes* them. Herein lies much of the potential of this kind of humor to be transgressive or to resist dominant ideologies: by revealing processes of iconization as *social* and *political* rather than *natural* truths. (2016, p. 98; emphasis in the original)

Jaffe's claim is relatively simple, despite the heavy theoretical apparatus deployed: by drawing attention to and making fun of stereotypes, comedians highlight the fact that the stereotypes are social constructs (hence political) and not natural categories. To use a different metaphor, making fun of ideology robs it of its transparency (invisibility). Mocking it draws attention to it and hence makes it visible, that is, reveals its presence. This is well expressed by Snyder:

> The average White American is not conscious that Whiteness shapes his worldview—not to mention his life and life prospects—in particular and problematic ways. Indeed, such an idea is out of keeping with a central tenant of the typical White lifeworld: that Whiteness is unimportant. By marking Whiteness, this White lifeworld—the naïve belief that race is no longer salient, the blind faith in colorblindness, the problematic conviction that racial equality has been established—is laid bare for Whites to see and demonstrated to be a particular perspective rather than a universal one. The framework through which the world

is interpreted is brought from the realm of the uncontroversial into the contestable. (Snyder, 2015, p. 298)

Here we see an example of the peculiar view that attributes to humor the power to "subvert" or "transgress" "dominant" ideologies. With these sort of ideas comes the view that humor is essentially progressive. However, as we will discuss in Part 4 of the book, the emergence of right-wing humor shows that humor is not necessarily progressive. It can be employed in subverting and transgressing any ideology, including the one that values democracy, egalitarianism and respect for any race, gender and sexual orientation.

## What Is SWPL About?

SWPL is literally about race, which figures in the title of the blog, and thus necessarily addresses it, in the sense that SWPL forces its readers and commenters to focus on the usually invisible fact that race is relevant, indeed central in the life of non-whites. However, as discussed previously, I also think that Walton and Jaffe (2011), Grzanka and Maher (2012), Snyder (2015) and Jaffe (2016) fail to fully appreciate or refuse to address the fact that SWPL is not really about race but about class and social values.

French (2010) notes that white subgroups have often been satirized: Jeff Foxworthy's mid-1990s "You might be a redneck if…" jokes, for example, or the "white trash" jokes analyzed masterfully by Davies (2010), the "bohemian bourgeois" described by Brooks (2000; see also Moss, 2017), the yuppies ("young, urban, professional") of the 1980s, satirized by Piesman and Hartley (1984) and discussed seriously by Ester and Vinken (1993), who find that they are culturally progressive and liberal, contrary to the popular characterizations. Rednecks and white trash are obviously the "poor whites" (and note in passing how the term "white trash" presupposes the existence of "black trash"). What yuppies, bobos and SWPL "white people" have in common is that they are/were affluent, educated and liberal/progressive. In short, making fun of a group of white people is a common phenomenon. What seems to have been different with SWPL is that, for the first time, the subset of highly educated, affluent, liberal elite was reduced to a racial identification. Much like essentialist racial classifications such as Black, or Asian, flatten the individual experience and the internal subdivisions of these groups, SWPL reduces all white people to the educated, affluent, liberal elite. Obviously, that's part of the joke. If nothing else, the authors who are targeting and thus othering the "white people" in SWPL see themselves as different. So, even if *ab absurdo* we assumed that Lander and Valentin really believe that all white

# Chapter 8

# DOGECOIN, THE JOKE CURRENCY

Sometimes a joke can take a life of its own. This is the tale of Dogecoin, a joke-currency that became worth $80 billion; yes, that is a "b" at the beginning of the word... (Serrels, 2021). The joke currency is probably the most internet-specific, never-heard-before, genre of humor ever. It most certainly was unheard of. Sure, due to hyperinflation some central banks were forced to print banknotes of unlikely values, such as the German 5 billion Marks banknote printed in 1923, by the Weimar Republic. However, there was no humorous intention at all. The Dogecoin instead was started as a joke. There are multiple confirmations of this fact (Kochkodin, 2021; Salzman, 2021). So what exactly is the story?

Dogecoin was started in 2013 by Jackson Palmer and Billy Markus. Palmer made a mashup between two memes. The first one was the Doge meme (https://knowyourmeme.com/memes/doge) which represent a Shiba Inu dog and its inner monologue. An example can be found in Figure 8.1.

Doge (a misspelling for "dog" according to Nani, 2022) memes started around 2012, on Reddit and 4chan. The second meme of the mashup was Bitcoin. On December 8, 2013, Palmer announced Dogecoin (Figure 8.2), on the Bitcoin Forum (https://bitcointalk.org/index.php?topic=361813.0). Note how the style of the multicolored snippets of inner monologue is respected, as well as the "doggie" syntax/spelling, reminiscent of LOLCats talk. Bitcoin is a lot harder to explain than the doge meme, so we need to do a little digression here and discuss cryptocurrencies.

Billy Markus saw the announcement on the web page and decided to create a "fun cryptocurrency." He modified preexisting code, for example replacing "mine" with "dig" (because dogs dig...), but also introducing some technical improvements, such as having more Dogecoins than Bitcoins. The point is that it was not a particularly complex process, and some of it was done, according to Serrels (2021), during Markus's lunch breaks.

**Figure 8.1** A Doge meme.

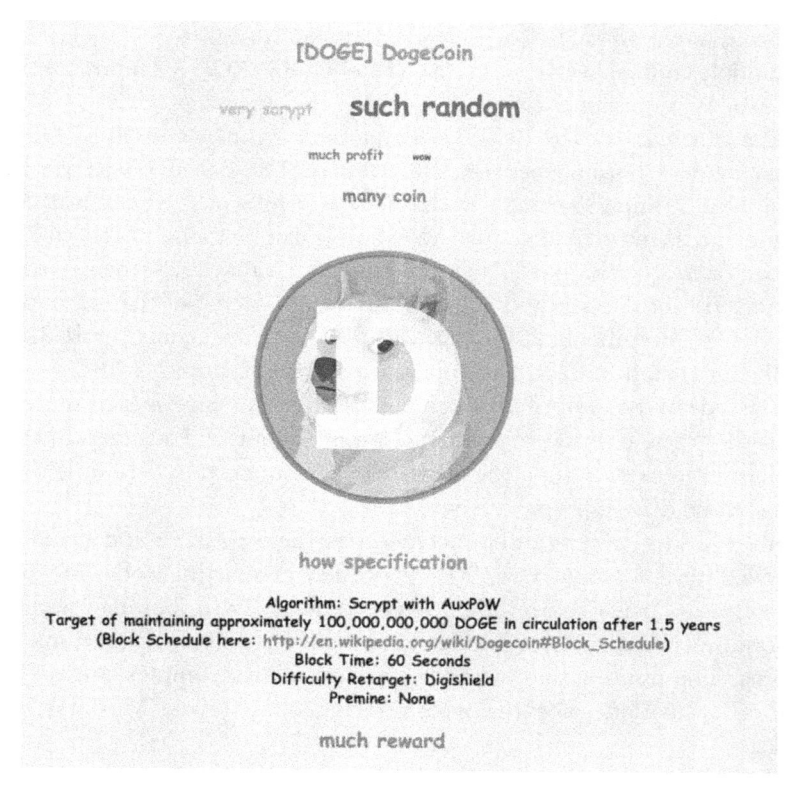

**Figure 8.2** The Dogecoin announcement.

## Bitcoin: The Cryptocurrency that Started It All

What is a cryptocurrency? Well, what is a currency? A currency was an agreement between a government and people that in exchange for a piece of paper the government would give you a certain amount of gold or other precious metals (e.g., silver, platinum). This was known as the gold standard. The government took great pains to ensure that only government-approved institutions could print the special pieces of paper and otherwise to ensure that the appropriate reserves in gold were kept. The obvious advantage to trading in bullion is that paper is easier to carry and can be printed in any multiples one desires. It would be rather complicated to carry nuggets of gold weighing 0.0002 ounces (5 hundredths of a gram) to insert in a parking meter. For a number of reasons, world currencies abandoned the gold standard after the First World War and, despite some returns to it, for example in the United States between 1945 and 1971, most currencies are now fiat currencies. A fiat currency is a currency which is worth whatever the government says it's worth (hence "by fiat" which is not the Italian automobile company, but the subjunctive form of the verb "to do" in Latin, so it translates to "let it be done"). Finally, when you take your money to your bank, or your employer deposits it there, no actual money changes hands. What happens is that your employer and your bank exchange some messages in which your employer agrees to lower its ledger of how much money they have by the amount of your salary and the bank raises the number in your checking account by the same number. It's obviously more complicated than that (otherwise you could call your bank pretending to be your employer and ask then to put double your salary in your account—nice try!) but that is the basic idea. In other words, in fiat currencies, that is, in all currencies nowadays, money is just an agreement between parties that we will all follow the rules and behave as if there is an actual value there. Because fiat currencies are backed by the police, the military, the banking system, etc., if you wish to operate within an economy, you need to follow these rules (and if you do not, the police, the military, etc., will take action against you.)

What would happen if you did not wish to operate within a state-run economy, using a fiat currency? That is essentially the question that Satoshi Nakamoto asked himself in 2008. I say asked himself loosely, as no one really knows who Nakamoto is/was. There are various theories, such that he may be a group of people, or a British citizen, summarized in the Wikipedia entry on Nakamoto (https://en.wikipedia.org/wiki/Satoshi_Nakamoto). In order to create a currency that was independent of fiat currencies, Bitcoin uses a blockchain, a ledger, just like your bank uses, but with one major difference, this one is publicly available. Essentially, each Bitcoin miner is a node in a network and the blockchain ledger is published to all the nodes every 10 minutes. This allows the blockchain to keep track of who has which Bitcoin, with all transactions encoded in a block. Each block contains encrypted information of all the transactions that goes all the way back to the original block (zero) issued by Nakamoto. The encrypting of the information is called "mining" a Bitcoin. One keeps Bitcoins in a "wallet" which is essentially a repository protected by a password that lets you access your bitcoins. Lose the password, you've lost your Bitcoins.

What is the point of all this? Well, for starters, if you wish to transfer money across borders, Bitcoin will do it much faster and more cheaply than doing it via your bank. Bitcoin can also be used for all sorts of transactions online that you would not want your bank, your government or your mother to know you engage in. Bitcoin was an enormous success. According to Bybit (https://learn.bybit.com/crypto/21-million-bitcoin-limit-mined/), there were about 19 million Bitcoins in circulation, as of June 2022, which would have made the total worth of Bitcoins roughly $630 billion (each Bitcoin is worth roughly $30,000 at the time of writing). Since then the price of Bitcoin and of all cryptocurrencies has dropped. Karif (2022) reports that 12,100 cryptocurrencies have stopped trading since the crypto-crash of 2022, which gives us an interesting measure of the width of the cryptocurrency market, in terms of different offerings. Karif reports that there are 64,400 cryptocurrencies, of which only 13,800 had had any activity, as of October 2, 2022.

## Dogecoin's Success

So, by the end of 2013, Bitcoin was already quite popular, but the price of a Bitcoin at the time was about $754. Nice, if you'd bought on January 1, 2011, at $0.30, but not quite mind-blowing as when you consider that by 2021 Bitcoin traded above $60,000. To put it in terms that are comprehensible, if you had bought $100 of Bitcoins in January 2011 (i.e., about 334 Bitcoins) you would have made a staggering 20 million dollars.

Dogecoin was always worth a fraction of a penny (remember, it was a joke) but in April 2021 its price suddenly spiked and reached $0.63 on May 7. If you had bought $100 of Dogecoin in January 2018 (i.e., roughly 10.000 Dogecoins at $0.01) your Dogecoin wallet would have been worth $6700. Enough to buy a used car, which is what Markus did, when he stepped away from the project and sold his Dogecoins. At the time of Salzman (2021) writing, Dogecoin was the fourth largest cryptocurrency, worth a breathtaking $80 billion. Nani (2022) claims that, at its peak, Dogecoin was worth 88 billion. I was unable to confirm that valuation.

What caused the surge of interest in Dogecoin? Recall that this is a joke currency that people are buying with *real* money. In order to understand this apparently mysterious phenomenon, we need to go back to the summer of 2021. Here too we see the creation of a social community, like the ones described by Tsakona (2020), with the difference that this community is closer to the GameStop phenomenon. GameStop is a company that sells videogames, in physical stores. In the age of the internet, where video games are downloaded or streamed, this seemed particularly ripe for failure (much like Blockbuster, the video rental chain). In January 2021, a group of internet stock traders banded together to perform what is called a "short squeeze." It is too complex to go into the details of how a short squeeze works, but essentially if one thinks that a company's stock price is going to fall, one borrows the stock and waits to return it at a much lower price, thus potentially making a lot of money This is called "shorting" the stock. The danger lies in the fact that in order to short a company you must borrow the stock and usually this is done by putting down collateral for a fraction of the price. This makes sense: otherwise one could just abscond with the stock, so the collateral is a guarantee for the lender. If the price of the stock goes up, the lender will want more collateral because they are now facing greater risk (if you borrowed $10,000 with a collateral of $2,000 (i.e., 20 percent), if the stock price doubles, your collateral is now only worth 10 percent. If something like that happens you need to provide more collateral (this is called a "margin call"). Now the fun part: by buying large amounts of a stock the price will go up. When the price gets up, the shorts need to buy back the stock to close their shorts, but this causes the price to go even higher, thus causing further margin calls. This is called a short squeeze. In January of 2021, led by a group on Reddit, a short squeeze of the GameStop shorts raised the price of GameStop stock from $5 to $483. This move by a crowd-sourced group shocked the financial world.

Shortly after that, interest in Dogecoin peaked, in part fueled by Elon Musk's tweeting about Dogecoin, as well as other celebrities endorsing it, such as Snoop Dogg (Chohan, 2021), but largely through a crowdsourcing word of mouth. This may also have been helped by several fundraising initiatives, such as "disadvantaged Olympians attempting to attend the Sochi Winter Olympics (2014) or raising money to build wells in developing countries on World Water Day" (Chohan, 2021, p. 5; Serrels, 2021). We recognize here the same "prank" effect of flash mob that we analyze in the Boaty McBoatface phenomenon (chapter 13). As Nani (2022) points out, the wide recognition of the Doge meme made Dogecoin accessible to people who otherwise would not have been familiar with cryptocurrencies. In fact, Nani argues that the viral nature of Doge and Dogecoin may provide the basic for building a "community large enough to sustain the value and usability of its own money"

(p. 1729). Recall, the currencies are essentially social conventions. Hence, if enough people start using Dogecoin to exchange payments, then Dogecoin will be a de facto currency. In fact, the success of Dogecoin was such that the sales of Shiba Inu dogs, the real-life actual animals, surged (Ballentine, 2021).

In 2015, Palmer distanced himself from Dogecoin and later denounced the whole cryptocurrency idea (see his remarks an interview in Wilson, 2022). Markus likewise distanced himself from the project at that time. Serrels (2021) has a revealing account of some of the issues that led to both founders abandoning Dogecoin. A company called "Moolah" (a slang term for "money") started a cryptocurrency exchange, that is, a repository to facilitate the purchasing and selling of Dogecoin. Moolah ended up scamming over $300,000 from the Dogecoin community and was revealed to be run by a man who was later convicted of rape and was found to have engaged in similar scams before.

**What Makes the Dogecoin Funny?**

First, obviously, the Doge meme itself is humorous. That is fairly easy to explain as we have a simple incongruity, much like in the grumpy cat memes (Chapter 13), of the anthropomorphic dog to whom the memes attribute an inner monologue. Most of the numerous mashups that constitute the derived memes involve a mashup with other memes (images) thus resulting again in an incongruity. For example, in Figure 8.3 we have an image from the Halo video game with the helmet revealing that inside is Doge. Note in passing the ironical text, in the Doge font/colors.

**Figure 8.3** Doge and Halo mashup.

Another aspect of the Doge meme is that it tends to combine an animal with funny facial expressions, with relatively higher status memes, as in the example above, in which we have Doge and the oh-so-serious Mark VI armor. If you doubt that Halo players take this seriously, I challenge you to find the slightest hint of irony or humor in the Halopedia (https://www.halopedia.org/MJOLNIR_Powered_Assault_Armor/Mark_VI). This is the recipe for disparagement humor, that is, a high/low status opposition (Chapter 3).

So, the connection between a humorous anthropomorphic, generally disparaging meme and a cryptocurrency is itself incongruous. Needless to say, naming a currency after a dog is also a high/low status script opposition. In the case of Bitcoin, a further target of humor is the fact that after Bitcoin's success cryptocurrencies proliferated. After Bitcoin, we get Litecoin, Namecoin, Peercoin and of course Dogecoin. Then we also get Ethereum, Tether, so called for being theoretically redeemable one-to-one in US dollars, Binance coin, Cardano, Polygon, Polkadot (no, seriously) and, confusingly, Shiba Inu (which is not Dogecoin). For a list of cryptocurrencies, see https://en.wikipedia.org/wiki/List_of_cryptocurrencies. So the joke here was that after four or five X-coin, why not have a Dogecoin?

Interestingly, Nani (2022) points out that several other joke cryptocurrencies did not achieve the success of Dogecoin: PepeCash, Cthulhu Offerings, Ponzi Coin (Minor, 2018), Loser Coin, Sad Cat Token, Stalwartbucks (King, 2021), Dogelon Mars (with a joke on Elon Musk's interest in Mars) and HODL (Reutzel, 2022). Cthulhu is a monstrous character from H. P. Lovecraft stories. Ponzi, as in Ponzi scheme, after Charles Ponzi who became widely known for defrauding a large number of people in the United States in the 1920s using the approach (which he did not invent). The joke here is that cryptocurrencies have been widely derided as Ponzi schemes. We will discuss Pepe in Chapter 22. Loser Coin and Sad Cat Token are self-explanatory, unlike Stalwartbucks, which is the personal cryptocurrency of Joe Weisenthal (Weisenthal, 2014), a journalist at Bloomberg. HODL is a rallying cry of meme stocks characteristically misspelled for "hold" meaning someone who holds on to their stock rather than selling at the first sign of dropping price (with the retronym "hold on for dear life"). Even more dog-themed cryptocurrencies are listed in Dogendorsed, (2021).

**Conclusions**

There is not much academic research on Dogecoin as a meme. Nani (2022, p. 1727) claims that "Dogecoin became a tangible representation of buying into the meme economy." Choan (2021) is a history of Dogecoin. The rest of the sources are merely journalistic accounts. There is no question that

Dogecoin has been the most successful joke cryptocurrency. There is also no question that a joke crypto currency is a uniquely internet-centric kind of humor genre. However, the sources of humor, the anthropomorphic Doge, the incongruity between a dog and finance, the opposition between low status, non-serious Doge and the high-status financial world are nothing new. The crowd-sourced community that comes together for a project and the social ties that emerge from the process (see Chapter 13) are perhaps the most significant aspect of the phenomenon as is the fact that the goodwill that leads people to donate Dogecoins to send a Jamaican bobsled team to the Olympics or to dig wells is also easily abused by scam artists. In this internet communities can reveal the best and the worst of people.

# Chapter 9

# THE SPOILER ALERT

According to Zimmer (2014) and McCool (2015) the term "spoiler" started out in the 1970s. McCool reports that in 1971 Doug Kenney, one of the founders of the *National Lampoon*, had a feature called "Spoilers" in which he revealed the ending of such films as *The Godfather*, *Citizen Kane* and *Psycho*. McCool also reports the use of "spoiler warning" in a column in the sci-fi magazine *Destinies*. As for the actual term "spoiler alert," both sources agree that it first occurred in 1982, in a Usenet post (on Usenet, see Chapter 1), apparently in the context of a discussion of *The Wrath of Kahn* (a Star Trek movie).

A "spoiler alert" is essentially a courtesy warning to the reader/viewer/hearer that one is about to reveal something about a show, book, game, etc., that is a significant plot point (for example, who wins the game). Thus if one wants to avoid having the plot spoiled, one should stop reading/watching, etc. The interest in spoiler alerts comes from the fact this is very much a contemporary phenomenon and that jokes and memes have been using the term. If one searches for "spoiler alert" on the internet, one will find that numerous articles have the phrase "spoiler alert" in the title as a clever way of conveying the point of the article. For example, the title of Viega and Thompson (2012) is "Ten Years On, How Are We Doing? (Spoiler Alert: We Have No Clue)". I will provide an extended example by analyzing a short 2015 comedy video by Key and Peele titled "Spoiler alert" which makes fun of the topic.

As we can see from the Google n-gram, in Figure 9.1, the earliest mention of the term begins in the 1990s, but the term does not really "take off" until the 2000s. So we can safely say that the spoiler alert is a practice (I hesitate to call it a genre) that is truly exclusive to the digital world. Now it is obvious that "spoilers" have always existed, at least potentially. It is easy to image someone saying, "Dante makes it out of hell and into heaven" to a reader in AD 1321 or a reader saying, "Aeneas makes it to Rome" to a would-be reader of the Aeneid in 18BC. I myself spoiled *In the Realm of the Senses* for a friend in the 1990s (the film appeared in 1976). That's not the point.

The spoiler becomes a cultural phenomenon when popular culture is no longer consumed synchronically by the public in a broadcast model. While

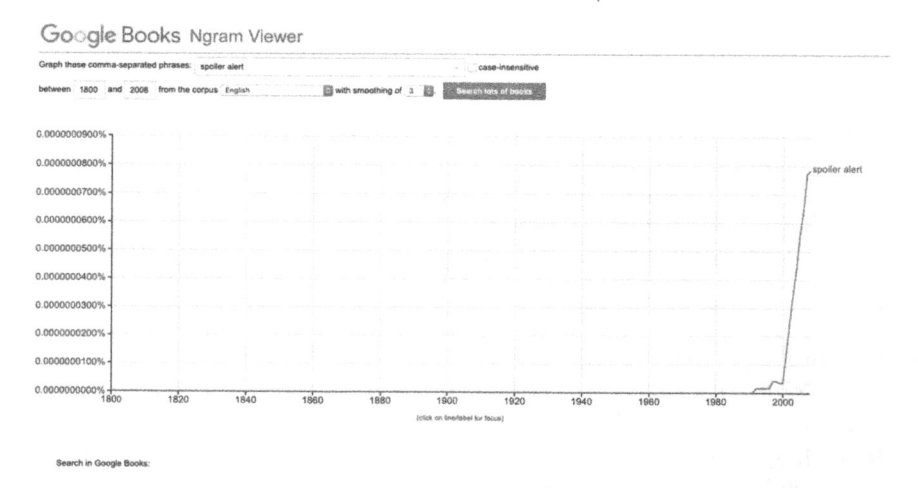

**Figure 9.1** "Spoiler alert" Ngram.

a movie may last a few weeks in a theatrical run, after the run is over it was assumed that anyone interested had seen it and so it was OK to discuss "spoilers." If today I mentioned that (spoiler alert!) Elizabeth Bennet eventually marries Mr. Darcy, it would hardly be a spoiler, since *Pride and Prejudice* was published more than 200 years ago (in 1813 to be specific). What happened in the 1990s is that "time shifting" was introduced. Time shifting is not time travel, but in the world of broadcasting it might as well be. With the introduction of recording devices (first the video recorder, then digital video recorders) and now streaming and the related practice of binge watching, in which one watches an entire series or season thereof in a sitting (or in a few close blocks) the time of consumption of popular culture is unmoored from its "release" or "broadcast." The viewer can watch a show or another cultural artifact whenever they want or it becomes available. However, there is no guarantee that others will have watched the show at the same time. As Perks and McElrath-Hart (2018, p. 148) put it, "By taking temporal power from broadcasters, time shifters have entered a new struggle with fellow viewers who are watching at a different pace."

More significantly, however, it reflects a significant cultural shift, brought about by the internet. In pre-internet times, only a small number of individuals had access to movies, books, TV shows and the likes, ahead of the mass population they potentially targeted. An even smaller number of these individuals was in a position to communicate in the media (newspapers, TV, radio, etc.) about these works. They were known as critics, reviewers or intellectuals. They were generally trained professionals, and therefore they were aware of and respected implicitly a code of conduct that banned spoilers. Revealing the identity of the killer in a review of a detective novel will lead to diminished sales of the novel, but also of the newspaper in which it is published, as the act of producing a spoiler is presumably wanted neither by the author/publisher of the work nor by the potential audience. With the internet and especially social media, literally anyone with access to Facebook or Twitter can provide their review of a movie or book they have just seen or read. Hence the necessity to flag potential spoilers: amateur reviewers may inadvertently reveal too much of the plot, or they may not be able to make their case for or against a given work, without reference to plot points that are spoilers. By flagging their post or tweet with a spoiler alert warning, they elegantly solve the problem by pushing the onus of avoiding the spoiler onto the reader/viewer. In other words, the spoiler alert is only necessary in a situation in which amateur, untrained "reviewers" who have access to a public (e.g., Twitter) or semi-public (e.g., Facebook) audience need to protect themselves from the potential accusation of spoiling their audience's experience. Prior to the internet, there was simply no need of spoiler alerts.

## Deliberate Spoilers

A different case is malicious spoilers in which participants in an internet forum are trolled by people who want to antagonize the members of the fan site, etc. In particular the death of major characters is chosen to be revealed. (https://knowyourmeme.com/memes/death-spoiler-reveals) So, for example, in the "Snape kills Dumbledore" spoiler in the Harry Potter series, that important plot point was revealed (https://knowyourmeme.com/memes/snape-kills-dumbledore). Of course it is also possible to fabricate false spoilers in which one pretends to be delivering a spoiler but in fact does not. Perks and McElrath-Hart (2018) also report that some viewers (their study is limited to television) deliberately seek out spoilers. They find that this correlates with a lower level of involvement in the show. Curiosity about the show may be one of the reasons for this behavior. Johnson and Rosenbaum (2015) review the psychological literature on spoilers and viewers preferences and report on several studies that show that spoilers may enhance the experience of a narrative, although their experimental evidence is not consonant with that idea.

## The Spoiler Alert Video

*Key & Peele* is the title of a sketch comedy show on Comedy Central, created by Keegan-Michael Key and Jordan Peele. There have been five seasons from 2012 to 2015. Comedy Central also has a YouTube page for the series.

*Key & Peele* has received several awards. The sketch comedy format is similar to the *Chappelle's show*. The "Spoiler alert" video was posted in 2015 and has received 11 million views as well as several thousand comments. Key and Peele's comedy is generally very much about race issues (Bradbury, 2018), but in this case, all the characters on the sketch are black and race does not figure prominently in the skit.

The video opens with two couples, sitting in an outdoor patio, eating dinner and having a casual conversation. The first male speaker says, "What did you think of the season finale of *Game of Thrones*?" and the two women seem very excited to discuss the topic, but the second male speaker stops him and states, "I am reading the books." Banter ensues, but everyone agrees that the topic is off limits. The first woman brings up a Russell Crowe thriller, but the second woman stops her saying she and her husband are going to see the movie the next day. So, again, they all agree the topic is off limits. The first woman makes a "zip up my lips" gesture. The next topic brought up by the first male speaker is "who won the game" but of course the second speaker says he's going to watch it later. A long pause ensues. One of the women brings up the weather, but the other woman nixes the topic because they are having a barbecue and she does not want to "stress about the weather." An even longer pause ensues. One of the men starts commenting on the food but one of the women stops him because "she has not tasted it yet." At this point, several of the characters try to come up with some topic of conversation, but stop themselves after a few words, when they presumably realize that they would be producing a spoiler. After another long pause filled with phatic noises, one of the men comes up with the topic of cheesecake. There is general agreement that cheesecake is good. The first man emphatically say that he has been watching his cholesterol, but "What the hell, we're all gonna die some day anyway, right?!" To this statement, all the other guests react as if he had just produced a massive spoiler, and one of them says, "You just ruin it every time!" The last line, as the other three guests walk away is, "How would you not know that that was taking place?"

The humor of this piece is, at one level, quite simple: Key and Peele take a real concern, not spoiling someone's pleasure in reading a book or watching a movie or sports event, and exaggerate it to increasingly unlikely topics: the weather, the food and eventually human mortality. However, at another level, the skit harks back at the satire of the upper class we saw in Chapter 7. As you will recall, I argued that *Stuff White People Like* is not primarily about race but targets the educated upper middle class. Here too, I believe that this is the case. First, let's note that race is effectively neutralized by the fact that all four participants are black. Indeed, the topic never comes up in the discussion.

However, from the setting of the video, the couples are clearly quite affluent, they eat *al fresco*, they drink wine in fancy wine glasses, they speak standard English and they have middle-class tastes (*Game of Thrones*, Russell Crowe). Their exaggerated sensitivity to the courtesy of avoiding spoilers is entirely in line with the "woke" esthetics of *Stuff White People Like*, albeit it this would be "stuff white people do *not* like."

# Chapter 10

# SATIRICAL NEWS WEBSITES AND FAKE NEWS

Consider the following headlines:

1) Louisiana Man Arrested for Possession of Too Many Sharks, Meth in Bayou
2) Drunk Partygoer Falls Off Roof Attempting To Jump Off Roof
3) Embryos can be listed as dependents on tax returns, Georgia rules
4) Police Did Great Job, Police Say
5) Upset over LGBTQ books, a Michigan town defunds its library in tax vote
6) Study Finds Fewer Millennials Choosing To Become Good Parents
7) Meta warns its new chatbot may not tell you the truth
8) Biden: U.S. Won't Rest Until Brittney Griner Returned Home To Serve Marijuana Possession Sentence

Which ones are real headlines from real newspapers and which are fake headlines published in the *Onion*, the famous satirical news website? The answers are in this footnote.[1] The very fact that a quiz like the one above is possible and the very real probability that you—dear reader—will get some of the answers wrong is one of the biggest differences between humor in the digital age and humor "before the internet." But before we get to this, let's back up a little and start by defining what defines satirical news as opposed to fake and real news.

Wikipedia's definition of Satirical News Website is as follows:

(…) satirical news websites (…) have a satirical bent, are parodies of news, which consist of fake news stories for mainly humorous purposes. The best-known example is The Onion, which was started in 1996.These

---

1 The odd numbered items are real news; the even numbered ones are fake.

sites are not to be confused with fake news websites, which deliberately publish hoaxes in an attempt to profit from gullible readers. News satire is a type of parody presented in a format typical of mainstream journalism, and called a satire because of its content. News satire is not to be confused with fake news that has the intent to mislead. News satire is popular on the web, where it is relatively easy to mimic a credible news source and stories may achieve wide distribution from nearly any site.

https://en.wikipedia.org/wiki/List_of_satirical_news_websites

Wikipedia gets it right: satirical websites pretend to be the news to satirize the news or the newsmakers. Fake news websites pretend to be the news to trick their readers into believing something false or misleading and/or profit from their attention, either through advertising exposure (ads on the same page) or pay-per-click payments.[2]

## What Do Fake News, Urban Legends, Memes, and Jokes Have in Common?

What do satirical news, fake news, urban legends, memes and joke share? First of course is their virality: they spread, they are repeated, re-tweeted, reposted. Second, the assumption of tellability (i.e., the fact that the text is worth telling, has an intrinsic interest). Fake news, urban legends and the rest are intrinsically interesting, unheard of, novel, remarkable, at least on the surface. They are also fictional, hence not real.[3]

By definition, urban legends and fake news put the teller in a position of one-upmanship toward their audience who cannot have heard the item before (since it is a legend/fake) or, alternatively, if the audience has already been exposed to the legend/fake news they face two radically different paths: (1) confirming the story, which means mutually reinforcing the belief of the

---

2 Pay-per-click is revenue stream in which "an advertiser pays a publisher (typically a search engine, website owner, or a network of websites) when the ad is clicked" (Wikipedia, https://en.wikipedia.org/wiki/Pay-per-click).

3 We need to be careful here: in the original sense of meme, as defined by Dawkins, a meme is any bit of information, factual or not. So for example, the meme that being hit by lightning is dangerous is factually correct. In the internet sense of meme, memes are fictional, even if they may be based on actual events. For example, Kanye West did in fact interrupt Taylor Swift at the MTV Video Music awards 2009 show, but of course the "Kanye Interrupts" memes (https://knowyourmeme.com/memes/kanye-interrupts-imma-let-you-finish) are fictional remixes. In passing, a mashup version in which Kanye interrupts Hitler's tirade in the bunker (see Chapter 17) is my personal favorite.

teller and their audience or (2) challenging the veracity of the story, which requires considerable effort (fact checking is of course more expensive than making something up or repeating a story one has heard). Jokes and memes require a certain degree of "work" in order to "get" the joke or meme. Often all that is required is familiarity with the format of the text and knowledge of some stereotypical information; in some cases more advanced inferential processing is required. In any event, all these types of texts share a certain, admittedly small in some cases, advantage to the first mover (the teller).

It is well known that urban legends possess a moralistic undertone: "Consumers circulate urban legends in order to communicate negative information involving moralistic stories possessing an ironic twist" (Donavan et al., 1999, p. 23). Memes attract attention to their subject, as we saw in Chapters 4 and 6. Jokes reward the hearer with amusement. What is the point of satirical fake news?

Before we answer that question, we need to disentangle the complex knot of the expression "satirical fake news." Each of the three words is, by itself, a conundrum. Together they are a conundrum, wrapped into a riddle, encased in mystery. Just to make our lives easier, let's assume that the "fake" and "news" parts of "satirical fake news" are non-controversial. To be clear, they are not, especially the fake part and people have distinguished between misinformation and disinformation,[4] but we need to simplify. So, we will assume that "news" is some information about the world, that is somehow determined to be worthy of sharing (i.e., it's tellable) and that "fake" means it did not happen in the real world. This leaves satire.

Satire is famously hard to define, possibly undefinable (Condren, 2012). However, some general points can be agreed upon, at least on the current understanding of the concept: (1) satire involves a humorous component; (2) satire involves a critical attitude toward a target; (3) satire is often associated with social criticism (Simpson, 2003). We can add that satire is often associated with irony and sarcasm, but does not have to be. So the purpose of satirical fake news would be to amuse by satirizing society, through the creation of fake news, which often involves an ironical stance, but don't have to do so.

Satirical news, memes and jokes are popular. Readers/viewers seek out memes and jokes, as the many collections that can be found online attest, and as we know, contribute to their distribution. Clearly satire is also in much demand, as evidenced by the commercial success of the *Onion*, *The Babylon*

---

4 Misinformation is information that is factually incorrect, but the person producing it may believe that misinformation to be factual; disinformation is misinformation knowingly and deliberately propagated (Guess & Lyons, 2020).

*Bee* and many other websites. In fact, I collected from various sources a list of satirical news websites, worldwide. The list is 132 entries long. It is available here: https://salvatoreattardo.substack.com/p/the-rise-and-fall-of-satirical-news. Even allowing for the fact that 46 of the entries were no longer active, that leaves 86 active satirical news websites, which is a clear sign that there is a strong demand for satirical news. Moreover, despite my best attempt, it is likely that the list significantly undercounts existing websites, especially outside the United States. Another trend that seems to emerge from the data is that increasingly satirical news websites are targeting niche markets: for example, sports, air travel, the mennonites, the military, the medical profession, etc. Another, possibly related trend is the appearance, especially after 2015, of right-wing satirical news websites. We will tackle this aspect in Chapters 22–23.

We are now in a position to tackle the question of how the digital age and the consequent move of culture largely online have affected the boundary between real and satirical news. Brodie (2018) argues that fake news items are hoaxes or practical jokes or more plainly lies, because they "employ [...] the form of the newspaper article, for centuries our default public genre for describing objective reality both through its explicit adverting to sources and data and through the aridity of its disinterested prose style" (p. 452). Brodie here goes back to the point that humor is violation of the principle of cooperation, albeit a short term one, in this case of the maxim of quality which suggests that speakers should tell the truth, if they wish to communicate effectively. However, the humorist satirizing the news wishes to communicate humorously, not effectively. In other words, they are willing to sacrifice the truth of what they say to make a point or just to get a laugh, while pretending to be news, by utilizing the stylistic and rhetorical trappings of serious/real news.

## That Time that the *Onion* Fooled China's *People's Daily Online*

The story referenced in the title of this section is in fact true (CNN, 2012). On November 28, 2012, CNN reported that the *People's Daily Online*, a Chinese online newspaper, had reprinted parts of the *Onion* article followed by a gallery of pictures. They subsequently removed the article, but the CNN story shows a screenshot of the page. This is not an isolated case: there are many examples of *Onion* stories that have been taken at face value (i.e., have been read as true news). Holland and Levy (2018) report also examples from the Iranian press, the *New York Times*, and Fox News. Brodie reports the Westboro Baptist Church (a notorious hate group in the United States) and a Republican senator. Wikipedia has a long list of other such cases: https://en.wikipedia.org/wiki/The_Onion#Print_edition_(1988–2013).

Brodie (2018) argues that the shift from a print newspaper (which is the format in which the *Onion* appeared originally), to a website, to finally links in Facebook or other sites brings about a decontextualization of the item, which makes identifying the satirical intention more difficult: when a story appears along other obviously fake stories, we can determine pretty easily that the story is fake, but if it appears alone in a friend's feed, the only cues to the satirical intent are internal and are thus much easier to miss. In fact, these examples of confusion, in which the reader misses the satirical nature of the text (or in other words "failed humor"), are so common that there exist entire subreddits cataloguing the mistakes of various sizes: for example, https://www.reddit.com/r/AteTheOnion/ (which has 550,000 members, as of August 13, 2022) and https://www.reddit.com/r/theonionfacepalm/ (1,200 members).

This erosion of the fact/fiction boundary constitutes then a significant difference between satirical news in the pre-digital era and satirical news in the Web 2.0 era.

Johnson et al. (2010) and Skalicky (2019) report that sometimes people struggle to identify satire. For example, Skalicky reports that people with more knowledge about the world do better. Leporati and Jacklosky (2021, p. 25) argue that their college-age (Gen-Z) students struggle with satire because "they inhabit a world where it is increasingly difficult to tell the intention of a piece of writing, where it seems increasingly difficult to distinguish truth from 'fake news'." They are not alone: Skalicky and Crossley (2019) find that satire in *Onion* titles is harder to process and moreover that older people have much more trouble than younger people. The above highlights the need to be part of the in-group in order to get the joke: if you are too young or too old, or just not in the know, you are more likely to miss the cues and hence the humor.

A further consideration is that in the past few years reality has taken a turn for the worse and things that would have seemed impossible a few years ago are now commonplace. Indeed, there is an active subreddit https://www.reddit.com/r/nottheonion/ that lists true news stories that are so absurd that they seem to have been invented by the *Onion*. For example, on August 4, 2022, a story by the title of "Houma man arrested in possession of too many sharks, meth in Oyster Bayou, LDWF says" was published by the WAFB9 channel website in Louisiana. https://www.wafb.com/2022/08/04/houma-man-arrested-possession-too-many-sharks-meth-oyster-bayou-ldwf-says/?fbclid

One could be forgiven for thinking this was a satirical headline. It is not.

## Follow the Money: The Case of *The Daily Currant*

There is further twist on the issue of the fake/true news and satire: as it turns out, the road from satirical news to clickbait is short and paved with money. If one is willing to uncooperatively state an untruth for fun, they may be just as willing to do so for money. As early as 2014, according to Rensin (2014), some satirical news websites had started cashing in by further blurring the boundary between satirical fake news and plain fake news. Rensin described *The Daily Currant*, which is no longer active, as "a fake-news site (…) entirely devoid of jokes. (…) an ad-driven clickbait generator." Essentially, what the *Daily Currant* did was create a fake story that may be taken equally as a joke or a serious bit of news, with the purpose of generating revenue through clicks (which are counted as traffic and indirectly generate revenue through ads). An example reported by Rensin is indicative: "Obama Pledges $700 Billion Bailout of VA." This is false, because the president Obama did not in fact do so, but it is also laughably false because, as Rensin informs us, the entire VA budget was 139 billion in 2013. Is it satire? Is it funny? Rensin reports that the article itself was not very funny. In any event, the point is that it does not matter as the title is designed to catch the eye of an anti-Obama reader, who will be outraged and is likely to click on the link or share it further on social media.

Rensin may be right about the lack of humor of that specific story, but the *Daily Currant* did hit several comedic home runs. While the site is no longer operative, the Wikipedia web page dedicated to it reports several very amusing examples: in 2012 they reported that Rick Santorum, a notoriously homophobic Republican politician, had been caught using Grindr, the gay dating app. That's not that funny (although it has a script opposition and a logical mechanisms of reversal, so the fundamentals are there), but the *Daily Currant* caps the joke by claiming that Santorum justified himself saying he thought the app was used to find the nearest coffee shop, which plays on the "grinder" ambiguity. The silliness of the excuses echoes the widely ridiculed "wide stance" excuse proffered by Larry Craig, another Republican senator, who was caught soliciting homosexual sex in a bathroom stall at the Minneapolis airport (https://en.wikipedia.org/wiki/Larry_Craig_scandal). With all due respect to Rensin, that's funny.

Other similarly amusing fake news included George Bush accidentally voting for Obama, because he could not figure out the voting machine, economist and Nobel prize winner Paul Krugman filing for bankruptcy (a nice reversal mechanism at work there) and "Marijuana Overdoses Kill 37 in Colorado on First Day of Legalization" which includes quotes from *Breaking Bad* characters passed off as real people. So was the *Daily Currant* (or rather its editor Daniel Barkley) satirical or not? It may be that the intention was there but that it failed to come across, due to the lack of markers. Ultimately, according to Thomas (2016) who quotes an interview with Barkley, it was the negative criticism that led him to discontinue the website. In the interview, Barkley claims he even contacted some academics (humor scholars) to check with them whether what he was doing was satire or not. So Barkley may have been genuinely trying to be funny—or he may have been lying about that too. If we recall the finding that young people and older people struggle to understand satirical news, we may be inclined in believing Barkley was indeed sincere.

Gillin (2017) contains further analyses of other websites, including RealNewsRightNow.com, also no longer active and quotes sources that claim that a fake news site can generate up to $40,000 a month in revenue. With these sort of fake news websites pretending to be satire (it is tempting to call them fake fake news), the humorousness is merely a fig leaf to be able to claim that they are not, in fact, simply lying. It is significant that Zeng et al. (2020), for example, include these types of websites in their study of "ads [that] use misleading, deceptive, and in some cases illegal practices—impacting users financially, wasting their time and attention, and spreading scams, misinformation, and malware."

## The Cues for Satirical News

How do we identify satirical news? An important cue is exemplified in the *Onion*'s telling of trivial stories as if they were newsworthy. This is seen most vividly in the "area man" stories. This type of news violates the tellability of the news. Take the following example:

Area Man Locked In Protracted Battle With Sweatshirt Neckhole
https://www.theonion.com/area-man-locked-in-protracted-battle-with
 -sweatshirt-ne-1819577252

Obviously, this is a commonplace incident which happens all the time. It is also trivial in the extreme. It does not even make it to the level of irrelevance of the famous journalistic aphorism of "dog bites man." Yet, the *Onion* treats it as newsworthy: it gives it the same treatment of "real" news: the title, a location (Gary, IN) emphasized (here in all caps), a date and time (12/01/14 2:40PM), the use of sources ("sources said"), the use of cliches such as "at press time." Brodie (2018) argues that this constitutes "moving [the story] from private to public discourse."

Exaggeration is a common trope. For example the following story

U.N. Mysteriously Disappears After Criticizing Russia https://www.theonion.com/u-n-mysteriously-disappears-after-criticizing-russia-1849574232

exaggerates the stories of Putin's critics disappearing or been found dead under mysterious circumstances by having the whole UN headquarters and its 193 representatives from member states disappear.

Incongruity, as always, is a common technique. Consider the following story:

Man At Strip Club Buffet Pays Extra To Get Private Time In Backroom With Buffalo Wing https://www.theonion.com/man-at-strip-club-buffet-pays-extra-to-get-private-time-1849435938

Here we get the incongruous opposition between two scripts: eating at a buffet and having sex with a stripper in the backroom of a strip club. This is further strengthened by some of the details in the story, for example, at the end the patron is seen with "a large obvious stain on his pants from ranch dressing" (ranch dressing vs. sperm).

Of course, among the cues of fake news are irony and sarcasm, that is, in their simplest form, saying one thing and meaning something contrasting with it, often its opposite. Consider the following rather subtle headline:

Shoplifter Always Gets Little Adrenaline Rush After Stealing Basic Necessities For Family https://www.theonion.com/shoplifter-always-gets-little-adrenaline-rush-after-ste-1849436522

In order to catch the irony of the title, one need to be familiar with the stereotype that teenage shoplifters do it for the excitement (there are in fact many other motives). The introduction of the "basic necessities for family" is not congruous with the teenager-doing-it-for-excitement expectation, but is consistent with shoplifting because of poverty (being unable to provide the basic necessities for one's family) instead. Therefore, there is an ironical opposition between the stereotype (shoplifters are teenagers doing it for the rush of adrenaline) asserted in the first part and the assertion in the second part of the headline that this shoplifter does it because she cannot feed her family (the image under the headline shows a woman putting a milk bottle in her purse). Finally, stealing for fun and stealing out of necessity evoke, again implicitly, without stating it overtly, a contrast between rich (or at least financially stable) people (stealing for fun) and poor people (stealing out of necessity). The fact that the opposition is merely evoked inferentially and the implicit critical stance toward those who hold the view that shoplifting is only done for excitement are the components of the irony in this case. On the production of irony in the *Onion*, see Waisanen (2011, p. 509), who argues along the lines above that the videos (but the argument can be extended to the written news articles as well) achieve "ironic iconicity" by juxtaposing a realistic depiction and a "slightly fantasized" version of reality.

## Conclusions

What can we conclude from the research on the *Onion* and other satirical news sites? First, and foremost, that academics cannot resist a pun on "peeling the onion."

More seriously, the impact of satirical news (on TV and on the internet) on communication has been significant. However, the boundary between real and satirical news is labile, context-bound and subject to renegotiation as behaviors that would have been unthinkable a couple of decades ago are now commonplace. For example, the news that Ted Cruz, a Republican senator, was "seen fist bumping Sen. Steve Daines on the Senate floor after [Daines] voted against advancing [a] bill" for veteran's health care (Choi, 2022) could very easily be mistaken for a satirical news item. It is not. Finally, because, by definition, satirical news are deceptive (they violate the principle of cooperation, see Chapter 3) in the sense that they "mascarade" as real news and because the markers for humor and especially satire and irony are not always obvious, detecting the satirical intent, especially out of context, can be difficult. This has led to spectacular failures to "get the joke" particularly from those who are not in "the know." This may include foreign journalists, who are literally in the out-group, but also extremists, like the Westboro Baptist Church, who hold beliefs that are "out of bounds" relative to the standards of society, or at least to the standards of the educated, sophisticated writers of satirical news.

The difficulty of figuring out what the point of satire is has a darker aspect. In Chapters 21–23 we will explore how the alt-right deliberately exploits this "grey area" to cloak its white suprematist and fascist propaganda. Relatedly, in this chapter we have not focused on right-wing satirical news, a more recent development of the genre. We will take up that topic in Chapter 21 as well.

# Part 2

# MEMES AND MORE MEMES

Part 2 is concerned with memes, arguably the most Web 2.0 innovation in humor. The section is bookended by two slightly more technical chapters, in which I deal with memetic drift and with virality and its staying power, or lack thereof. The other chapters deal with more "fun" topics, such as Boaty McBoatface, Grumpy Cat, Pastafarianism and the Chuck Norris facts.

# Chapter 11

# MEMETIC DRIFT OR THE ALLITERATION ARSONIST

In this chapter, we will describe the "Cheryl's she shed" meme cycle. The term "meme cycle" is a deliberate calque on "joke cycle" the term used by folklorists to describe groups of jokes, usually thematically related. The theoretical purpose is to engage the concept of memetic drift, which we introduced in Chapter 2, in more detail and to go beyond it by introducing the idea of semantic bleaching and considering memes as syntactic constructions as the end result of memetic drift.

**Joke Cycles**

Consider this example:

> How many Polacks does it take to screw in a light bulb? Five—one to hold the bulb and four to turn the ceiling (chair). (Dundes, 1987, p. 143)

This was the "original" light bulb joke, variants of which swept the United States in the 1960s and 1970s. Light bulb jokes were centered around the "changing a light bulb" situation, which, as everyone knows, is normally performed by one person climbing on a ladder or chair and manually screwing in the light bulb in the socket. In the jokes, an unusually high number of people were required (e.g., six or seven), which is of course incongruous, and this incongruity was partially (very partially!) justified by the fact that they engaged in a very unorthodox way of doing so, which introduced another incongruity, for example by having one person stand on a table and the other six turning the table (or worse, the ceiling). The invited inference was of course that the group of people changing a light bulb in such an inefficient and counterintuitive way must be stupid, which was confirmed by the mention of the ethnicity of the group (Polish, in the original joke). The stereotype for stupidity was thus both confirmed and served as resolution (justification) of the incongruous behavior. I discuss light bulb jokes in some detail in Attardo (2001). For the shallow nature of such groupings, see Hempelmann (2003).

What made lightbulb jokes interesting to me, as a linguist, was not so much that these jokes targeted originally Polish-Americans, and the reasons behind this and other ethnic jokes, masterfully explored in Davies (1990). Rather, I was interested by the fact that if you looked at all the variants (and there were a lot of them) you could group them in three classes:

1) the basic jokes, like the one we just described above, with many variants. Clements (1969) reports 28 versions, prior to 1969. By "variants" we mean different versions of the same joke, so for example, in the version reported by Dundes we already see two variants: in one the four men turn the chair the fifth one is standing on and in another they turn the ceiling. The variant I first heard has them on a table. The total number of people may vary or some of the word choices. However, the joke remains fundamentally unchanged.

2) a set of derivative jokes, which keeps in place several of the components of the one, what linguists call the knowledge resources of the joke, such as the question and answer structure of the text, but crucially changes several others. In particular, the targeted group may change in these jokes, so that the light bulb changing is now done by Californians, or graduate students, etc. The activity itself (changing the light bulb) may be replaced by an equally trivial activity (in other words, the situation may change). However, some of the knowledge resources remain unchanged. Indeed, there must be a way for the hearer to recognize the format of the light bulb joke, because otherwise the text would not make a lot of sense. Because of this fact, I dubbed this category "intertextual" jokes, that is, they require a reference to the original light bulb joke to be fully appreciated. An example of intertextual joke would be

> How many lawyers does it take to screw in a light bulb? Fifty-four. Eight to argue, one to get a continuance, one to object, one to demur, two to research precedents, one to dictate a letter, one to stipulate, five to turn in their time cards, one to depose, one to write interrogatories, two to settle, one to order a secretary to change the bulb, and twenty-eight to bill for professional services.

3) a second set of derivative jokes that played on the expectation of a light bulb joke, but ended up delivering another joke entirely. These are called meta-jokes, because they pretend to deliver a light bulb joke, but in fact deliver another one, thus they violate the expectations of the script for light bulb joke, in a clear metatextual move.

How many lawyers does it take to screw in a light bulb?
How many can you afford?

Here the first line looks exactly like the first line of an intertextual joke, in other words a light bulb joke about lawyers, rather than Polish-Americans. Instead we do not get the expected resolution (i.e., an impractical way of performing the activity, as we saw in the previous example, where 54 lawyers are needed to change a light bulb). The frame for the joke is interrupted by another joke, one that refuses to deliver the expected conclusion and instead delivers another joke (by coercing a less salient reading of "How many does it take?" from "What is the number required to do X?" to "How many lawyers can I get to do X" and then delivering a punch line that implies greed).

## Meme Cycles

When I started looking at memes, I immediately realized that those categories that had emerged from the data 20 years before were at play in the same way, in a different set of data. With memes as well, we get an original meme (called the anchor or founder meme, see Chapter 1) which is then replicated with changes. The changes can respect the original organization of the meme (intertextual memes) or they can subvert it to create a new meme (meta memes).

Of course, I am not the first to notice that memes "travel in packs." Shifman (2014b) uses the term "group." Segev et al. (2015) use the term "families." The presence of "constants" across meme cycles has also been discussed before (see Attardo, 2020b, for a review of that literature). In Attardo (2020b) I analyzed a joke cycle called Sheryl's She Shed, which went viral in 2018–2019 (https://knowyourmeme.com/memes/sheryls-she-shed). Without going into too much detail, let's recap my conclusions there.

The anchor meme is in fact a commercial for State Farm, an insurance company. In the commercial, we see a couple, Cheryl (the name is spelled in several ways) and Victor. They look at a shed in their backyard which is on fire. The wife is on the phone with an insurance adjustor and says: "It finally happened, somebody burned down my she shed." Victor, the husband, who is holding a water hose, says: "Nobody burned down your she shed, Cheryl." He shows no affect, throughout the video. He adds: "The shed was struck by lightning," again without any affect. The agent then states that the shed is covered by State Farm. Cheryl then says: "Did you hear that, Victor? I am getting a chichier she shed." Victor says "Chichier?" with a dejected look. Cheryl replies "uhuh." and Victor responds by saying "That's wonderful news" still without affect.

While the commercial "sell" was presumably to show that Cheryl was unaffected by the fire, due to her having been insured, the viewers latched onto the lack of feeling in the husband's delivery, and the ineffective water hose he was holding. A "conspiracy theory" emerged, arguing that Victor had burned down Cheryl's she shed. Obviously, this was a "joke conspiracy" but the YouTube users responding to the video amused themselves by finding reasons for Victor's guilt. To be fair, he does look guilty, and as some of the posters on YouTube, Reddit and Facebook point out, there is no trace of a lighting storm. There were several other, just as silly, conspiracy theories. I argued that the Cheryl's she shed conspiracy theories were parodies of serious conspiracy theories, mockingly adopting "a conspiracy theorist stance in what is clearly a) fictional and b) a trivial matter." While particularly amusing, the conspiracy theory aspect of the meme cycle is not my central point. Likewise, I will ignore the fact that most of the memes are still images from the video and so are examples of trans-mediation (Jenkins, 2006; Jenkins et al., 2013).

A significant number of the memes played with various reasons why the shed burned down: that it contained meth lab, that Cheryl wanted to meet hunky firemen, etc. Some version got political, blaming either the Democrats and the Republicans for the fire. In the cases of these political versions, there is obviously an additional target that changes the otherwise politically neutral meme into a biased one. However, all these versions are still fairly close to the original meme, with the proviso that it has been trans-mediated.

Other memes are far more distant from the original. In several intertextual memes, which as you will recall present a different joke, while retaining some aspect of the original anchor meme, we see mashups with Quentin Tarantino's film *Pulp Fiction* with *Star Wars*, etc. These mashups are incomprehensible without a reference to the anchor meme.

Finally, a mashup of the Cheryl's She Shed meme and of the Disaster Girl meme achieves meta meme status. (Figure 11.1)

What starts out as a Cheryl's She Shed meme turns out to be a Disaster Girl meme. The resolution of this incongruity comes from the affordances of the original disaster girl meme (Figure 11.2), from 2007 to 2008, in which the girl is seen smiling in the vicinity of a fire.

## Memetic Drift

In order to account for the increasingly distant nature of the memes, I postulated a process of memetic drift in which an anchor meme progressively is surrounded and possibly displaced by other derived memes. The scale looks as follows:

# MEMETIC DRIFT OR THE ALLITERATION ARSONIST 115

**Figure 11.1** A meta meme: Mashup of the Cheryl's She Shed meme and of the Disaster Girl meme.

**Figure 11.2** The Disaster Girl meme.

$$\left. \begin{array}{lll} \text{anchor} \quad > \quad \text{virality (reproduction)} \quad > & \text{new memes (from the anchor)} \\ & > & \text{intertextual} \\ & > & \text{meta} - \text{textual.} \end{array} \right\} \text{memeiosis}$$

On the left we have the anchor meme. If it is reproduced it goes viral. If it is reproduced with changes we enter memeiosis (the creation of new memes). This is already some way away from the anchor. Memeiosis can then become intertextual or finally in the most distant form from the anchor meme, a meta meme. Whether this scale is psychologically real, that is, does it match the speakers' intuition on the subject, is a good question, but not one for which I have an answer.

However, I think that in perhaps a broader sense, memetic drift is very real: As I put it in my 2020 paper:

> During the process of memetic drift, memes are remixed, parodied, mashed up and altered to reflect the concerns of the culture in which the users engaging in memeiosis operate. When the rather innocuous story of Cheryl's arsonist husband is turned into political aggression (as in the anti-Democratic and anti-Republican variants of the meme), or when someone connects the completely extraneous idea of a meth lab to the suburban settings of Cheryl and Victor's home, (...) we see more about what the users are thinking about, than about the original meme. We could argue that the original meme is merely an excuse or a pretext to raise political, cultural, or otherwise newsworthy concerns.

## Semantic Bleaching

Just to be clear, I am not saying that there is a linear process through which every meme goes sequentially. What I am claiming is that through a process of accretion, in which numerous instances of an anchor meme are repeated and remixed, which is definitely not linear, eventually the original meaning of the meme is essentially lost. This process is called semantic bleaching. Bybee (2015, p. 132) puts it very clearly: "The lexical meaning is *bleached* of specificities of meaning, or generalized as specific components of meaning are lost." Her example is the Old English word "cunnan" (to know) which becomes "can" in modern English (compare "cunning" which is also etymologically related to "cunnan"). The original meaning included that "a subject possessed mental ability or knowledge" (know how). What happened is that during Middle English, the intermediate stage between Old English and present-day English, the mental aspect was lost and what remained was just the meaning of "capacity." Semantic bleaching is due to repetition and use within expanding contexts. As we have seen, memeiosis provides plenty of both.

## Grammaticalization and Constructions

Grammaticalization is the end-of-the-line in semantic bleaching. A good example is the formation of the future tense ending in Italian (and in other languages derived from Medieval Latin). In Latin the future was indicated by a verb ending: *cantabo* means "I will sing" (the suffix "-bo" is added to the root "cantar-"). These endings were lost during the Middle Ages (they were in the dark, someone put them somewhere and the rest is history). So people started using a periphrastic expression (much like one does in English saying, "I am going to sing") using the word "habeo" (I have to). So one would say "cantare habeo" (I have to sing, hence I will sing). Slowly, over centuries, the verb "habeo" in this context lost its specific meaning (was bleached) and merely retained its grammatical meaning of "future" and eventually became a suffix that now appears attached to the verb "canterò" (I will sing). So, essentially, a word that undergoes semantic bleaching, if the loss of meaning is very high, becomes so general that it becomes a grammatical marker.

Constructions are among the most abstract type of grammatical marker. For example, in English the position of a noun before or after the main verb of a sentence tells you whether the given noun is a subject or an object. In *Mary loves John*, the only reason why we know that it's Mary who's doing the loving is the position of "Mary" in the sentence. There are slightly less abstract constructions, such as *X let alone Y*, as in *Mary doesn't exercise let alone run a marathon*. The (very abstract) meaning of the *X let alone Y* construction is that there is a scale of intensity between activity X and Y and that since the subject does not engage in X they definitely do not engage in Y (Fillmore et al., 1988). Let's look now at an example of a meme's progressive semantic bleaching until it reaches the grammaticalization level.

## The "For the Better, Right?" or Clueless Padme Memes

The "For the Better, Right?," a.k.a, Clueless Padme, is based on a scene from the 2002 film *Star Wars: Episode II – Attack of the Clones* in which Anakin and Padme are having a picnic. The lines as they are stated in the meme do not actually occur in the film (much like "Play it again, Sam" does not occur in Casablanca) which means that the anchor meme is already different from the original film dialogue. However, according to Know Your Meme (https://knowyourmeme.com/memes/for-the-better-right/) the meme is "based on the film's overall theme of Anakin's progression to becoming an evil Sith" so it is fairly close to the spirit of the movie. The first instance of the meme (Figure 11.3) was posted on April 2021, still according to Know Your Meme. The dialog actually reproduces a prior meme (posted in 2019) in which the characters are a turtle and a frog. So, our anchor meme is in fact a mashup. While this is interesting, we are not concerned with that aspect.

The meme went viral and Know Your Meme catalogs about 200 different instances of remixes. In these we find the same intertextual and meta patterns we have seen in Cheryl's She Shed and in the Bernie memes. Thus for example, we get a Netflix version, a topical version concerning the Russo-Ukrainian war and a rather surreal Stalin-Lenin version. In the latter, while

**Figure 11.3** The Anchor meme "For the better, right?"

the organization in four squares and the smiling patterns are respected, obviously the characters are completely changed, but the underlying meaning is still intact: the second character (Padme, in the anchor) comes to realize that the first character (Anakin, in the anchor) has sinister intentions (script opposition good vs. bad). We find the same patterns in the following instances, but the memetic drive and corresponding semantic bleaching has gone further. In Figure 11.7, we find a "rage comics" (Chapter 22) version, in which the "sinister intentions" implications are absent. In Figure 11.8, we see a meta version, where not only the "sinister intentions" implications are absent, but the meme "fails" to deliver a properly formed "for the better" meme. In Figure 11.9, we find a meme that not only does not have any "evil" implications, does not respect the gender (as the Stalin/Lenin version did as well), but deliberately inverts the gender roles and replaces the script opposition with a sex/no sex opposition.

Finally, in Figure 11.10, we find a "yassified" version. The "yassification" meme (https://knowyourmeme.com/memes/yassification) is complex, and in

**Figure 11.4** Netflix remix.

**Figure 11.5** Russia Ukraine War.

**Figure 11.6** Stalin Lenin version.

**Figure 11.7** Rage comics version.

**Figure 11.8** Meta version and fail.

**Figure 11.9** Sex/no sex opposition version.

**Figure 11.10** Yassified version.

fact probably conflates two separate memes, but here we are only interested in one aspect of it: the use of image filters (here blending Hayden Christiansen and Natalie Portman's faces). With this final version, it is my contention that we have reached a purely syntactic use of the meme (note the absence of text), which is used merely to provide a construction order that carries a vague allusion to the anchor and the script opposition that generates script incongruity is between the anchor see and the yassification meme (which carries a gender-fluid connotation, or as one of my students put it, LGBTQ-adjacent).

In short, the meme has become a syntactic construction.

# Chapter 12

# THE SAGA OF BOATY MCBOATFACE

In 2016, the British Natural Environment Research Council (NERC) decided to let the Internet suggest a name for a $287 million polar research ship. The poll went viral and among other hilariously inappropriate suggestions Boaty McBoatface was the winner, with 124,109 votes. The sore losers at NERC did not follow the poll, and named the ship Sir David Attenborough, but in a sop to the masses named one of the autonomous submarines on board Boaty McBoatface. The whole PR fiasco is chronicled in the Wikipedia page on Boaty; see also Rogers (2016), Golshan (2016) and Phillips and Milner (2017, pp. 164–168). What interests us in this little story is, first of all, that the risk of the PR stunt of having an open poll was predictable. This strategy is a good one, in theory: that 125,000 people might even be aware of the existence of NERC is a PR major feat, with zero cost. A publicist's dream. Indeed, Golshan (2016) reports that the NERC spokesperson was "delighted" by the fracas. The whole story itself went viral, as attested by the press coverage, including an article by the *NY Times*, *NPR*, the *Guardian* and many more. It got to the point that a British minister took a position in favor of Boaty. Of course there were numerous complaints about the refusal of the NERC to follow the results of the poll and name the boat after Sir David Attenborough. My favorite comment on the subject was the suggestion that Sir Attenborough change *his* name to Boaty McBoatface.

### Antecedents to Boaty

As I said, the risk was predictable. There had been several antecedents of attempts by various authorities to harness the internet as cheap public relations. In 2012, Slovak lawmakers in Bratislava rejected an online vote to name a bridge after Chuck Norris: "Despite 12,599 votes for the Norris name in a two-month online poll, Bratislava regional assembly decided to call the bridge spanning the Morava river and Slovakia's border with Austria the 'Freedom Cycling-Bridge' in memory of people killed attempting to escape communist eastern Europe." (Reuters, 2012)

The use of the Chuck Norris meme to mock the choice of the Bratislava Regional Assembly, which received only 457 votes, was not however the first or the largest such case. In 2011, Austin, TX, announced an internet poll to determine the name of its waste management department. The "Fred Durst Society of the Humanities and Arts" was the top pick with 29,796 votes, followed by "Department of Neat and Clean" with 2,069 votes and by Ministry of Filth, with 1,361 votes. Fred Durst is the lead singer of Limp Bizkit, the rap rock nu metal band named after a uniquely American practice consisting of a group of men masturbating over a cookie (Urban Dictionary). Durst tweeted: "I want to thank all of you who are helping me in Austin. I hope we win." (CNN Blog, 2011). His hopes were to be dashed, however. The city of Austin must have felt that was too much over the top even for a city that prides itself on being "weird" and went with the boring Austin Resources Recovery moniker (COAUtilities, 2022). Another, more disturbing, example also took place in 2012, when Mountain Dew, the successful soft drink company famous for its "Do the dew" slogan, launched a poll to determine the name of its new apple flavored soda. The poll was labeled "dub the dew" (they like alliteration, apparently). The poll was hijacked by 4chan who propelled clearly inappropriate slogans such as "Gushing Granny" and "Fapple" (a portmanteau word between "fap" [jargon for masturbation; chapter 4] and "apple") to the top 10. However, the winner of the poll was the slogan "Hitler did nothing wrong" a much less amusing option, if equally inappropriate (Huffington Post, 2012; Rosenfeld, 2012). We will return to 4chan's neo-nazi tendencies in Chapter 23.

What these examples share is (a) a successful attempt to ridicule some sort of institution wishing to harness an internet poll to generate free PR; (b) the mockery is achieved by proposing clearly inappropriate names (hence a basic script opposition between appropriate vs. inappropriate name or good vs. bad); (c) one or more of the inappropriate proposals goes viral and therefore easily wins the poll; (d) the institution disregards the results. Point (d) is important, because it shows that the perpetrators of the prank are punching up, since the institution holds all the real power and exerts it by ignoring the results of its own poll.

Incidentally, these cases are very good examples of "ideological targets" (Attardo, 2020) that is, groups or organizations which may not have a distinct membership: normally a target is someone identifiable (say, the president, or the guy falling down on the stairs, see Chapter 5). What makes a target ideological is that it is a non-specific entity, such as "marriage," or "the patriarchy," or "woke people." In our example, it is doubtful that anyone who participated in the Boat McBoatface poll knew, or cared, who the members of the NERC were or for that matter what NERC does. The only thing that matters here is that the target is institutional.

## Variations on the Boaty McBoatface Meme

Once the Boaty McBoatface saga went viral, memeiosis kicked in and remixes of the meme started appearing. Wikipedia lists a few examples, from which I have chosen my favorites, but of course there are many more:

Horsey McHorseface (Racehorse)
Trainy McTrainface (Swedish transport)
Ferry McFerryface (Australia)
Mega McMegaface (Megabus UK bus)
Floaty McFloatface (Floating bridge, Isle of Wight)
Parsey McParseface (Google grammar parser)
Electro McElectroFace (Electric racing car)
Gritty McGritface (salt truck, Shropshire)
Bossy McBossface and Swordy McSwordface (Videogames)
Skatey McSkateyface (skate part, Southend on Sea)
Stabby McStabface (sword in Minecraft) Wikipedia, https://en.wikipedia.org/wiki/List_of_Mcface_spoofs]

As you can see, this is very formulaic and works very much like a template for a visual meme: all you have to do is insert a noun, preferably in the diminutive -y form (Bob vs. Bobby), followed by "Mc," a second instance of the noun, and -face. I toyed with Booky McBookface as the title of this book, until the publisher sent me a strongly worded email... In other words, it does not take a comedic genius to generate these variants.

The story has been covered enough. We will therefore turn to trying to understand what makes the Boaty McBoatface phenomenon work and why it is perceived as funny. I think that the categories that are most relevant to understanding these questions are (1) the flash-mob and (2) the collaborative prank.

## Flash Mobs

In 2003, 100 people gathered in Macy's in New York and asked for a rug. This is reportedly the first flash mob event. It was organized by Bill Wasik to satirize New York hipster culture. By 2004, "flash mob" was in the OED, which defines it as "a public gathering of complete strangers, organized via the Internet or mobile phone, who perform a pointless act and then disperse again" ("Flash mob," n.d.). An aspect of flash mobs that the OED ignores is the element of surprise: a large part of the fun of a flash mob is to surprise the passers-by. A publicly announced flash mob is a contradiction: there has to be an essential divide between the in-group, who has been alerted to the flash mob performance and the out-group (the passers-by) who are unaware and thus surprised.

I would argue that flash mobs are a form of street art performances. In some cases, they literally involve the performance of a musical or dance piece, but can entail pantsless subway rides, pillow fights, silent raves or discos and much more.[1] Obviously, flash mobs can be used for political or even criminal purposes, but in its original form a flash mob shares the crucial features of being organized on social media, having no external purpose aside from the performance itself, with the exception of surprising the onlookers and being performed in a public space. In this respect, online flash mobs such as the Boaty McBoatface movement only differ in that the "performance" does not take place in a physical locale but in an online public space (a poll). The campaigns to rename a boat or a bridge are likewise organized on social media (I use "organize" loosely, essentially someone posts about them and they go viral), are open to all those who want to participate and provide the all-important in-group feeling, while surprising and mocking the out-group. In this latter aspect, they are akin to pranks.

## The Collaborative Prank

Folklorists have done very useful work on practical jokes and pranks. We will follow Dundes (1988) and Marsh (2015). Dundes provides us with a handy list of the folklore of practical jokes and pranks, these include April's fool, still commonly practiced, fool's errands or wild goose chases (in which a young or inexperienced person is sent off to fulfill an impossible task, such as finding a left handed wrench), and archaic popular customs such as the French charivari, which dates back to the Middle Ages, of which the American shivaree is a reflection (pranks on newlyweds), *diable à quatres* (Medieval plays in which four performers pretend to be devils and cause mayhem). What makes these practical jokes as opposed to verbal jokes is that they involve "action or activity of some kind" as well as a "butt" or victim (Dundes, 1988, p. 7), what we have called the target of the joke. Dundes further establishes three roles in the performance of a practical joke: the prankster, which performs the practical

---

1 Examples: musical piece (https://www.youtube.com/watch?v=kbJcQYVtZMo), dance piece (https://www.youtube.com/watch?v=-bnYpCiwV2Q), pantsless subway rides (https://commons.wikimedia.org/wiki/Category:No_Pants_Subway_Ride_by_city), pillow fight (https://en.wikipedia.org/wiki/Pillow_fight_flash_mob) and silent raves or discos (https://www.youtube.com/watch?v=4NX2vKf0GUU).

joke, the dupe (the victim) and finally the audience (although it is not strictly necessary). It is easy to make a connection with the practices of the Carnival, in particular the common role reversals (Bakhtin, 1965), although Dundes does not quote him.

Marsh's analysis is based on Goffman, an influential sociologist who has had a profound impact on sociolinguistics and pragmatics. Marsh defines pranks as "unilateral play" that is, "scripted play activities in which one protagonist is unwittingly contained in the play frame" (Marsh, 2015, p. 6). What does all this mean? Usually, unless it is solitary, play involves all participants to be aware of the play frame. A frame is, in this context, a way to construe a situation, what we have called a "key" (Chapter 3). Recall the example of monkeys playfully biting each other. For this situation to work as play, both monkeys have to be aware that they are not really fighting or the unaware one might bite for real which would collapse they playful key. The way there can be unilateral play is of course through deception: if one of the participants (the dupe or target) is not privy to the playful key, that is, has been deceived as to the nature of the exchange, then they may be in a play key (as far as the joker(s) and possibly the other participants, the onlookers) while they believe themselves to be in a serious key. Marsh provides several excellent examples of pranks analyzed in this framework.

Flash mobs are pranks, because they share the prankster/dupe/audience structure, even though they lack the element of deception (Marsh, 2015, p. 29). There is no deception in deciding to ride the subway without pants on. Marsh classifies flash mobs as "stunts" along with the MIT students who place various objects such as a police car, a replica of a cow or a replica of the Lunar Landing module on top of a dome 150 feet off the ground (Figure 12.1).

## A General Theory of Boaty

Poll swampings for the purpose of funny naming are disruptive of the process and antagonistic to the ultimate goal of the institution running the poll (i.e., securing cheap PR). Indeed they are rejected by the authorities, as the pranksters must have known would happen (it is particularly obvious in the "Hitler did nothing wrong Mountain Dew" flavor example, but we must not forget that Boaty McBoatface started out as a joke name). The takeovers are the equivalent of flash mobs, but in the digital domain (online). In this sense, they harness the undeniable organizing power of the internet, and specifically social media, for the purpose of creating the flash mob whose "performance" is the vote. The solidarity and sense of "belonging" (however diffuse) that comes from participating in the prank is of course an important aspect of the appeal of the performance for those who take part in it. For the onlookers, the

**Figure 12.1** A MIT prank.

incongruity of the name, the targeting of the institution and the surprising (partial) success of the prank are probably enough reasons for the undeniable interest that the Boaty saga has generated.

A significant aspect of the Boaty McBoatface phenomenon is that it shows just how porous the barrier between digital and real life is. After the kerfuffle of the naming died out, the little submarine named Boaty McBoatface went into service and was used in serious research, reported in Kennedy (2019). There is now a coin celebrating Boaty (Starck, 2018). There is a video of The Duke and Duchess of Cambridge and Sir Attenborough at the official naming, with Boaty in the foreground (see Figure 12.2). (Spillett, 2019)

In short, because of a successful prank, the real non-play world is different. Obviously, the boundary between fiction and reality has always been porous: we buy with real money real merchandise because it is associated with fictional characters, such as Pixar movies (think of Buzz Lightyear). One can order mugs or t-shirts with memes on them. This level of interplay is not surprising. We have come to expect it. This sort of phenomenon long predates the internet: just think of the iconic Che Guevara poster, created by Jim Fitzpatrick in 1968, that graced many a student bedroom, or the black cat drawn by Théophile Alexandre Steinlen in 1896 for Rodelphe Salis' Chat Noir cabaret, which is still popular. All these images are memetic. The process is simple: a bit of reality gets selected, reproduced and becomes iconic and thus enters the world of art/fiction. A bit of fiction becomes iconic and gets reproduced and thus enters reality. The difference here is quantitative not qualitative. It's the size of the impact of the meme on reality that is remarkable.

**Figure 12.2** News coverage of the Boaty events.

**Two Questions of Ethics**

Why is the Boaty prank funny, unlike the trolling of Justin Bieber fan site? One of the factors is that the Boaty activists were punching up, against an official arm of the British government, which eventually decided to disregard entirely the results of their own poll and name the boat after Sir Attenborough, thus demonstrating very tangibly where the power dynamics lay. Conversely, harassing teenagers who are presumably naive about the internet is, well, a cheap shot, that clearly punches down.

What do we make however of the fact that the Research Council decided to name a small submarine after the name they rejected for the vessel itself? I think the most plausible interpretation is that while the institution holds most of the power it does not hold all of it: in theory ultimately these institutions are funded in the public interest and therefore indirectly they answer to the public. Hence being wildly unpopular is not a prudent move for most public institutions (the Internal Revenue Service being the one exception). Therefore a prudent move is to humor the taxpayers who may be among those who participated in the poll.

The most significant aspect that the Boaty-type flash mobs is the capacity to aggregate a number of otherwise independent and unrelated participants into collective action. However, this capacity takes a negative turn, when the same tactics are harnessed for brigading (a form of harassment in which group of people coordinate an attack against someone, for example of Reddit; see Dictionary.com, 2022), or worse forms of outright harassment such as doxxing (revealing personal information, such as the residence of an internet user, which can then be used to send death threats, etc.) or swatting (a form of doxxing, by calling law enforcement against someone). These practices are collectively known as "trolling" and will be analyzed further in Part 4 of the book.

# Chapter 13

# A GENERAL THEORY OF GRUMPY CATS

The job of the humor scholar is to tackle difficult questions, which other scholars shy from. In this chapter, I will address the issue of why is Grumpy Cat funny?

## Anthropomorphism

Grumpy Cat, the feline named in the title of this chapter, was an internet celebrity. The actual name of the cat was Tardar Sauce (note the spelling). It lived for seven years (2012–2019), according to Wikipedia (https://en.wikipedia.org/wiki/Grumpy_Cat). Grumpy Cat's death was reported by the international press, for example, *The NY Times, The Guardian, Le Monde* and *Die Frankfurter Allgemeine Zeitung.*

The cat has its own website (https://www.grumpycats.com) where one can buy merchandise with the cat's likeness, such as a calendar (Figure 13.1). By any standards, Grumpy Cat is an internet star, according to Wikipedia, "As of March 5, 2019, Grumpy Cat had 8.3 million total followers on Facebook, 2.4 million followers on Instagram and 1.5 million followers on Twitter."

Having established that Grumpy Cat is better known than most people, we need to attempt to explicate the source of the animal's fame. Unquestionably its "grumpy" facial expression was the starting point of its fame. Apparently, the grumpy facial expression was the result of an underbite and feline dwarfism (Wikipedia). Be that as it may, it is unquestionable that the cat's expression looks grumpy. Here a possible explanation seems to have *prima facie* (pun intended) credibility: people recognize the expression of the cat because it matches the facial expression that in humans is associated with bad (grumpy) mood.

Now it is the case that facial expressions in non-human animals exist and have been investigated (see for example a review in Waller & Micheletta, 2013) and in the case of mammals bear remarkable similarity to the facial expressions of humans or are functionally equivalent to them, for example in

**Figure 13.1** The Grumpy Cat website.

primates the bared teeth expression is equivalent to the human smile, indicating benevolence.

The fact that some animals may display facial expressions and express emotions and desires that are recognizable to humans is probably the ultimate source of anthropomorphism, that is, attributing human-like characteristics to animals. I am taking the Grumpy Cat–type memes to be the quintessential expression of animal anthropomorphization.

Of course the anthropomorphization and human fascination with cats (and other animals, domestic and not) did not begin with the internet. Since the cat's domestication, which probably took place in Egypt before 2000 BCE (Rogers, 1998, p. 7) people seem to have been fascinated by the idea of cats (and other animals) doing "human" things. Rogers (1998, p. 10) reports that humorous anthropomorphic cats are found between the 13th and 11th centuries BCE in the Valley of the Kings: "one cat, upright on its hind legs, carries a jar and a basket; another herds ducks, another, holding a fan and a napkin, presents a roasted goose to a seated lady rat dressed in a fine pleated garment." (Figure 13.2)

This trend continued in the Middle Ages; there are plenty of anthropomorphic visual representations of cats in medieval manuscripts (see for example, Figure 13.3).

However, the cultural associations around cats were quite different, as cats were often seen as demonic creatures. In this sense, then, the grumpy cat phenomenon is truly culturally unique, in that it could only happen in a late

**Figure 13.2** Anthropomorphic cat herding geese. Egyptian Museum, upper floor, room 24, JE 63801 (Height = 11 cm), ca 1120 BC.

**Figure 13.3** Anthropomorphic cat dressed as a nun; French prayer book, ca 1490.

capitalist phase in which the practical role of the cat as mouser has largely disappeared and the existence of significant numbers of childless family units means that anthropomorphized animals (cats, dogs, etc.) can re-interpret them as members of the family. It is not uncommon in the United States to see pets being referred to as "(furry) children."

The Grumpy Cat meme flourished in the general internet-cultural milieu of LOLcats. Börzsei (2013) attributes the popularity of LOLcats "to them being a digital reimagining of anthropomorphic animals traditionally in folk culture." Animal fables were, and largely remain, a common trope. Miltner (2011) claims that people identify with LOLcats; they often see themselves in the animals, and in the situations they are facing. So, to understand our Grumpy friend, we need to understand LOLcats.

## LOLcats

As we have seen in many cases, what seems like a quintessentially internet-related phenomenon, in fact predates it. This is the case for LOLcats, as well. In 1905, Harry Whitter Frees produced captioned cat images, which were quite popular (https://knowyourmeme.com/memes/image-macros). Whittier Frees photographed other animals as well, but his preference was for kittens (Weeks, 2016).

On the internet, the LOLcats meme originated in 2006 (Rutkoff, 2007; Borzsei, 2013). On the LOLcats memes, see Buchnel (2012, pp. 38–41). Obviously LOLcats is a compound between the acronym LOL (laughing out loud) and the word "cat." LOL dates back to the early digital chat rooms. Much has been written on the semantics (the meaning) and the pragmatics (how it's used) of LOL (see Chapter 4 for a short summary).

The LOLcat memes share some typical characteristics: aside from visually representing one or more cats, they have typically some text, written in a non-standard variety that includes childish spellings and/or grammar errors; and last, are written in the same font (Impact, part of the standard Windows distribution). This is one of the reasons that memes tend to share the same "look." It is interesting to see how a series of unrelated events ended up determining the esthetics of memes.

First, in 1965, long before the Internet was a twinkle in Tim Berners-Lee's eyes, Geoffrey Lee, a British designer, designed the font Impact. The font was designed for use in titles and thus for maximum legibility and, well, impact. Initially the font was released in actual metal type. Eventually it was digitized, and the company that owned it sold it to Microsoft. In 1992, Microsoft released a digital version of Impact for its operating system, Windows.

The second event was that in the mid-1990s, Microsoft's operating system and browser (Explorer) were the clearly dominant force and so when in 1996, the World Wide Web Consortium and the Internet Engineering Task Force, two of the standards organizations that govern the internet, recommended a set of core internet fonts, the fonts in Microsoft were chosen if for no other reason for compatibility with the majority of computers. In short, those fonts became the standard fonts one could assume would be available for a web page or document. (Brideau & Berret, 2014). This is important because at the time, if your computer lacked the right font, the text would not display at all or would display as weird boxes or meaningless characters.

The third, unrelated event was the creation of image macros. According to McCulloch (2019) and to Know Your Meme (https://knowyourmeme.com/memes/image-macros) the first image macros were produced in the Something Awful online forum (https://en.wikipedia.org/wiki/Something_Awful). Originally an image macro was not an image at all: it was a set of coded instructions that could be "called" by entering a short cut (much like control-c = copy and control-v = paste). This made calling up images on the forum easier. Using the same process, overlaying text onto an image could also be automated.

These unrelated events, coincided with LOLcats memes going viral and as a result the format of the LOLcats memes, produced by image macros, became the assumed format of many memes that followed (advice animals, etc.). Image macro metonymically became the name for its products (the memes).

A final consideration which also explains the success of the Impact font in image macros is how legible it is (Brideau & Berret, 2014, p. 310; McCulloch, 2019, p. 142). That fact that it is white type bordered in black makes it legible in any background color and since the font was designed for short texts, such as titles, it is quite an apt choice for what are necessarily very short texts.

Perhaps the quintessential, and original, LOLCat meme is " I Can Has Cheezburger?" (https://en.wikipedia.org/wiki/I_Can_Has_Cheezburger%3F). On LOLcats' English, see Brubaker (2008); Leigh (2009); Gawne and Vaughan (2011); Miltner (2011); White (2020); Maddox (2022). For those who live in the eternal present of the internet, it may be difficult to conceptualize that LOLcats are passé (Sewell & Keralis, 2019). White (2020) distinguishes three "eras" of internet cats: the webcam and personal blogs period (1995–2004), the meme era (2005–2011) which includes LOLcats and the celebrity cat (2011–present), of which our buddy Tardar Sauce (a.k.a., Grumpy) is the prime representative.

Humor scholars have long claimed that human-acting animals are "endearing" and "amusing" (Critchley, 2002, p. 32; Chiaro, 2018, p. 27, 151). We will explore this through the lens of "cuteness."

## Baby Animals Are Cute (and Lucrative)

The field of cute studies (Dale, 2016) stems from research by Lorenz (1943), the founder of ethology and Nobel prize winner, who established that animals, children and more generally objects are perceived as cute if they have "large head and round, soft body; short and thick extremities; big eyes and chubby cheeks; small nose and mouth, and a wobbly gait" (Dale, 2016).

Page (2016) argues that cute animals in general are a form of "relief" from the drudgery of everyday life and that the central factor is "cuteness." In Maddox's (2023) view, the posting of cute animals is a reprieve from "doom scrolling" that is, the practice of looking at one's feed (such as Facebook) and becoming depressed because of the negative news, and more generally the social and political landscape of the 2020s (p. 94). In this sense, cute funny cats would be a form of humor relief (see Chapter 2).

While that position unquestionably reflects reality, I think it is too narrow. I would point to the widespread, at least in the United States, practice of considering one's pets as children, not merely metaphorically, but in treating them as such (e.g., dressing them up, sleeping with them, referring to them as "furry children," etc.). I would argue that much like parents and grandparents display pictures of their (grand)children, these displays of pictures (posts) have the same "boasting" function.

As Dale (2016) puts it, cuteness is not merely a biological instinct with obvious evolutionary advantages (if seeing an infant triggers a cute reaction one is less likely to harm said infant); it is also culturally mediated. In particular, this mediation comes through Japanese culture. According to White (2020, pp. 48–49), Japanese culture has had a long fascination with anthropomorphic cats, dating back at least to 1842, when artists started producing pictures of anthropomorphic cats to get around a ban against prints of kabuki actors and gheisha. The other aspect of this Japanese "connection" is the "girl culture" exemplified by the Hello Kitty character. Created in 1974, it represents an anthropomorphic cat. Aside from the anthropomorphic nature of the character, we need to only note the unquestionably "cute" features: big eyes, pastel colors, etc. In Japan this is referred to by the term "kawaii" which means "charming, vulnerable, shy and childlike" (https://en.wikipedia.org/wiki/Kawaii). There are, needless to say, all sorts of issues with gender characterization, especially when post-pubescent young women (and men) adopt kawaii looks and attitudes. Just to name one example, the so-called "Lolita fashion" consists of young women dressing as children.

Hello Kitty is owned by the Sanrio corporation and is widely commercialized. According to Wikipedia (https://en.wikipedia.org/wiki/Hello_Kitty) in 2008 there were 50,000 products with the Hello Kitty brand. Originally meant to target young women, the character expanded its reach to children and adults. According to Wikipedia, by 2014 Hello Kitty generated $8 billion revenue.

Thus the monetization of cuteness can be serious business. Anyone familiar with phenomena such as Hello Kitty and the "kawaii" culture should not have been surprised by the emergence of cute animals' memes and eventually celebrities. Patently, cuteness sells. Just consider again Tardar "Grumpy cat" Sauce's celebrity status, which is actively monetized by its owners. White (2020, p. 91) even claims that many of the most famous cats, including Grumpy Cat, share the same manager, one Ben Lashes (https://www.linkedin.com/in/benlashes/). There is even a Wikipedia page about internet cats (https://en.wikipedia.org/wiki/Cats_and_the_Internet).

## Advice Animal Memes

Not all animals are cute. I am not referring here to "nature red in tooth and claw," but to a category of memes in which an animal is seen with text above and below the image and garish background colors. We already mentioned advice dog, socially awkward penguin and philosoraptor. There are quite a few more: Confession Bear, Foul Bachelorette Frog, Insanity Wolf, Paranoid Parrot, Anti-Joke Chicken and others (Maddox, 2023, pp. 142–143). These animals share the anthropomorphization of Grumpy cat and its ilk, but not the cuteness. For example, Socially Awkward Penguin behaves in socially awkward ways that resonate with similarly socially awkward people.

Anthropomorphism has a distancing effect: by having an animal enact the human behavior there is the relative "safety" of having the behavior be mediated by the animal (Maddox, 2023). Another distancing effect comes from the fact that these are mostly cartoons of animals, although there are exceptions. Cartoons are mostly associated with children and/or teenagers (despite the existence of very mature comics—we will not address this issue which would take us too far afield) and of course the association with children brings cuteness back into play. However, cartoons are also stylized representations: they are not realistic. Mickey Mouse does not much resemble a household pest.

The trifecta of cuteness, anthropomorphic and cartoonish representation has been harnessed by the alt-right to further their agenda. In a famous example, Pepe the Frog, a cartoon character originally innocent enough, has been transformed into a vessel of racist ideology. We will discuss this in Chapter 23.

Summing up: Tardar Sauce, a.k.a., Grumpy Cat is funny because of the basic script opposition between human vs. animal (anthropomorphism) and in many cases adult vs. young, which goes back to the dawn of Western civilization and in any case long predates the internet. Because of this association with humor and lightheartedness Grumpy Cat, and many other videos of

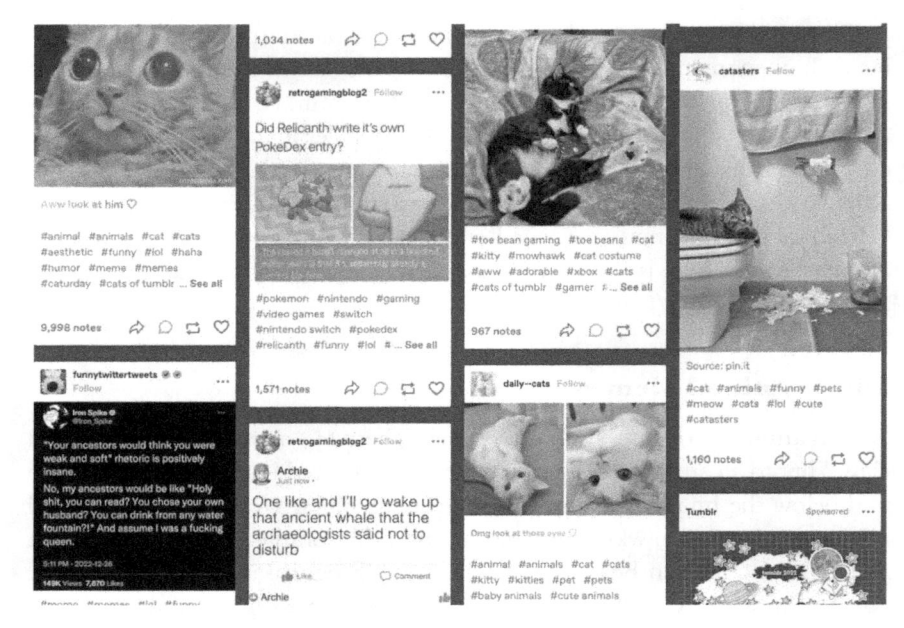

**Figure 13.4** Tumblr search for #funny.

cute animals, provide a form of relief from "doom scrolling," that is, the practice of spending excessive amounts of time absorbing negative news or posts and more broadly from the alienating effects of modern life. The escapist nature of internet cats is inscribed, or resonates to use a different metaphor, in a context in which the cuteness, "kawaii" culture and generally the infantilization of women, provide a general frame of non-seriousness or play.

As we saw, the consensus is that cats on the internet are passé. But are they? To this day, if you type #funny into Tumblr, the hip, social justice aware, LGBTQ and BIPOC-friendly platform favored by teenagers and gen z users, what you get is largely funny pictures of cats (Figure 13.4).

# Chapter 14

# THE PASTAFARIAN MEMEPLEX: JOKE RELIGION AS A SYSTEM

A memeplex is a cluster of memes. The significant aspect of a memeplex is that the memes that form it are mutually supporting. For example, in the traditional patriarchal society we have a meme that considers husbands to be dominant over wives. We also have a meme that only men are allowed to be priests or preach. Clearly, then, these two memes mutually support one another and thus it becomes easier for both memes to replicate. At the upper end of the spectrum of complexity a memeplex is an ideology. At the lower end, trends in popular music or fashion are often a memeplex: think of the early Beatles' music, their hairdos and their clothing. By providing a complete "image" their memes could spread more easily.

Pastafarianism is a humorous religion which has developed a series of related memes that support each other. Let's start from the beginning: in 2005, Bobby Henderson founded the religion to demand that Pastafarianism be taught along with evolution and intelligent design, in Kansas schools. The Kansas Board of Education had voted that "intelligent design" should be taught along evolution. Henderson's point was that if a religious viewpoint, which has no scientific standing, was going to be taught in schools, then why not teach that the Flying Spaghetti Monster (FSM) had created the Earth, fossils and all? The FSM creation myth parodies the biblical creation narrative, but includes a beer volcano and mentions that Adam and Eve live in the Olive Garden of Eden (Olive Garden is a pseudo-Italian food chain, quite popular in the United States).

Henderson posted his letter to the Board of Education on his website, where it went viral (https://web.archive.org/web/20070407182624/http://www.venganza.org/about/open-letter/). In 2006, he published *The Gospel of the Flying Spaghetti Monster*, which has sold over 10,000 copies and been translated in several languages. Other books include *The Loose Canon* (http://www.loose-canon.info/Loose-Canon-1st-Ed.pdf) and *The New Testament of The Flying Spaghetti Monster: Dinner 2.0* (https://unitarianchurchofpasta.files.wordpress

.com/2018/06/for-free-here3.pdf). Henderson still maintains an active website (http://venganza.org). According to Bauer (2018), Pastafarianism has "tens of thousands" of adherents, primarily in Western countries (North America, Western Europe, Australia and New Zealand). However, there are reports of Pastafarians in Russia, China, Japan, South Africa and Nigeria, so I suspect that Pastafarianism has reached worldwide.

Pastafarianism has undergone many legal challenges. In 2021, the European Court of Human Rights rejected the claim that Pastafarianism was a religion (Brzozowski, 2022). Venema and Alm (2022) discuss negative judicial opinions in the Netherlands and Austria. Bauer (2018), Spaschi (2021) and Venema and Alm (2022) review several other cases as well. Scholarly treatments of the FSM include Knobel and Lankshear (2007), Cusack (2010), Maćkowiak (2016), Quillen (2017) and Spaschi (2021).

**Why Is Pastafarianism Funny?**

At one level Pastafarianism is a parody of intelligent design and of Christian beliefs. However, there are many more script oppositions operating within the memeplex. It would be impossible to review all the sources of humor in the memeplex, but we can certainly trace some themes: We will focus on (1) pasta and noodles, (2) pirates and (3) religion.

Obviously, pasta occupies a central role in Pastafarian theology: let us note first that the term "Pastafarian" is a portmanteau word between "Pasta" and "Rastafarian" (a religious movement originating in Jamaica). The concatenation of the words is facilitated by the fact that "pasta" and "rasta" share four out of five phonemes. This formal similarity is then elevated to semantic connection, as is common in puns and other wordplay, and thus provides a modicum of resolution (logical mechanism). This whole process establishes a script opposition between food vs. religion, at an abstract level. From this original (rather feeble) joke, the Pastafarian canon has built a panoply of pasta-related jokes. For example, the books (chapters), in which *The New Testament of the Flying Spaghetti Monster; Dinner 2.0* is divided, are titled as follows:

The Holy Book of Lasagna; Introduction to the Church
The Holy Book of Soba; How to Worship
The Holy Book of Lo Mein; The Physical Churches of Pastafarianism
The Holy Book of Tortellini; Dos and Donts

and continues for another 12 pasta-themed chapters. Numerous appellations of the FSM involve pasta-themes references, such as "His Noodliness" and "Divine Carbohydrate." Worthy of particular mention is the "Noodly

Appendage" with which the FSM interacts with the physical world: this is how the FSM changes the carbon dating results to make it appear as if the Earth is billions of years old, for example. Many prayers end with the word "R'amen" a pun between the Japanese word for "noodle soup" (Ramen) and the Hebrew word "amen" (truth) used in ecclesiastical Latin. Figure 14.1

Another key element among the pasta-related themes in the memeplex are colanders. Obviously, colanders are part of the pasta script since they are the most common way of extracting the pasta from the boiling water, outside of professional kitchens. However, in Pastafarianism they are religious headgear. In other words, Pastafarians wear colanders on their heads. See Figure 14.2 below.

Here the humor is slightly more complex: on the one hand we have the basic opposition between cooking utensil vs. headgear (or to be simple, "hat"). Using a cooking utensil as a hat is a very basic opposition. The fact that the shape of the colander more or less resembles that of a hat (insofar you can fit your head in it) is a partial resolution of the incongruity. However, at a deeper level, we have a high prestige vs. low prestige opposition as well: religious head covers are semiotically "marked" (i.e., they are different, they stand out: think of the miters worn by Catholic bishops, or the epanokalimavkion and kalimavkion of Orthodox Christian monks, the Mexican feather headdresses, etc.). The point is to make the wearer stand out and signal their status. By replacing a high-status head cover with a low-status cooking utensil one is then also indirectly ridiculing the status claimed by the wearer of the high-status headdress and by extension of the source of that presumed exalted status.

**Figure 14.1** "Touched by His Noodly Appendage" Parody of Michelangelo's Creation of Adam. *Source*: Niklas Jansson (2015).

**Figure 14.2** Pastafarian wearing a colander. *Source*: Image by Giovanni Dall'Orto.

Specifically, the colander is one of the most controversial aspects of Pastafarianism because in many countries photos for IDs must be taken without head coverings, but exceptions are made for religious headgear. Thus the Pastafarians insist that they too should be allowed to wear a colander on their ID. In some cases, they have been successful. According to Steinhart (2017), "California, Massachusetts, Oklahoma, Texas, Utah, and Wisconsin permit residents to wear colanders as religious headgear in drivers license photos."

The presence of pirates in the memeplex is more puzzling, since after all pirates are not known to eat pasta. However, the central role of piracy in the Pastafarian Weltanschauung dates back to the ur-document of Pastafarianism Henderson's 2005 letter to the Board, in which he demonstrates the statistical negative correlation between growth in average temperature and number of pirates. In other words, Henderson argues that the decrease in number of pirates causes the increase in global temperature. This is accompanied by a graph that clearly demonstrates the linear correlation. From there pirate gear has become a common apparel at FSM events (see, for example, Figure 14.3).

## Two Decades of Pastafarianism

Interest in Pastafarianism has been fairly steady since 2005, with a couple of spikes, the largest one surrounding the victory by Lindsay Miller who was

**Figure 14.3** A screenshot from https://www.spaghettimonster.org a Pastafarian website, reporting on Pastafarians in Australia. Note the pirate hats.

allowed to wear a colander as a religious headdress on her driver's license, in Massachusetts (Durando, 2015). See Figure 14.4.

This distribution through time is an interesting difference from other memes. Let us compare the Pastafarianism interest graph, from Google Trends, to the same graph for the Grumpy cat meme (Figure 14.5).

Here we see a peak of interest around 2012, when Grumpy Cat went viral, followed by a quick drop, mitigated by a few later spikes which attest to a resurgence in interest. The largest, and final, spike is tied to the death of the cat, which was widely reported in the media. After about 2020, interest is minimal.

If we compare the level of interest for some of the memes we have examined so far, beyond Grumpy Cat, Woman Yelling at Cat, Chuck Norris Facts, Stuff White People Like and Boaty McBoatface, we see that all the above memes show a typical pattern, that is, interest in them peaks very fast (they go viral) and decays just as fast. See Figure 14.6.

Graphically this is represented by a very steep rising curve, which peaks and comes back down equally fast. We will discuss the "exponential" nature of the growth in memes that go viral in Chapter 16. It should also be noted that each meme is in fact a family of memes, that is, a meme cycle (there are hundreds of variants of "Woman yelling at cat," just to name one example).

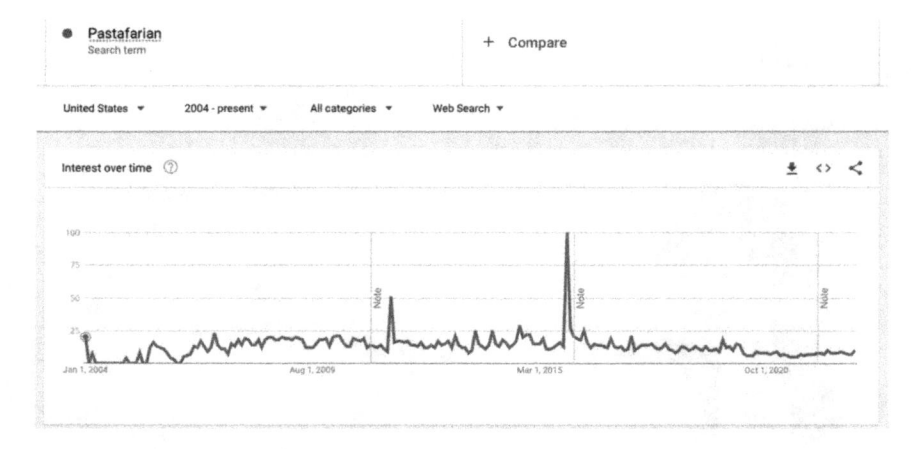

**Figure 14.4** Interest in Pastafarianism 2004–2022 (Google Trends).

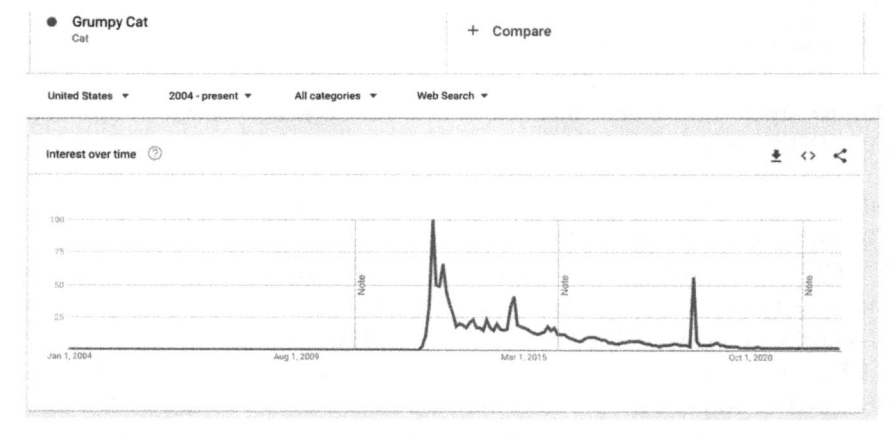

**Figure 14.5** Interest in Grumpy Cat 2004–2022 (Google Trends).

As can be seen, all the internet memes in this admittedly limited sample share the initial peak of interest followed by a sharp decline, whereas the Pastafarian memeplex shows a fairly consistent pattern of interest over the past 17 years, with a few spikes, tied to news stories.

Let's recall the distinction, introduced in Chapter 1, between Dawkinian memes, that is, memes in the original sense of "ideas that spread in the culture," and internet memes in the primary sense of humorous image accompanied by text which spreads on the internet (and beyond, of course). Even though we did not discuss this in particular detail, Dawkinian memes can be humorous. Indeed, canned jokes as they were told in social context and

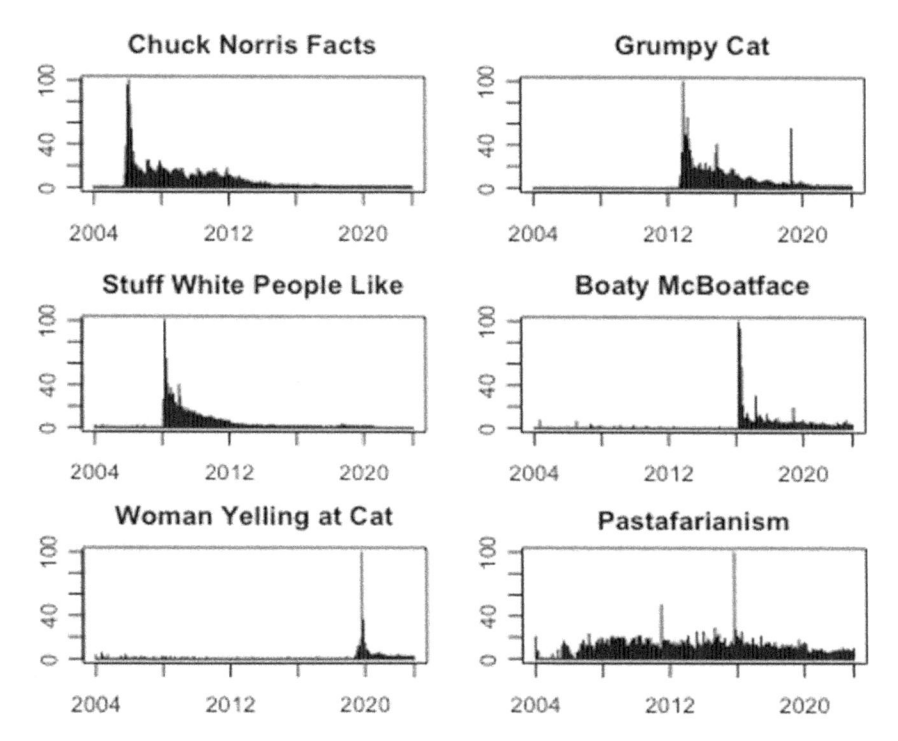

**Figure 14.6** A comparison of the chronological distribution of interest for several memes (Google Trends).

recorded by folklorists were a good example of Dawkinian memes. So, what is the difference between a humorous Dawkinian meme and an internet meme? Let's assume that both spread via the internet (again, there is nothing preventing Dawkinian memes from spreading on the internet). I wish to suggest that the difference lies in the fact that internet memes are fads (Chapter 2).

We may speculate what the difference between the two kinds of memes are. The internet memes are characterized by steep spikes in interest and correspondingly steep decline in interest, with some delayed interest, for example caused by new facts which cause a renewed surge of interest, as in the death of Grumpy Cat or the deployment of Boaty. The Dawkinian memes and the memeplex of the Pastafarian church, in particular, seem to show that, unlike internet memes, Dawkinian memes are not just fads, that is, they establish a sufficiently persistent interest such that they keep being actively present in the cultural environment. In other words, a memeplex such as the Pastafarianism one, because it consists of a cluster of mutually supporting memes, can build a sufficiently diversified set of sources of interest such that it persists, in the Pastafarian case for almost 20 years and counting. A slightly different interpretation is provided by Maćkowiak (2016) who claims that the source of the interest in Pastafarianism comes from the "conflicts and comparisons" (p. 94) with the opponents of the church, primarily Christianity but also Islam. (She reports that Turkish Pastafarians critique Islam.)

## Other Parody Religions

Pastafarianism is far from being the only parody religion. It should be noted right at the offset that I do not mean to define as "parody" a religion in a reductive sense (i.e., it is *just* a parody) but merely as a descriptive label (the religion includes a parodic element). I follow in this the example of Quillen (2017), who identifies the philosophical antecedent of the FSM in Bertrand Russell's example of the "china teapot" orbiting the sun which is undetectable by telescopes but is not therefore assumed to exist, unlike in the first-cause argument in favor of the existence of god, proposed by Thomas Aquinas. Essentially Russell says, if from my claim that there is a tea pot orbiting the sun you cannot conclude that it's actually there, from the claim that a creator exists you cannot conclude that it actually exists. (Kant had already reached this conclusion, incidentally.) Other "parody" religions, discussed by Cusack (2010) and Quillen (2017) include the Temple of the Invisible Pink Unicorn, The Church of the Subgenius (https://en.wikipedia.org/wiki/Church_of_the_SubGenius), Discordianism (which venerates the goddess Eris, whom we will encounter in Chapter 22, minus the religious aspects) (https://en.wikipedia.org/wiki/Discordianism) and many more. A list of parody religions can be found on Wikipedia (https://en.wikipedia.org/wiki/Parody_religion).

Quillen (2017, p. 206) argues that FSM is "an invented religion designed to look like a 'real' religion, to point out that all religion is, by means of the improvable beliefs that make up religion, invented." However, they do not exhaust their functionality in a negative critical stance: "They function as organizations in which like-minded individuals can associate and find commonality via shared doctrine, rituals, experiences, ethics, artistic expression, and mythology" (p. 206). Cusack (2010) argues that Pastafarianism (and many other invented religions) "rather than being exceptional and best classified as 'fake' religions are properly understood as the inevitable outcome of a society that values novelty" and consumerism (p. 141). A quick search for FSM paraphernalia on Amazon seems to bear out her claim.

## Is Pastafarianism a Joke? Pastafarianism vs. Religion

*Prima facie*, which is Latin for "face palm" or "on first impression," the question whether a religion whose deity is a plate of pasta (with meatballs) is real seems itself a joke. It certainly started out as one. However, and this is crucial, Pastafarians worldwide have fought for legal recognition of Pastafarianism as a religion, with the privileges that society attaches to that status (for example, in the United States, tax exemption). This crucially requires adopting the stance that Pastafarianism is a real religion.

The canonical texts of Pastafarianims deny that it is a joke. In a Question and Answer section of the Pastafarian website (https://www.spaghettimonster.org/about/), we read:

> *Q:* Is this a joke?
> *A:* It's not a joke. Elements of our religion are sometimes described as satire and there are many members who do not literally believe our scripture, but this isn't unusual in religion. A lot of Christians don't believe the Bible is literally true – but that doesn't mean they aren't True Christians.
>
> If you say Pastafarians must believe in a literal Flying Spaghetti Monster to be True Believers, then you can make a similar argument for Christians. There is a lot of outlandish stuff in the Bible that rational Christians choose to ignore.

Steinhart (2017, p. 1) is a serious essay by a philosopher arguing that Pastafarianism has all the tenets of a "real" religion: "Pastafarianism shares so many features with legally recognized religions that it both is a religion and deserves legal recognition." Among the features, we can list "public displays of community symbols," "perform social ceremonies" such as weddings and regular meetings, "perform charitable and philanthropic work," engage in proselytizing and seeking legal recognition for their practices. According to Spaschi (2021), "All the five criteria [delineated by the cognitive science of religion] are successfully satisfied by the Flying Spaghetti Monster religion."

Referring to a case in which a federal judge rules Pastafarianism was not a "real" religion, Feldman, a law professor at Harvard, states: "The court may not have gotten this case right. Yes, Pastafarianism was born as a parody. But that parody came to be accompanied by rituals, adherents and beliefs. Those are some of the key sociological factors that go into a description of religion." (2016). Spaschi (2021) concurs: in his view the FSM "has, from the point of view of the cognitive science of religion, a similar formal structure as the great historical religions of humanity."

Steinhart concludes his essay, which is a lengthy discussion of the legal case and the criteria used in the legal opinion to determine whether something is a religion, as follows: "I have shown that Pastafarianism shares many salient features with other religions. These features are not merely superficial; on the contrary, they are theologically deep. Pastafarianism is a real religion. It deserves legal recognition" (2017, p. 10). In conclusion, since Pastafarianism is indistinguishable on theological, social and legal grounds from any other religion, then it follows that it is just as "real" as any other religion.

Leaving aside the legal status of Pastafarianism, since after all the number of religions that have not been recognized by states is probably the same as those that have been, we will briefly address the real thorny question of what differentiates Pastafarianism from other religions, if anything.

A naive assumption is that quite simply Pastafarianism is not a revealed religion, whereas Christianity, Islam and others are so. Of course this begs the question, because we have no evidence of the revelation from outside the revelation itself. It should be noted that the question is not of whether a historical Jesus, Mohammed, Mani, Bahá'u'lláh or Joseph Smith existed, but whether some divine entity manifested themselves to them and "dictated" a message or teaching for them or their followers to write down or convey orally. In short, if you believe in the existence of a god with the quality of personhood, which is necessary to "manifest/speak" themselves, then you can believe a revealed religion. However if you do not, then nothing in the texts of a revealed religion can convince you that you should accept it, since the very foundation of the revelation is missing.

The parodic aspect of Pastafarianism is not necessarily an issue: Venema and Alm (2022) pointedly ask, "Might Jesus not have been regarded a parodist by first century Jews?" Indeed there is plenty of mockery in the Bible. For example when Jesus states that it's easier for a camel to go through the eye of a needle than for a rich man to go to heaven (Matthew 19:23–26) the blatant impossibility is humorous (and indeed the disciples are "astonished"). After all, Jesus could have said "it's unlikely." Why go to the trouble of using a metaphor, if not to mock the pretension of the rich man asking how to get into heaven? Another example is Jesus's "snappy" line against the Pharisees when they question the fact that Jesus's followers are gathering food and "He said to them, 'Have you not read what David did when he was hungry?'" (Matthew 12:3). Here King James's version softens the blow; the Greek is "anagignotes" that is, "don't you remember?" Recall that the Pharisees were experts at interpreting scriptures. To ask them if they have not read or do not remember a Biblical passage is the purest sarcasm, that is, mocking irony. In short, the criterion of humorous or mocking scripture cannot be considered a priori disqualifying for a religious text.

## Conclusion

In conclusion, we have seen that Pastafarianism belong to a surprisingly large number of new fictional religions that have emerged in the past 60 years. Whether the consumerist nature of these churches is the defining aspect of the phenomenon, as argued by Cusak (2010) or whether the parodic aspect predominates, as Quillen (2017) argues, it remains that the memeplex nature of the Pastafarian/FSM memes strengthens and facilitates their diffusion and retention. Pastafarianism seems to have endured long enough to have established itself as not just a faddish meme but as part of the cultural tapestry of Western culture. Certainly by the complexity of the belief system, the rich set of texts and references, the numerous groups, which we have barely hinted at, Pastafarianism has developed enough cultural heft to endure. Currently, Pastafarianism is not considered a "real" religion, at least in most legal systems and in common parlance. However, when we approach the matter from a dispassionate, non-partisan stance, Pastafarianism is not easily differentiated from other religions. Whether this is seen as an indictment of the "serious" religions or as a success of the "joke" religion, remains to be seen.

# Chapter 15

# WHEN CHUCK NORRIS IS WAITING, GODOT COMES

The Chuck Norris Facts are a cycle of jokes/memes which revolve around Chuck Norris's invincible, superhuman strength. It can be seen as the latest incarnation of the "tall tale" of the American hero, such as Paul Bunyan, the gigantic oil driller/lumberjack of Western folklore, John Henry, the African-American steel-driver who beat a steam-powered drilling machine, and of course Davy Crockett. However, we will argue, that while the tall tale spirit is still present in the Chuck Norris Facts, a more complex analysis is needed.[1]

Chuck Norris starred in *Walker, Texas Ranger* a TV series inspired by the film *Lone Wolf McQuade*, also starring Chuck Norris as a member of the Texas Rangers. The series aired between 1993 and 2001. The series is known for its corniness and its main attraction seems to be that of seeing Chuck Norris/Walker kick criminals in the face. (https://en.wikipedia.org/wiki/Walker,_Texas_Ranger#cite_ref-12). In 2010, then governor Ricky Perry made Chuck Norris an honorary Texas Ranger for bringing "renewed attention to our Ranger corps" (https://www.texastribune.org/2010/12/02/gov-perry-designates-chuck-norris-honorary-ranger/).

### A People's History of Chuck Norris Facts

The fundamental ambivalence of the Chuck Norris Facts is evident from the very beginning: in 2004, NBC, the TV network on which the show *Late Night with Conan O'Brien* aired, acquired the rights to *Walker, Texas Ranger*. This inspired the *Late Night with Conan O'Brien* to run a gag in which Conan would

---

1 A collection of tall tales, including Davy Crockett, John Henry and Paul Bunyan stories, can be found in Osborne (1991) and Blair (2018). Felton (1947) is a collection of Bunyan tales. See Quam-Wickham (1999) and Edmonds (2010) on Paul Bunyan. On John Henry, who was called the black Paul Bunyan, see Dorson (1965) and Nelson (2006). On Davy Crockett, see Lofaro (1985).

play a clip from *Walker, Texas Ranger* by pulling a "Walker, Texas Ranger Lever" (a comically red and yellow stick). Know Your Meme describes the clips as "comically over-the-top scene[s]." It is clear from Conan's introduction and the laughter from the audience that the intention here is to ridicule the show, not to aggrandize it. The skit continued for a while and Mr. Norris even appeared on *Late Night with Conan O'Brien* firing a prop gun at Conan O'Brien.

In 2005, the Vin Diesel movie *The Pacifier* was released. The premise is that a Navy-SEAL is tasked with protecting five children. The film was not a success. It has a Rotten Tomatoes score of 21 percent (see Figure 15.1).

According to Know Your Meme, Something Awful forum member ScootsMagoo started a thread titled "Post Your Vin Diesel Facts." Heavily driven by the laughable premise of the film, many members of the forum chimed in on the thread with a slew of tongue-in-cheek factoids, glorifying the actor as the archetype of a modern-day tough guy.

Examples of Vin Diesel facts include: When Vin Diesel gets pulled over he lets the cop off with a warning; Vin Diesel coded the Google search engine in his sleep; Vin Diesel has two speeds: walk and kill. Vin Diesel played Russian Roulette with a fully loaded gun and won. It is easy to see that these are essentially Chuck Norris facts, before they existed. According to Know Your Meme, the Vin Diesel Random fact generator garnered over 10 million hits in one month.

In Figure 15.2, we can see the earliest capture of the Vin Diesel Random Fact generator, as captured by the Wayback Machine, on February 11, 2006. (http://www.4q.cc/index.php?pid=fact&amp;person=vin ) The Chuck Norris fact generator was a spinoff of the Vin Diesel generator, as can be seen from the number of facts: in 2006 there are 4,633 facts in the Vin Diesel generator, 3,128 in the Mr. T generator and a mere 2,892 in the Chuck Norris generator. Of course, the Chuck Norris Facts went viral around 2006 and maintained a certain amount of interest until the mid-2010s, whereas the Vin Diesel Facts or the Mr. T Facts are now forgotten. This can be seen

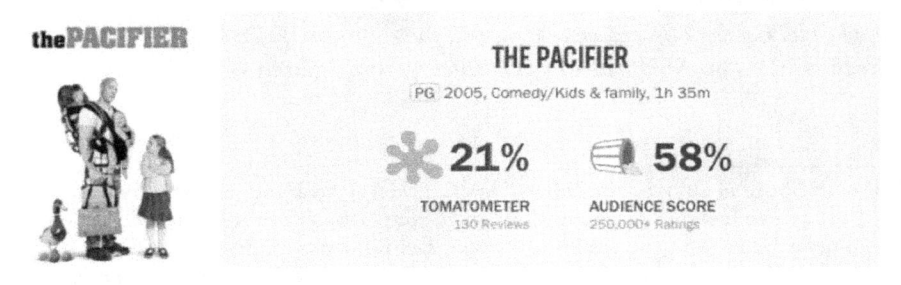

**Figure 15.1** *The Pacifier* (2005).

WHEN CHUCK NORRIS IS WAITING, GODOT COMES    153

```
We have facts on many people. Currently you can read facts about these people:
4633 facts in the Vin Diesel database.       Top 100 facts about Vin Diesel
3128 facts in the Mr. T database.            Top 100 facts about Mr. T
2892 facts in the Chuck Norris database. Top 100 facts about Chuck Norris
Browse all Facts in Database                 All Time Top 100 Facts
```

**Figure 15.2**  Facts about Vin Diesel, Mr. T and Chuck Norris, in 2006.

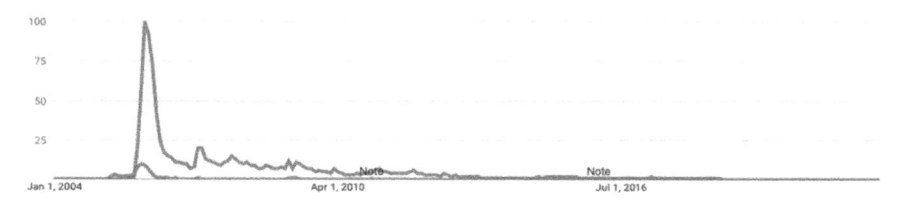

**Figure 15.3**  Interest in Chuck Norris (blue) and Vin Diesel (red) facts.

in Figure 15.3 below, from Google Trends, where the popularity of Chuck Norris Facts (Blue Line) peaked in January 2006 (that's what the 100 score represents). The red lighter line is the Vin Diesel Facts. The taller blue line crosses over the red line in October 2005.

After the popularity of a meme peaks, the meme becomes "dank." This means it's been overused, or just that the trend is past. The fallout of favor is just as fast as the viral spread in the popular phase. The meme is no longer "cool." However, this does not mean the end of the life of the meme. Mainstream media and other "uncool" agents may use the meme. In the Chuck Norris Facts case, there is strong evidence that the meme had gone "dank."

According to Know Your Meme, two factors determined that the Chuck Norris Facts had lost its cool. First, *Family Guy*, a relatively mainstream TV show, in the episode "Boys do cry" had a cameo by a cartoon Chuck Norris, in which the Dad (Peter) repeats a Chuck Norris fact ("Chuck Norris is so tough that there is no chin under his beard, there is only another fist.") Brian (the dog) replies "That's ridiculous" and gets punched by Chuck Norris' chin/fist. (The clip is available at https://www.youtube.com/watch?v=8WtZxZzFs58.) Significantly, the gag is introduced by Lois (the mother) who shows a *Walker, Texas Ranger* needle point she was given. This clearly shows the dank nature of the memes at this point. It is worth mentioning that the entire episode is a satire of Texas, so *Family Guy* seems to be making fun of the memes.

Second, in 2008, a Republican candidate, Mike Huckabee, aired an apparently serious ad in which Chuck Norris endorses him. Huckabee is seen saying that his border plan consists of two words: "Chuck Norris." He also repeats the chin/fist joke and other Chuck Norris Facts. The entire ad can be seen here: https://youtu.be/MDUQW8LUMs8. Clearly, being used in a political ad is as mainstream as you can go.

This was not yet the end of the line for the Chuck Norris Facts. In 2017, Chuck Norris Facts started circulating in which the bottom line of the meme had been cropped out. This is an example of meta humor: the memes become funny because they do not deliver the expected joke (see the meta-humor discussion in Chapter 11). An example of these cropped memes appears on Imgur (https://imgur.com/gallery/Qute8) with the title "Chuck Norris memes are 100X funnier without the bottom caption," as can be seen in Figure 15 4.

Summing up, the Chuck Norris Facts meme cycle is great example of memetic drift, that is, the change process whereby the original context and meaning of a meme is progressively lost as the meme becomes more abstract.

phase 1: Chuck Norris Facts memes: hyperbolic statements of strength and power and/or mockery of the Walker, Texas Ranger character.
phase 2: Chuck Norris Facts memes jump the shark (use in TV series, Huckabee's political ad, etc.). The memes can be used to comment on any issue of interest to the users (detachment from original meaning).
phase 3: Chuck Norris Facts memes without the bottom line (the memes achieve complete meta-status). See Figures 15.4 and 15.5 below.

As an example of basic memetic drift, we can consider this recent meme (Figure 15.6). Obviously, since the meme was produced almost 20 years after the 2006 peak of Chuck Norris Facts memes, this is a revival of the original memes; however, it fits in very closely with the original memes: the

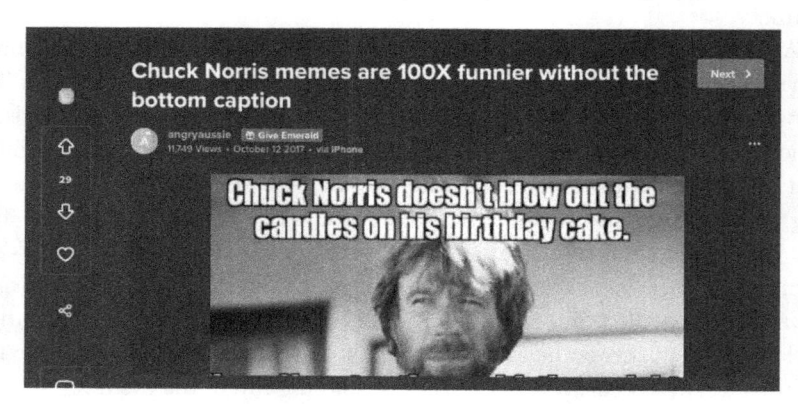

**Figure 15.4** Cropped Chuck Norris fact.

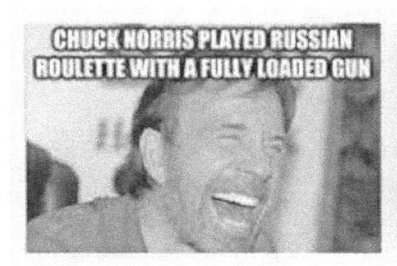

**Figure 15.5** Examples of Chuck Norris Facts Without the Bottom Line.

**Figure 15.6** Chuck Norris and Covid-19.

theme is Chuck Norris' extreme strength/resilience. An analysis in terms of the GTVH (see the section on the General Theory of Verbal Humor, in Chapter 3) would look as follows:

*SO:* strong vs. weak + normal vs. abnormal + possible vs. impossible
*LM:* exaggeration + role reversal
*SI:* COVID-19 pandemic
*TA:* Covid virus

*NS:* Micronarrative (setup/punchline); meme
*LA:* irrelevant (but enhancers[2]: "quarantine," "virus," "exposed," and "COVID-19")

Fundamentally, the joke plays on the role reversal between virus and patient. This is the incongruous script opposition. In a normal situation, if a person has been exposed to the COVID-19 virus the person has to quarantine for 14 days. Here, because Chuck Norris is so deadly/powerful/strong, the roles are reversed, and the virus has to quarantine. Obviously, no human being is that powerful and even if one were extremely powerful, viruses cannot quarantine themselves, so the incongruity is only partially explained by the logical mechanism that it is an exaggeration and possibly even a touch of nonsense (an impossible situation of a virus quarantining itself). The target of the joke is the virus, but this is not a prototypical target (i.e., not a human). The textual organization (labeled "NS," Narrative Strategy) is a micronarrative, that is a very short text with a setup/punchline organization, in this case a meme. It is similar in this respect to one-liners. The image just reinforces the text. The language is mostly irrelevant structurally, but is used as an enhancer, as the use of terms such as "exposed to," "quarantine" or "virus," which belong to a medical register, reinforce the plausibility of the situation: this is a joke about the COVID-19 pandemic.

Let us now widen our scope. On a social level, the joke can be seen as trying to reaffirm a degree of human control over the pandemic. By using Chuck Norris as the epitome of the powerful human, the joke playfully claims that humanity can control (quarantine) the COVID-19 virus. In order to develop this more fully, we would now need to broaden our scope to other COVID-19 jokes.

Consider the Woman Yelling at Cat meme in Figure 15.7, from the https://knowyourmeme.com/memes/2020-cant-get-any-worse meme series. Without going in to the details, at the height of the pandemic, this meme series jokingly suggests that things are going to get worse, by having various monsters/aliens, etc., attacking Earth. This instance of the meme has Smudge-like aliens in flying saucers attacking the women in the yelling woman meme and destroying a car. Indeed, a terrible way to go…

The point here is that, like with all gallows humor, by exaggerating the badness of the situation, one exerts a modicum of playful control over it.[3]

---

2 "Enhancers" are unnecessary details that however "improve" the joke.
3 During the COVID-19 pandemic, humor, especially online, emerged as an important coping mechanism (see the relief function of humor, in Chapter 3). As one of the

WHEN CHUCK NORRIS IS WAITING, GODOT COMES            157

"There's no way it's getting
any worse, right?"

April 2020:

**Figure 15.7** A surreal variant of Woman Yelling at Cat.

With this COVID example of the Chuck Norris Facts we observe the first step of memetic drift: the focus is no longer on Chuck Norris, but on the COVID pandemic. The same is true of the following facts: "Chuck Norris mines bitcoin with a pen and paper" (this does not require strength or resilience) or "When Chuck Norris tips the waiter, the waiter falls down." (This is a pun and the Chuck Norris Facts are not.) Both of these examples come from https://ponly.com/chuck-norris-jokes/

As new themes are brought into the meme, by remixing it or by parodying the original memes, the drift increases. As we saw in the Cheryl's She Shed memes case (see Chapter 11), topics and themes that have no connection with the original meme are brought in (e.g., Bitcoin, Covid-19) and eventually, a mere intertextual reference to the form or the content of the meme is left. In the Chuck Norris Facts case, this happens with the Chuck Norris Fact without the second line (i.e., without the punch line). These memes can only be understood if one knows what the meme are supposed to look like (i.e., gets

---

anonymous reviewers put it, "Covid-related internet memes have taken humor's relief potential to a whole new level as suggested by recent studies, showing that creating and sharing humor on the internet helped people cope with negative emotions during confinement while also enabling a much-needed sense of connection and community belonging." See for example, Bischetti et al. (2021).

the intertextual reference) and then they are funny by incongruously failing to deliver the expected punchline.

## Blending Reality and Fiction

An interesting observation is that the memes are known as "Chuck Norris Facts" not as "Cordell Walker Facts" (Cordell is the first name of the character). While Mr. Norris is a martial artist, holds several black belts and won several martial arts championships in 1967–1974 period (according to Wikipedia), there are no serious reports of extraordinary accomplishments, similar to those in the Walker TV series. Thus the "tough guy" imagery of the Chuck Norris Facts seems to come primarily from the Walker Texas Ranger show. In other words, in popular culture, Mr. Norris is identified with the fictional character he plays. It is significant, for example, that none of the Chuck Norris Facts mentions his philanthropy or his right-wing conservative political stance.

In fact, Mr. Norris may be encouraging this blending himself, for commercial purposes, as can be surmised from the following screenshots details from the chucknorris.com website: in Figure 15.8, we see a visual blend of the real Chuck Norris (center) and caricatures drawn from the Walker character (left and right; note that he is wearing cowboy boots).

In Figure 15.9, we see Mr. Norris in character, with the background on an American flag, used to sell a silver coin.

## Two Levels of Chuck Norris Memes

The Chuck Norris memes can be read at two levels. So far we have mostly taken the memes at face value: Chuck Norris is seen as powerful and strong,

**Figure 15.8** Blend of caricatures (left and right) and photo.

WHEN CHUCK NORRIS IS WAITING, GODOT COMES 159

**Figure 15.9** Chuck Norris silver coin.

which are positive qualities. In this sense, one can see these memes and their exaggerations as ridiculous, childish projections of omnipotence fantasy. In psychoanalysis, children are commonly assumed to go through a phase of "infantile omnipotence" in which they consider themselves to be omnipotent. Superheroes, like Superman or Wonder Woman, allow the same kind of fantasy. When delusion of omnipotence persists in adulthood they become pathological signs of superstition and magical thinking (the idea that something is a certain way because we wish it to be so).

However, as we have anticipated, there is a possible second reading, that is to mock those who attribute these magical qualities to Chuck Norris. In other words, the joke here is on those who believe that Chuck Norris is superhumanly strong, resilient, etc. Schematically, we can attribute these types of readings to two model readers: a naive, marginally educated, conservative reader and a sophisticated, highly educated, progressive reader. Now consider the following joke: When Chuck Norris is waiting, Godot comes.

The naive reader, who may be barely aware of the title *Waiting for Godot* but who has most likely not read/watched the play, will interpret the joke as "Nobody keeps Chuck Norris waiting" and derive the usual superiority effect. The sophisticated reader will get the reference to Beckett's masterpiece and will most likely be aware that Godot is a metaphor for god or more generally for a transcendent meaning to life, so that the joke is saying that Chuck

Norris provides a transcendent meaning for life, which is of course a ridiculous claim, which can be read only as a parodic mockery of the naive reader's satisfaction in the fantasy of power and control.

The table below summarizes the analysis. Note that the only differences are the target of the joke and the source of the incongruity (script opposition).

|     | *Naive* | *Sophisticated* |
| --- | --- | --- |
| SO: | strong vs. weak | low brow vs. high brow |
| LM: | exaggeration + role reversal | exaggeration + role reversal |
| SI: | waiting for Godot | waiting for Godot |
| TA: | N/A | Chuck Norris memes and their audience |
| NS: | Micronarrative (setup/punchline) | Micronarrative (setup/punchline) |
| LA: | irrelevant (but enhancers: "Godot," "waiting") | irrelevant (but enhancers: "Godot," "waiting") |

Let's focus on the fact that the two audiences are literally reading/hearing a different joke/meme. The naive audience sees this joke as merely another example of the template "Chuck Norris is so strong/powerful that…" with the SO being strong (Chuck Norris) vs. weak (Norris' opponent). The sophisticated audience instead sees a joke about the juxtaposition of low-brow culture (*Walker, Texas Ranger*) and high-brow culture: Beckett's theater is considered one of the high marks of modernism: *Waiting for Godot* was voted most significant play of the 20th century in a Royal National Theatre poll (https://en.wikipedia.org/wiki/Waiting_for_Godot). Note that while everything else remains unchanged, the target of the joke shifts from an empty slot (since Godot is a fictional character, about which we know next to nothing) to the TV series from which the memes emanate, and metonymically, to the memes and their audience. The sophisticated audience feels superior to the naive audience that either will not understand the joke at all or will "mis-read" it as another Chuck Norris meme.

Thus we can detect two different and contrasting readings of the Chuck Norris Facts memes: a naive one, in which the audience endorses the fantasy of control of the superhuman agent, and a sophisticated one, in which the audience mocks that fantasy. Of course, no reader will either assume the literal veracity of the Chuck Norris Facts or will completely reject the information (for example, by claiming that the real-life Norris faked his martial arts degrees, etc.). In other words, the attitude toward the Chuck Norris Facts will range on a continuum: some readers will be closer to one end of the scale, and some will be closer to the other. Much has been made of the ideological divisions of this age. It seems that even these modern versions of the traditional American tall tale reflect these differences. Even if we laugh at the same subject, we see them through different lenses.

# Chapter 16

# THE HALF-LIFE OF A MEME: THE RISE AND FALL OF MEMES

This chapter discusses the life span of memes or, to put it differently, how long do memes last? The answer is that generally speaking humorous memes' life span is rather short and is characterized as a very fast gain in popularity ("going viral") followed by a very fast loss of popularity. As you will recall from Chapter 2, memes are fads. The term "fad" is usually rather derogatory, in the sense that it implies that the interest is short-lived and possibly excessive (for example, *Webster* defines fad as "a practice or interest followed for a time with exaggerated zeal"). Here we consider the faddish nature of memes as merely descriptive. Berger and Le Mens (2009) make the case that the faster a fad is adopted, the faster it disappears. It should be noted that their work involves names, which are less mediated by tech, but as we will see their analysis applies fully to internet memes.

## Memes as Viruses

As we saw the term "meme" itself was born as a metaphorical analog of genes: genes are to physical organisms as memes are to cultures. However, another metaphor, also from biology and largely unrelated to genetics, has "colonized" the conceptualization of memes. Namely that memes are viruses and spread like diseases. Indeed, the very term "going viral" is an expression of this metaphor. Virality, i.e., meme diffusion, has been the subject of much discussion. In what follows we will review the reasons why memes "go viral" but we will also examine the much less discussed reason why memes go out of fashion. We will also briefly address why both the rise and fall of interest in memes is so fast.

## The Birth of the Cool

A key concept to understanding the rise and fall of memes is that of "cool." Cool comes from African American English, through jazz music. The sense of "general approval" is attributed to Lester Young (1909–1959), the famous saxophone player. "Cool" is seen as "desirable" (Danesi, 1994). Blommaert (2015) argues that memes have open, indeterminate meanings, but index (connote) "cool": using a meme is cool. The motivation for users to share a meme would thus be to associate themselves with this positive connotation (technically this is called indexing by association or enregisterment, Chapter 2).

Blommaert further argues that memes cease to be cool when "people attempt to construct memes intentionally—there are several 'meme generators' and 'make your own meme' systems available online—they are 'uncool' (2015, p. 22). So, in Blommaert's view, memes spread when they are cool and they stop spreading when they become uncool, which happens when memes are produced "intentionally."

This cannot be quite right, because memes are generally produced intentionally by individuals (with or without meme generators). It is possible that someone may say or do something that inadvertently becomes a meme, for example, the woman who knit Sanders's mittens reported significant interest in them, which she obviously had no intention of generating. However, a more common situation is that someone says, records or designs something with the intention of expressing an idea and thus potentially with an interest in this idea spreading as widely as possible. So it makes more sense to look for social-interactional reasons.

## Social Network Models

There have been a variety of models of memetic virality, including Heylighen & Chielens' (2009) model of diffusion in a social network. The starting idea is that mutations and recombinations of existing ideas will produce a variety of memes that compete with each other for the attention of people (Heylighen & Chielens, 2009, p. 3). Diffusion takes place in a social network, which is a scale-free, that is, a network in which there is a power distribution of the connections (i.e., Pareto's 80–20 law: 80 percent of the connections come from 20 percent of the nodes). In simpler terms: some nodes have a lot of connections, but most don't. Heylighen and Chielens (2009) go back to Dawkins' (1976) idea of "fecundity": "the faster the rate of copying, the more the replicator will spread." (Heylighen & Chielens, 2009) propose to model fecundity mathematically as "meme fitness" (MF) defined as the number of memes at time t+1 divided by the number of memes at time t (Heylighen & Chielens, 2009, p. 12). Obviously this number may go up or down, or be stationary. If the number of memes is the same at both times, that is MF = 1, the situation is stable and there is no change. However, if MF > 1 we have exponential growth, and if MF < 1 we have exponential decay.

The idea of exponential growth and decay is crucial to understanding virality, so we will need to explain it in some detail. The basic difference is between exponential and linear growth. Linear growth is relatively easy to conceptualize. Suppose that you sell ice cream. For each ice cream cone you sell, your profit is $2. If you sell 10 cones, your profit is $20, if you sell 50 cones, your profit is $100; if you sell 100 cones, your profit is $200, etc. The increase in sales matches the increase in profits: you simply multiply the number of cones sold by the profit for the individual cone. This can be modeled by a straight line, geometrically, hence the name linear growth. Exponential growth is different: here each step up is not a multiplication, but a power (which is indicated by an exponent—the little number above a number in mathematical notation—hence the name). You sell the first cone and make $2, the second cone nets you $4; the third cone nets you $8; the fourth one $16, etc. What is remarkable about exponential growth is how fast it is. If you sold 20 cones, you'd make more than a million dollars. A hundred cones would net you an amount of money so large that if you added up all the wealth of all the billionaires in the world, they would still look like paupers, compared to you.

This is fine and dandy if you are selling magical ice cream, but when epidemics spread with exponential growth this is very bad news, as the world learned recently again with the COVID pandemic. Essentially, for the first few days, only a few sporadic cases appear and then all of a sudden, everyone is sick, hospitals are overwhelmed, and the health care system breaks down. In passing, let's note that whereas linear growth is fairly intuitive, exponential growth is counterintuitive. This may explain, in small part, why people reject precautions such as wearing masks during a pandemic: they observe very few cases around them and therefore draw the conclusion that their risk level is low, whereas they are only a few days away from a massive outbreak.

## The Viral Model

As we mentioned, many models of social diffusion of memes are based on the idea of viral diffusion. The analogy between infectious disease, virality and memetic spread is, as we saw in Chapter 2, a metaphor. You start with one person with the disease (patient zero). That patient infects a few more patients. Each of those infects several more, until the vast majority of the population is infected. Like all metaphors, the metaphor of meme diffusion as viral diffusion falls apart under certain respects: specifically, with infectious diseases the length of the chains of infection is more or less unlimited: person A infects person B, who infects person C, etc. However, with memetic spread, the length of chains is generally much shorter, and there are individuals who are responsible for most of the spread ("influencers") (Goel et al., 2012, 2016). For example, when we discuss the life cycle of the meme, we will see that there is consensus that when a meme is the subject of mainstream journalism, it is past its prime. This is an implicit recognition that the broadcast model (i.e., a model of diffusion that relies on few, central nodes) inherently disrupts the pure memetic viral distribution.

During the COVID pandemic we found out about "superspreaders," individuals who could infect many more people than usual (apparently due to their higher production of aerosolized particles; Edwards et al., 2021). Superspreaders have an analog in social media and meme distribution. Suh et al. (2010) looked at 74 million tweets and found that a number of features predict retweeting: the strongest predictor of retweeting is the number of followers of the account (Suh et al., 2010, p. 183). Other features include the presence of a URL (indicating that one is likely to retweet a link to some information—a picture of a cat is information too, of course…); the presence of a hashtag, which suggests the retweet takes place within a social context, that is, other people have tweeted about this topic; and, how established the author of the tweet is (i.e., how long they have been on Twitter).

## A Meme Diffusion Model

Spitzberg's (2014) meme diffusion model stresses, as Heylighen and Chielens did, that the diffusion of memes is not determined by their adaptive properties alone (i.e., how interesting or novel they are) but also on the amount of competition they face (i.e., the presence of other memes in the same conceptual space). This is intuitively straightforward: if you are selling stoves and it's winter, your business will do very well. However, if you are competing with electric heaters, you will have a harder time. Furthermore, Spitzberg makes the important observation that

> memes are likely to compete for prominence within parts of the social network, but when a particular social network segment faces competition against rival social network components, the meme is more likely to survive and thrive to the extent it is ensconced within a cohesive and coherent frame of reference. (2014, p. 313)

which we could paraphrase as "strong memes travel in packs." An isolated meme has less of chance of survival than a meme that is part of a complex of other memes, all other things being equal. This is the lesson behind memeplexes, such as the Pastafarian religion (Chapter 14) or the Kek and Wojak memes (Chapter 22).

Spitzberg lists four features of memes that increase the likelihood of forwarding or remixing a meme: distinctiveness, redundancy, triability and media convergence. Distinctiveness is the degree of novelty and hence informativeness of a meme. Redundancy affords the preservation of the meme, through repetition. For example, a song that is being played continuously on the radio will be more likely to be learned, remembered and sung. Triability is a concept coming from the study of the diffusion of innovations (Rogers, 2003). It refers to how easy (or conversely, how complex and expensive) it is for someone to do a trial run of the innovation. Consider for example two memes. One has a meme generator template which allows users to create their own remixes with a few clicks and keystrokes, whereas the other requires that would be user to open Photoshop, import suitable images, create a text layer, etc. Obviously, the first meme is more likely to be remixed and thus propagated. Finally, media convergence indicates the availability of the meme in different media, e.g., textual and visual (Spitzberg, 2014, p. 319).

Moreover, Spitzberg makes an important point about "transmemic diffusion," that is, the fact that "events evoke memes that generate new memes, or memes generate new events" (2014, p. 328).

For example, in November of 2022, Elon Musk introduced in Twitter an authentication checkmark, priced at $8. This is an event in the real world. As a result, many users paid the $8 to acquire a false verified account, which they used to impersonate celebrities and athletes (Marcin, 2022a/b). In one case, a fake account impersonating the official account for pharmaceutical company Eli Lilly, tweeted "insulin is free now" which caused Eli Lilly stock to fall 4.5 percent. A fake Lockheed Martin account announced it had suspended the sales of weapons to Saudi Arabia, Israel and the United States, pending investigations of human rights abuses. A fake Chiquita account announced they had overthrown the Brazilian government. Another fake Chiquita account tweeted, "We apologize to those who have been served a misleading message from a fake account. We have not overthrown a government since 1954." As these examples demonstrate the direction of influence goes both ways. Moreover, many of these tweets were retweeted, forwarded on Facebook and on other social media.

## What Makes a Meme Go Viral?

There have been a variety of theories addressing what characteristics of memes cause them to go viral. Over a number of papers Heylighen (1993, 1997, 1998), Heylighen and Cielens (2009) have developed a long list of reasons why memes may spread. The list is too long and complex to reproduce in its entirety, but we can get an idea of the type of factors at play: for example, if a meme is not self-contradictory, it stands a better chance to be replicated; if a meme fits better with the knowledge that individuals already have it is more likely to be repeated. Other factors include (a) simplicity: short and simple memes are easier—less costly—to spread and (b) novelty: information that is unexpected will attract more attention (cf. Berger & Milkman, 2012). In some cases, memes that have no usefulness for the hearer (they are parasitic) still manage to spread: parasitic memes include hoaxes, chain letters and fake news. Obviously, parasitic memes may be very useful to the creator of the meme, for example in the case of propaganda and fake news: if I tell you that my "supplement" guarantees weight loss, and I sell it to you for $50, that's very useful to me and completely parasitic to you.

There is no question that useful information will spread more rapidly. There are plenty of videos on YouTube describing hacks and tips, which attest to their virality. In fact, there are so many that they have been satirized (see Chapter 21). Berger and Milkman (2012) found that informative and useful *New York Times* articles were more viral. Informativity is directly related with authority: generally speaking, expertise about a subject is defined as possessing highly informative knowledge about it. Thus if the source of a meme is particularly authoritative, this can facilitate the diffusion of the meme. By replicating a meme that originates with an authoritative source, one aligns one self with that source. In a study, Bischetti and Attardo (2023) found that among the responses to a tweet by Ricky Gervais a significant number consisted of praising Gervais's humor (we called these responses "plaudits"). Note that by praising someone's humor one implicitly establishes one's good taste as well, by the act of recognizing quality humor. While we cannot know the motivations of those who retweet or plaudit a comedian, it is clear that they establish an association between themselves and the comedian or at the very least a validation of the originator of the meme (a funny tweet in this case). Of course this is not restricted to comedians, but applies to politicians, public figures, etc. This leads us to the next significant factor: managing one's image. (Dafonte-Gómez, 2018) argues that one among the reasons for sharing memes on social media is self-presentation or "personal promotion." (p. 2139) Interestingly, this is connected to social media "snacking" (Costera Meijer & Groot Kormelink, 2015, pp. 6760–6671), that is, the practice of consuming news and media in "bite sized" fragments: "In snacking, the communicative value of news is often more important than its informational value. You snack news less to get informed than to have something to talk about" (p. 671). Dafonte-Gómez (2018) observes that sharing a link or a headline without even reading the content, let alone checking its validity, is "the perfect breeding ground for fake news" (p. 2141) because the "snacker" has no incentive to read the actual news to acquire information about it and since they are operating with extremely impoverished knowledge (a short paragraph, a headline, a simple image meme) they have no ground to assess the validity of the source and are therefore likely to fall back on what confirms their cognitive biases/ideology. Indeed, a study by Weeks and Holbert (2013) showed that users who were classified as partisans were more likely to share news. Song (2013) sums up her research arguing that social media sharing is "Charged with emotions; Bounded by self-image management, and also; By concerns over relationship with others."

## High Arousal Emotional Content

Berger (2013, p. 110) and Berger and Milkman (2012) show that high arousal emotions such as anger and anxiety, but also awe and mirth lead people to share. Guadagno et al. (2013) also find that strong emotional response is associated with intention to forward the video but they report even further that videos that produce anger are more likely to be shared if the source of the video is from the outgroup. This final observation pretty much explains why social media is awash in angry videos.

Negative tweets are retweeted more often, even the presence of a negative emoji increases the likelihood of retweeting. This parallels the depressing finding in psychology that negative facts are more salient psychologically (which explains, for example, why positive irony is harder to process). We are programmed, as human beings, to remember and focus on negative experiences (e.g., Baumeister et al., 2001; Rozin & Royzman, 2001). As Agent Smith, in the Matrix tells Neo, explaining why the first utopian implementation of the matrix in which everyone was happy failed: "As a species, human beings define their reality through misery and suffering." However, Berger and Milkman (2012) found that positive *New York Times* articles were more viral than negative ones.

The idea that emotionally arousing, both positive or negative, content is more likely to get shared is consistent with the Emotional Broadcaster Theory (Harber & Cohen, 2005) which posits that people across cultures have an innate compulsion to share personal experiences, especially if significant and traumatic. This certainly explains why people describe at length their surgeries and accidents, but it also explains why emotionally charged content gets shared on social media as well. This is true also for second-hand sharing, that is, if I hear a particularly emotionally arousing story from person A, I am more likely to share it with person C and so on.

It should be remembered, however, that mirth is also a high arousal emotion. This means that humorous (mirth-causing) memes will have a tendency to go viral. If we combine mirth and anger, for example by humorously attacking a common enemy, this can be a recipe for virality. Satirical news is one strategy to do so, and indeed it has been a very productive genre (see Chapter 10).

There are many reasons why memes go viral. However, it is crucial to remember that some of them have no connection whatsoever with the characteristics of the meme itself. For example, the prestige of the proponent of the meme is mostly unrelated to the validity of the meme, and yet there is solid evidence that people believe individuals (and hence are likely to repeat what they say). As Henrich et al. (2008, p. 128) puts it, "Otherwise-deleterious or unattractive ideas and practices often spread because they happen to be statistically correlated with attractive individuals or successful groups." Indeed, they argue that people use "cues of skill, success, health, prestige, and self-similarity (e.g., sex and ethnicity) to figure out who to pay particular attention to for cultural learning" (p. 131). We will return to this point in Chapter 22. Another explanation, also unrelated to content, is that weak ties networks (such as Twitter) are more conducive to engendering virality than strong ties networks (e.g., Facebook) (McCulloch, 2019, p. 39). "Weak ties" are defined as loosely affiliated people (but this applies to any kind of network, really) who do not interact often. Facebook has stronger ties because relatives and coworkers are likely to be your "friends," whereas on Twitter, as a default, anyone can see and re-tweet your posts. One can make one's post private, but that requires effort. Once again, affordances at work.

## Dank Memes: The Death of the Cool

According to the Slang Dictionary (https://www.dictionary.com/e/slang/dank-meme/) dank memes "refers to viral internet content that, due to overuse or passing trends, has lost its value or currency (...) Calling something a dank meme thus suggests a broader critique of the meteoric rise and fall of viral content. In other words, 'This meme was funny and cool until it got so popular.'"

Memes go through a phase of "cool" when they are used only by those in the know and once the use spreads too widely, they become "dank." In fact, predictably, there are memes about the cool/dank cycle of memes. Most agree the sequence goes as follows: Memes originate on 4chan and other "obscure" sites. At this stage they are 100 percent cool. They are then spread through Reddit and other less edgy sites, until they reach Instagram, Twitter, Snapchat or Tumblr. Around the time that the meme reaches Instagram or Twitter it gets an entry into Know Your Meme. At this point the meme begins to be overexposed. It has gone mainstream. Finally, the meme appears on Digg, Pinterest or Facebook (the kiss of death of the cool). The only thing less cool for a meme than appearing on Facebook is to appear in an academic paper.

Once a meme has reached dank status, it may be rescued by ironical uses. In this case, "dank" is also used antonymically as a positive term (as for example the term "bad" in some vernacular forms has a positive meaning). So, someone may boast of the "dankness" of their meme, much like dad jokes get their charm from being bad jokes.

## The Life Cycle of Memes

As we saw, the epidemiological and social diffusion models converge in that they both predict that memes spread at an exponential rate and they correspondingly disappear just as fast. Exponential growth followed by exponential decay is exactly what we see in the spread of contagion in epidemics or in bacterial growth. Let's look at Figure 16.1, from Kartono et al. (2021) which graphs the spread of Covid-19 in Saudi Arabia. Kartono et al. use a logistic growth, which is essentially exponential growth when resources are limited (here, people who can get sick). In the case of memes, obviously, the resource (i.e., people to reproduce the meme) is practically infinite: there is no reason to stop listening to a Taylor Swift song or using a fork to eat, and there will always be new people who have not been exposed to forks and/or Taylor Swift.

Notice the exponential growth starting slowly in April 2020, peaking in May and June, and after a short plateau beginning to decay just as fast until it tapers off in October. You may recall the curve of interest for the Mitten Bernie memes, discussed in Chapter 2, which looks just as symmetrical if much steeper (memes spread faster than viruses: we don't have to think about a meme for 10 days or so, before deciding if we want to forward it to our relatives—come to think of it, perhaps we should—but I digress). Let's

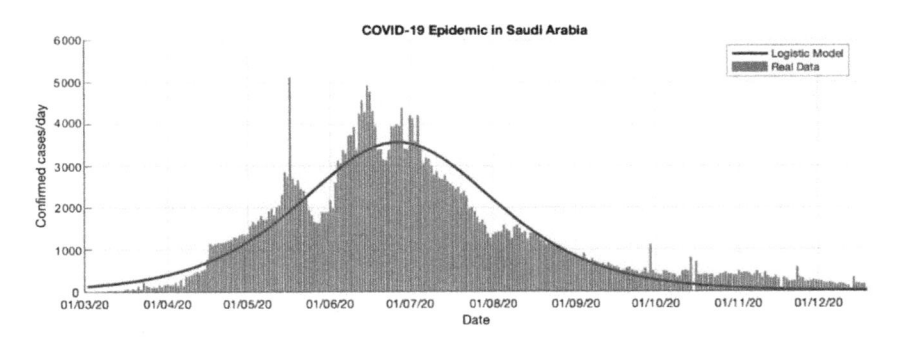

**Figure 16.1** Covid-19 in Saudi Arabia (figure from Kartono et al., 2021, p. 477).

compare this to a few more examples of meme cycles: Figure 16.2, Figure 16.3, and Figure 16.4, the Boaty McBoatface and the Woman Yelling at Cat, and Expanding Brain memes respectively.

What do these examples have in common? First they show the characteristic explosive exponential growth, as predicted by the epidemiological and social models, they show a peak and a short plateau, again as expected, but they show a "fatter" tail than predicted by the models. We can speculate that the age stratification of internet users (McCulloch, 2019) discussed in Chapter 1 is at play here: essentially, a new meme is created in the "cool" areas of the web (4chan, etc.) it spreads exponentially because other users

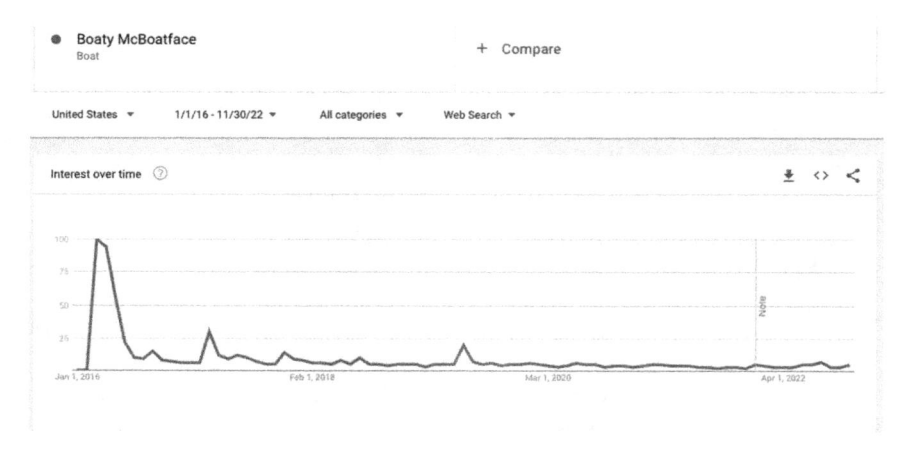

**Figure 16.2** The "Boaty McBoatface" meme cycle.

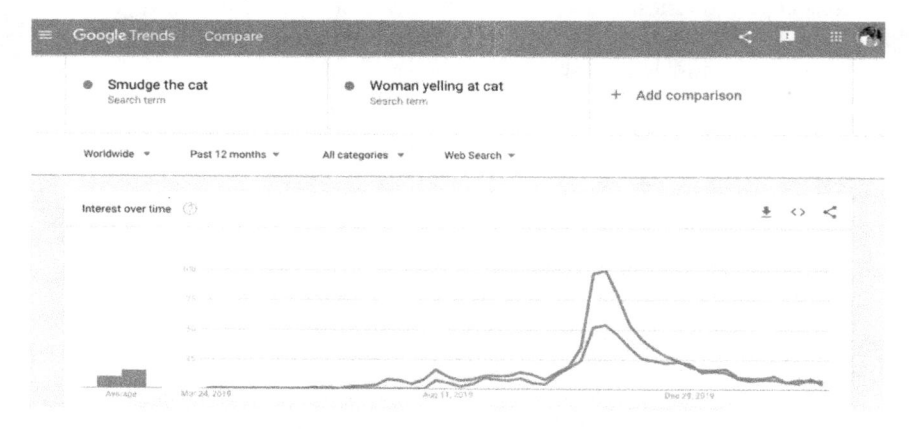

**Figure 16.3** The "Woman yelling at cat" meme cycle.

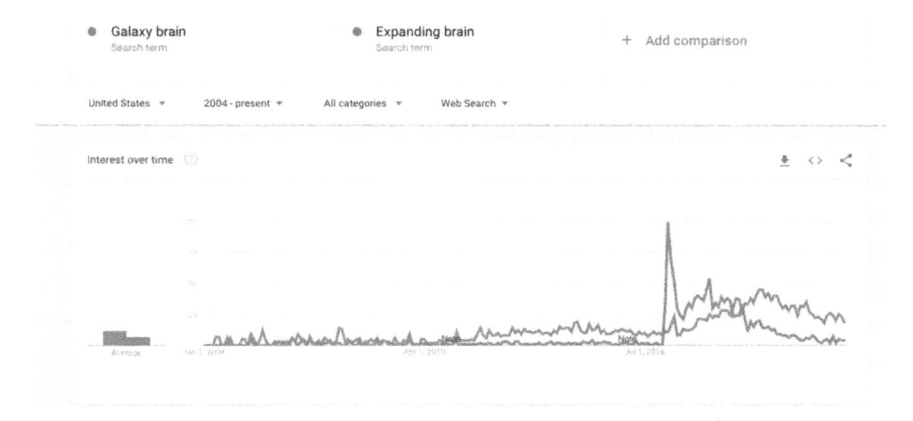

**Figure 16.4** The "Expanding brain" meme cycle (taller line); the lower line is the graph for "Galaxy brain," another name for the same memes.

wish to associated themselves with the cool content and thus display their coolness. This causes over exposure and therefore loss of cool. So far, this is what the epidemiological model predicts. However, the models did not take into account that the fathers and mothers, even the grandparents of the cool meme creators and early adopters, also are on the internet and they read about new memes that have spread on the mainstream press. They then *start using them themselves*—much to the dismay of the cool kids who realize their fathers and mothers are now laughing at the very same memes they found so cool a few (oh, so short) days before. In fact, when I started working on the "Woman yelling at cat" meme, my 20-something daughter informed me that "your memes are dank." To put it differently, I think that the asymmetrical nature of the curve (what statisticians call "skewness") of memes cycles comes from the fact that the uncool masses (and a few humor scholars) stretch the lifecycle of the meme by paying attention to them past their "expiration" date.

## Conclusion

Memes are fads: they spread very fast and fall out of fashion, mostly, just as fast, in a dynamic that can be modeled effectively as exponential growth followed by exponential decay, with a proviso for a certain degree of skewness (i.e., the fact that the meme decay slower than they spread). One of the reasons memes spread on the internet is that they evoke a strong emotional response, in our case mirth, or the sentiment of amusement. Strong emotional responses lead to increased sharing. The association of humor with other emotional triggers, such as cuteness, as in the LOLCats phenomenon (see Chapter 13), aggression, as in satirical news (see Chapter 10) and the desire to affiliate one self with perceived "prestigious" (cool) users further increases the potential virality of humor. These combined mechanisms largely explain why humorous memes are so successful and also why they can be used to spread pernicious information, as we will see in Part 4 of the book.

# Part 3

# MULTIMODALITY

Part 3 of the book addresses multimodal texts, i.e., texts that operate in the linguistic modality (they use language, in other words) and in some other additional modality or modalities. For example, film, video, or graphics are other modalities (visual, auditive, etc.). Gestures are another modality as well, including facial expressions, hand gestures, body stance, and eye gaze. In short, meaning, broadly intended, can be conveyed in many different ways, only some of which are linguistic. Of course in an image or a silent video no language is used and quite simply the linguistic modality is not used, and, as Seinfeld used to say, there's nothing wrong with that.

In particular we will consider in embarrassment comedy (also known as cringe comedy), one of the defining new genres of the digital age, photobombing, the quintessential visual and non-verbal genre, and the video parody. The latter is exemplified by the Hitler rants, an incredibly popular sub-genre, reaction videos, a parody of a music video by German metal band Rammstein done with legos, and the uniquely digital genre of the rant-to-music video, in which someone's rant is set to music.

# Chapter 17

# HITLER'S OPINION ON THE PARKING SITUATION IN TEL AVIV

Did Hitler have an opinion about parking in Tel Aviv? In 1945, Tel Aviv was under British rule (a League of Nations mandate, to be precise), and its population barely reached 183,000 in 1946, according to UN estimates. It seems unlikely that parking would have been an issue, at the time. Of course we know that Hitler did not really have an opinion on parking in Tel Aviv, especially not 70 plus years in the future. That's why the idea is funny, in part. Or offensive, depending on who you ask. Depending on who you ask, you will get very different answers as to whether it is funny or even OK to ask the question, what would Hitler's opinion have been? But before we can even try to answer these questions, we need to address the broader issue: Why are we talking about Hitler's opinion about parking in Tel Aviv? Here we need to take a step back.

Goodwin's Law of Nazi Analogies reads, "As an online discussion grows longer, the probability of a comparison involving Nazis or Hitler approaches one" (Goodwin, 1994). Goodwin observed, some 30 plus years ago, that the longer an internet discussion lasted the probability of someone mentioning Hitler as a comparison to someone or something in the discussion increased and so that if the discussion is long enough someone will end up using a Hitler analogy. Thus any sufficiently long discussion of humor on the internet must mention the Hitler Rant parodies.

This chapter therefore discusses some aspects of the meme variously known as *Hitler's Rants* or *Downfall* parodies.[1] The anchor text of the meme is the *Downfall* (*Der Untergang*) a 2004 film directed by Oliver Hirschbiegel, starring Bruno Ganz as Hitler. The parodies focus on a scene toward the

---

[1] My primary sources on *Hitler's Rants or Downfall* parodies are Know Your Meme and the Hitler Parody Wiki. https://hitlerparody.fandom.com/wiki/Hitler_Parody_Wiki. Most of the videos can be found on YouTube: https://www.youtube.com/c/hitlerrantsparodies

end of the movie in which Hitler is told that a counter-offensive on which he had pinned his last hopes to turn around the war has failed. Hitler explodes in a bout of rage, and his staff overhears the outburst and is seen reacting to it with apprehension. The parodies are done by adding subtitles but keeping the original German soundtrack. The first parodies appeared in 2005 or 2006 (Know Your Meme and the Hitler Parody Wiki disagree on the matter). However, there is agreement that they originated in Spanish. According to Google trends they peaked in popularity between 2010 and 2011, around the time that the copyright owner tried to have the parodies taken down. Hitler Rant parodies continue to appear currently (Figure 17.1).

An important matter that should always be kept firmly in the center of any discussion of these matters is that the character "Hitler" is not the historical Hitler, but rather an amalgam of what the average viewer is likely to recall. In other words, most people will know that Hitler was the dictator of Germany and that he had under his control Nazis and the SS. However, most people will not know the difference between a run-of-the-mill Nazi and a member of the SS, for example. For that matter most people will readily identify the situation as being during the final days of the 3rd Reich, in Hitler's bunker in Berlin, but they will not be able to provide an exact date. In other words, the information in the script available for Hitler is a much reduced one, relative to the historical script for Hitler, which would be available, say, to a historian. To be sure there is a direct, causal relation between these two scripts (after all, the folk script for Hitler is a simplification of the historical script) but we need to be prepared to accept that the reduction may be accompanied by possible distortions. In other words, we should not confuse Hitler the media icon, with

**Figure 17.1** A still from an example of Hitler Rant.

Hitler the historical figure. Media icons operate in some cases rather independently from their real-world referent (the historical character). For an example, see the Chuck Norris - Walker Texas Ranger "blend" (Chapter 15) in which the attributes of the Walker character are attributed to Norris. Gilbert (2013) defines the Hitler in the Downfall parodies as a "mobile signifier" that is, a carrier for meaning, or to put it differently an empty vessel in which the parodist pours their meaning (finding a parking space is hard, etc.).[2]

Furthermore, in order to be functional as a script in a humorous script opposition, the details of the genocidal regime responsible for the murder and death of millions of people must be backgrounded. The human aspect of the holocaust and of the devastation brought about by the Second World War must be absent from consciousness so that Hitler in the bunker is merely a cipher, a bad guy who is having a temper tantrum, about whom schadenfreude is perfectly acceptable. Hitler's rage can be funny, because we know who Hitler is but we are not thinking about the specifics of what Hitler did. Hitler's evil has been bleached away and all that is left is a functional role in a narrative. As Bergson (1901, p.18) put it, "The comic demands something like a momentary anesthesia of the heart." Indeed, Schwabach (2012, p. 1, n. 9) notes that some of those who objected to the parodies did so exactly on the grounds that they trivialize the horror of the Holocaust (see also Steir-Livny, 2017). Furthermore, as pointed out by Schwabach (2012, pp. 3–4), we are aware that the film is a fictional work: the actor Bruno Ganz is not really Hitler, he is merely impersonating him. This too provides emotional distance.

By itself, of course, Hitler's rage is not particularly funny. Certainly, there is not much to laugh about in that scene watching the original movie straight through. It becomes a humorous meme when it is combined with another subject matter. Then we have an opposition between Hitler's rage about losing the war and the new, added subject matter. The first conclusion our analysis reaches is that the new subjects are trivial and unimportant. For example, Laineste and Woolaid (2016, p. 35) define them as ranging from "topical events to trivial news or gossip." Let's look at the subjects that have been the object of Hitler's rage: "the lack of new features in the demo trial of Microsoft's Flight Simulator X" (this was the first use of the meme, in Spanish, in 2006), "Hitler finds out he has to go see *Don't Mess with Zohan*,

---

2 A different take, from Phillips & Milner (2017, p. 98), is to argue that Hitler here is "fetishized" not in a psychoanalytical sense, but in a Marxist sense, that is to say like Marx argued that consumer products hide the labor that was necessary to produce them and become fetishes, so we can argue that in laughing at Hitler's opinion on the parking situation, we focus myopically only on this aspect and conveniently ignore the rest of our knowledge of Hitler.

because tickets for all the other movie screenings are sold out," Twitter is down, the sub-prime mortgage crisis, Sarah Palin's resignation from governor, Kanye West's interruption at the VMA 2009, etc. Sometimes the same trivial matter is the parody subject repeatedly. Hirsch (2019) analyzes three versions of "Hitler finds out he's out of dope."

This gives us the first source of humor, an opposition between two topics (two scripts) that are brought together by the subtitling which literally overlays the second script on the original one. One script remains the same: the end of the Second Word War and German loss of the battle for Berlin, the other one is brought in by the subtitles.

Moreover, the additional subject is of low status (the features of a video game, parking, the availability of Twitter, etc.) whereas the other is, literally, a life-or-death situation and hence high status. This gives us a further source of humor the opposition between high and low status (this is the superiority theory of humor, which we saw in Chapter 3). There is a further incongruity between the variety of German spoken by Hitler in the film, which is rather formal standard German, with an Austrian accent and the low varieties used in the subtitles (Hirsch, 2019, p. 28). However, this aspect can only be recognized by those viewers who are sufficiently fluent in German to notice the difference (further on that below).

Is this all? No, there is more to it. Shifman (2011) uses the *Downfall* parodies to exemplify the "participatory culture" on the internet, that is, "the practice of reconfiguring content and publicly displaying it in parodies, mashups, remixes and other derivative formats" (p. 188). Indeed, the creation of the new subtitles is a parody, with a slight difference. Normally, a parody is a work that reproduces some of the features of the original text (be it a verbal text, a musical one, etc.). For example, *Shamela*, Fielding's parody of Richardson's *Pamela* preserves some aspects of the form of *Pamela*, for example, both are in epistolary form, that is, they consist of letters. The title itself is a good example of parody: while it keeps most of the name of the heroine (-amela), it replaces the initial "P" with a "Sh" thus creating a portmanteau word "Shame" + (Pame)la. Weird Al Yankovic's 1996 parody of *Gangsta Paradise* (by rapper Coolio, 1995) respects the music, but changes completely the lyrics (Amish paradise vs. gangsta paradise) and the visuals of the video: in the Weird Al parody we see Amish life scenes which contrast with the original scenes from gangster life intermixed with scene from the movie Dangerous Minds which included the Coolio song in its soundtrack. In the *Downfall* parodies, the original work is completely respected and present, but the parodic element is added by the subtitles.

This brings us to the fact that, in order for the joke to work, we must not consider the meaning of the German conversation in the soundtrack.

Even assuming that the audience is not German and has no knowledge whatsoever of German, the names of the suburbs of Berlin remain intelligible (Lichtenberg, Mahlsdorf, etc.) as do the names of identifiable persons: Stalin, Steiner, the German general on whom Hitler was counting to break the siege of Berlin, Keitel, Jodl, Krebs and Burgdorf, the four generals that Hitler retains in his office after the news that Steiner's attack was not delivered. Moreover, the map of Berlin is clearly visible with the name of the city clearly legible. In other words, for the joke to work, the audience must willingly suspend disbelief about the fact that the subtitles are not a faithful translation of the original. This requires a certain complicity between the audience and the author(s) of the parody.

This is implicitly acknowledged by the authors of the parodies: in some cases, the author of the parodic version employs careful editing and scripting so that the new text matches those recognizable feature of the original German:

> Working carefully on matches between the original dialogue of the scene and the Hebrew script (e.g. using the reference to Stalin at the exact moment Hitler says "Stalin" in the original scene, or translating words from German that most of the Israeli audience does not understand to curses in Hebrew that sound the same) increased the amusing feeling that Hitler was indeed ranting and raving about the parking problems in Tel Aviv. (Steir-Livny, 2017, p. 110)

Hirsch (2019) discusses several other examples of close matches of the parody with the original text. Obviously the authors of the parodies would not engage in that kind of concerted effort if they did not have the desire, as Steir-Livny points out, to pretend that Hitler is really ranting about parking in Tel Aviv. In other words, the authors of the parodic text are providing some resolution of the incongruity, by pretending that the subtitles actually match the original German.

In fact, I would argue that the *Downfall* parodies are examples of joint fictionalization, a term used for example by Tsakona (2020, p. 82) to indicate the shared construction of a narrative by a community. Not only, as we pointed out above, must the audience suspend disbelief about the German text, they must suspend disbelief about the impossibility of Hitler having an opinion about the traffic in present day Tel Aviv, or the features of video games, availability of Twitter, etc.

Even further, in the video Hitler reacts to his parody being removed for "hate speech" Hitler's anger is due to the fact that parodies of Downfall are being removed on YouTube because they violate the hate speech policy.

Hitler points out, quite accurately, that parodies of Nazis are not hate speech. The metanarrative plot in itself is a new source of incongruity: Hitler could not possibly be aware of parodies of the text he is in. This is a fairly common technique for humor; it is used for example by Mel Brooks in *Spaceballs*, as we saw in Chapter 2.

Humor in longer texts tends to be hyperdetermined (i.e., caused by multiple factors at the same time). Here too, as usual, small details introduce humor. For example, in the YouTube policy rant, when the subordinates are asked to leave, the subtitles say, "all those who disagree with You Tube's policies please leave" and therewith most people leave the room; a nice jab at the policy.

We are touching here another aspect of the humor of the *Downfall* parodies: within the larger text (each clip is about 4 minutes long) there are some embedded jokes, generally related to the original major opposition. For example, in the Hitler learns that Boris Johnson is the new Prime Minister parody, Hitler's reaction to the initial statement that Boris Johnson is leading in the polls is "Don't worry, there is no way that that clown will win." This joke works on two levels: (1) the audience knows that Hitler is wrong, as we know that Boris Johnson did in fact win the election, hence the audience experiences superiority toward him, and (2) the text calls Boris Johnson "a clown" and thus the audience experiences superiority toward him and the incongruity of the opposition between "clown" and "Prime Minister" (low status and high status, respectively). A little later, after he's been informed of the election of Boris Johnson, Hitler erupts: "THE UK NOW HAS ITS OWN TRUMP" (capitalization in the original). The jab works on two symmetrical levels: Boris Johnson is compared to Trump, thus mocking Boris Johnson and Trump is compared to Boris Johnson, who was just described as a clown. We could continue the analysis, as there are several more jokes about Boris Johnson and Trump, but the point has been made. The connection to the main theme of the parody is however not necessary. For example, at 00:30 in the video the original German is "Mein Führer" the English subtitle is "My Failüre" (*sic*); this is unrelated to the Boris Johnson theme, but is a little jab against Hitler, labeled as a failure, with the humorous spelling of the "u" with the umlaut (i.e., the author is transposing an orthographic sign from German into English spelling). In this version of the parody as well, the script manages to put in a reference so that the word "Stalin" fits in. Hitler produces a jab against Corbyn: "To defeat Johnson and Brexit we must sacrifice the UK to Corbyn, who would support STALIN" (2:20; capitalization in the original)

In conclusion, the *Downfall* parodies presuppose that the audience is willing to play along in the creation of a text that does not respect the assumption of realistic fiction. This too contributes to the distancing from the historical Hitler figure.

Another feature of the Hitler rant memes is that they show extreme productivity as they are adapted to all sort of topics, completely irrelevant to the original text. In fact, the lack of relevance is part of the fun derived from the incongruous opposition. For example, Hitler reacts to the trucker protest in Canada, the purchase of a video game company by Microsoft, his latest gas bill, Christmas, the COVID vaccine, etc. In other words, as we saw in the Cheryl's She Shed memes, memetic drift, that is, the progressive movement away from the content of the original meme to reflect the concerns of the new authors of the memes is the natural endpoint of the production of new memes (memeiosis). In fact, I would argue that one of the sources of humor is precisely the fact that there is a very large number of variations on the theme of the *Downfall* parody.

An important issue is that, naturally enough, different audiences will fill the Hitler-shaped vessel of the parody in with different things and will subsequently find their different things. According to several authors, Israeli parodies are different due to the unique position of the Holocaust in the collective memory of the community: Kotler-Fux (2018), Hirst (2019), Gal (2019). According to Steir-Livny (2017), Israeli parodists

> express how the Holocaust memory is an integral part of their identity. It is tattooed on their souls, and the anxiety it triggers pushes them to use black humour, not because they have detached themselves from the memory, but because they cannot detach themselves from the trauma. (pp. 117-118)

Others argue that it is impossible to eliminate the historical record: "One does not understand Downfall parodies or their topics outside the context of Hitler's wickedness" (Gilbert, 2013, p. 414) and as we saw, many object to the inherent trivialization of the Holocaust. Some, as for example Rosenfeld (2015), see these (and many other) memes as part of a process of "normalization" of Hitler and of Nazism.

I would argue that different audiences see what they want to see: Was Hitler's portrayal by Bruno Ganz too humanizing? Is it disturbing to think that Hitler was a human being and a mass murderer? Is it disturbing that Israeli parodists mock Hitler? When Mel Brooks's fictional producer Max Bialystock produces the worst possible musical "Springtime for Hitler: A Gay Romp with Adolf and Eva at Berchtesgaden" in *The Producers* (1968) is he being funny, or offensive, or both? Different audiences will react differently because their stances toward the humorous target will vary and most importantly the scripts that are available for humor will vary. Ultimately, a text is necessarily perceived in a context, which includes the feelings and attitudes of the audience. How they react depends on the text, but also on the audience. Thus it is impossible to try to pinpoint a single meaning for the *Downfall* parodies. Some will appreciate the humorous variation on a theme, some will appreciate the edginess of joking with a taboo topic and some will use humor in a sort of therapeutic fashion. And of course, some will not laugh at all.

# Chapter 18

# PHOTOBOMBING AS FIGURE GROUND REVERSAL

Photobombing derives its humorous nature from the incongruity of a forced reversal of the roles of the figure and selected aspects of ground in the image. The term "photobombing" seems to have been coined in 2009 (Wikipedia). It does not appear prior to 2008 in Google Ngram. Zimmer & Carson (2011, p. 473) narrow it down to a post on May 22, 2008. Most definitions of photobombing assume the intentionality of the act of photobombing: Know Your Meme defines photobomb as a practical joke. The top definition of photobomb in *Urban Dictionary* reads, in part, "Intentionally posing in other people's photos." As we will see that is not entirely correct; to be fair another definition on *Urban Dictionary* hits the nail on the head: "Any time the background of a picture hijacks the original focus."

Know Your Meme lists a large number of websites dedicated to photobombing and lists several particularly viral photobombs. Let us examine some examples, choosing among the viral cases. When the image of two copulating dogs appears in the background of a beachside picture of two friends, what should be an otherwise unremarkable detail of the background is brought to the foreground and the script opposition between the scene in the foreground (contextualized as such by the literal framing of the image) and the scene in the background. Consider that if the two dogs had been merely walking by, this would not be a photobomb. So, what should have been an unremarkable element of the ground becomes a figure, but a parasitic one: it is not the intended figure, which the photographer had chosen, framed the image around, etc.

The photobomb may be intentional or unintentional (see the contrasting definitions in Zimmer & Carson, 2011). In the former case, the gaze of the photobomber has to be directed at the camera. If the gaze of the photobomber is not directed at the camera, we have no particular reason to assume that the photobomb is intentional. A potential exception to this may be movie star Bill Murray, who is well-known as a photobombing aficionado. Notice that photobombs by animals fall within the same category. Animals have intentionality, just like humans. They may not know that the camera is taking their picture, but they know that the camera is an object and that they are gazing at it.

The cognitive mechanism of figure/ground reversal was introduced by Gestalt psychology and was then used in humor theory within the GTVH as one of the logical mechanisms that explain the resolution of the incongruity and in cognitive linguistics more generally. The basic idea is that perception, let's say in a visual scene, but this applies also to sound, for example, separates background information (say, a grassy field) and prominent focal information (say, a little girl running). Typically the background is largely undifferentiated, whereas the focal information is unique and stands out, often by moving, whereas the background tends to be static. We call the background the ground and the focal information the figure. You may be familiar with the image in Figure 18.1.

If you look at Figure 18.1, you may see a white vase on a black background or two black faces looking at each other on a white background. Going from one interpretation to the other is a figure/ground reversal. My claim is that in a photobomb we literally reverse the figure with an element of the ground.

If the photobomb is intentional, we can argue that we recognize the intentionality of the photobomber and infer the humorous nature of the prank: the intentional photobomber is deliberately "ruining" the picture by inserting themselves in it. Of course "ruining" is a relative term: when a celebrity

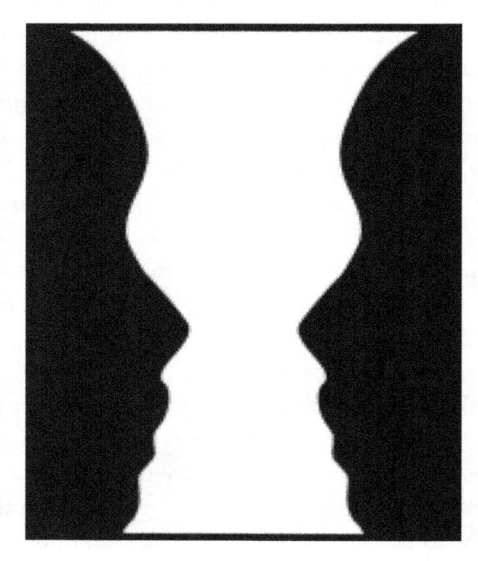

**Figure 18.1** Example of Gestalt figure/ground reversal.

inserts themselves in someone else's photograph, they may be argued to "increase" the value of the picture (certainly they increase its viral potential, since people are more likely to make celebrity-related material viral).

A good example of celebrity photobombing is documented in *The Guardian* (2014) when the Queen of England photobombed a selfie taken by Jayde Taylor, a hockey player, at a Glasgow game. Taylor posted the image on Twitter (Figure 18.2).

In fact the celebrity photobomb has become a genre of prank: several talk show hosts (e.g., Graham Norton, Jimmy Fallon) organize photobombs with celebrities who photobomb unsuspecting fans' selfies.

If the photobomb is unintentional, however, we cannot assume that we recognize the intention to prank in the photobomber (recall that in an unintentional photobomb there is by definition no intentionality, no desire to affect the image). The copulating dogs or the shirtless man who happens to be in the background of a wedding shoot did not place themselves there deliberately and may in fact be completely unaware of the fact that they are photobombing. So, where does the humorous key come from? First, there is an incongruity between the situation (figure) and the parasitic figure (the photobombing element). This is unexpected and possibly surprising. Second, the parasitic figure is either lower in status (shirtless man/copulating dogs) or higher in status (celebrity) than the figure. Third, the parasitic figure is

**Figure 18.2** Queen Elizabeth photobombing.

salient enough that it draws attention away from the original figure. This latter feature is the most significant one, because it introduces the "spoiler" effect of the photobomb. If I take a picture of a friend pretending to hold up the tower of Pisa, there will probably be hundreds of other tourists in the picture. However, we do not perceive them as photobombers. It is only if one of the tourists stands out enough to be remarkable (noticeable, i.e., salient) that we have the photobomb effect.

This is the case in Figure 18.3, where literally hundreds of tourists can be seen in the background, but they are not perceived as photobombing because they are not salient enough.

A common source of unintentional photobombs are animals. They can insert themselves between the camera and the subjects, thus becoming the figure. Two examples are a flying pigeon (see Figure 18.4 ) and a squirrel. In fact, the squirrel photobomb became so famous that the Banff National Park capitalized on it to produce a promotional video (Figure 18.5).

Another possibility is that the photobombing animal appear in the background but is salient enough that it captures the attention of the viewer (e.g., a whale or a shark emerging from the water behind someone on a boat).

Let us go back now that we understand the mechanism of the photobomb to the prank aspect of the photobomb. Obviously, unintentional photobombs

**Figure 18.3** Leaning Tower of Pisa tourist photo.

PHOTOBOMBING AS FIGURE GROUND REVERSAL     187

**Figure 18.4** Animal photobomb.

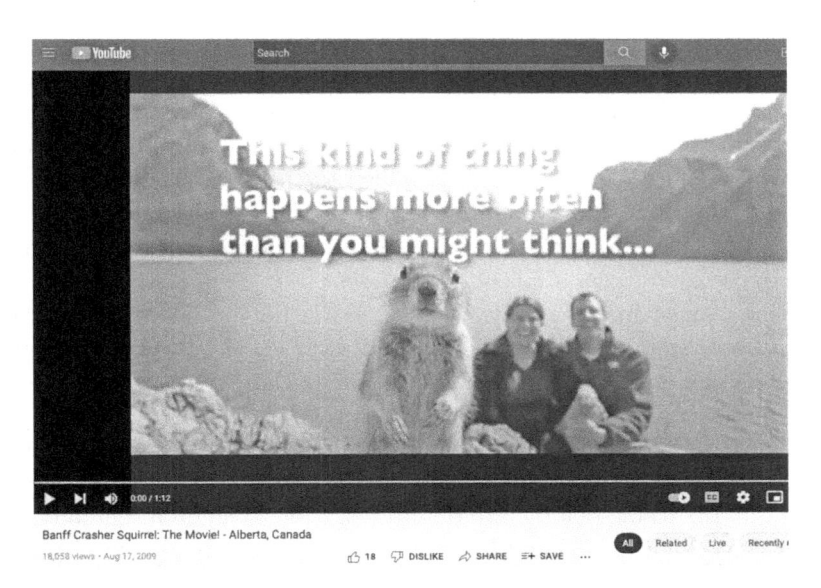

**Figure 18.5** Banff National Park promotional video (still).

**Figure 18.6** Stranger photobombs a group picture.

are not pranks. Neither are demonstrators holding up signs in the background of a reporter doing a live bit on the news. However, some photobombs are deliberate and done with the intention to "ruin" the photograph. This requires a certain amount of planning, as the photographer will not take the picture if they see an extraneous subject in the frame. Usually, this is done by jumping in the frame or by quickly moving behind or to the side of the subjects.

A good example of this sort of prank can be seen in Figure 18.6, which was taken at the Fort Worth Stockyards, which the author (seated left), his wife (sitting next to him) and two family friends (seated to the right) were visiting. A complete stranger (extreme left, standing) came over and inserted himself in the picture, to the amusement of all present.

What then of intentionality? If an innocent (in the literal etymological sense of "one who does not know") animal, such as a dog, or a manta ray, or a squirrel, can photobomb a picture, how can we claim that intentionality is a core component of the definition of photobomb? Intentionality is in the eye of the beholder—literally: it is the viewer of the image who attributes intentionality. Either as a matter of obvious inference, as when someone deliberately walks into the frame of a picture (Figure 18.6), or a playful resolution of the incongruity (Figures 18.4 and 18.5) whereby an animal happens to be in the frame at the right/wrong time. We know it was just an accident, but it's funnier to think it was not.

# Chapter 19

# "HARD TO WATCH": CRINGE AND EMBARRASSMENT HUMOR

Consider the following jokes. The first is by Sarah Silverman

(1) "I was raped by a doctor, (...) Which is so bittersweet for a Jewish girl." (quoted in Goodyear, 2005)

The second involves Tig Notaro and Natasha Leggero. A little background is necessary: in 2013, Leggero hosted a self-produced show on YouTube called "Tubbing with Tash" in which she "interviewed" comedians in her hot tub. In the following video
https://youtu.be/8YNtDkgxNG0

(2) Tig Notaro is sitting, fully clothed in a brown suit, in the tub, while Leggero and the other people present are wearing swimsuits. Leggero wears a bikini. Around 1:23, Leggero says: "I wanted you to wear a bikini." Notaro, pointing to her suit, says: "Close enough" and takes off the suit jacket. Leggero continues: "We're trying to get a lot of hits on this."

This may seem like an innocuous, if somewhat odd, exchange (why would Notaro wear a suit in a hot tub?). However, the video was posted October 30, 2013. Notaro had been diagnosed with breast cancer in 2012 and had had a double mastectomy without reconstructive surgery.
 I think that it is unnecessary to explain why considering rape "bittersweet" and asking a cancer survivor who has undergone a double mastectomy to wear a bikini in order to get more hits on YouTube is cringeworthy. These two examples have the advantage of being very short, but we will also examine part of an episode of the American version of the sitcom *The Office*, below. First however, we need to define "cringe humor" also known as "embarrassment humor."

We live in the "age of cringe" (Schwanebeck, 2021). Schwanebeck puts the beginning of the age of cringe as the early 2000s. Of course, awkwardness has existed since Adam and Eve had to cover themselves up—that's not the point. The point is that awkwardness, embarrassment and cringe are one of the defining themes of humor from the 2000s onward.

Cringe humor is defined as humor in which the hearer experiences vicarious embarrassment on behalf of one or some of the participants in the humor (Hye-Knudson, 2018; Schwanebeck, 2021).

Embarrassment is commonly considered a "social" emotion (as opposed to the "basic" emotions described for example in Ekman, 1992), that is, it is related to the assessment of one's violation of a social convention or loss of status in a social context,[1] as can be seen by the fact that embarrassment is seldom experienced when one is alone and when solitary embarrassment occurs an imagined audience is evoked (Tangney et al. 1996, p. 1266). Already Goffman had noted that "when an individual finds himself in a situation which ought to make him blush, other present usually will blush with and for him, though he may not have sufficient sense of shame or appreciation of the circumstances to blush on his own account" (1956, p. 265). The size of the audience and their relative social distance also increases the sense of embarrassment (Tangney et al. 1996, p. 1266) presumably because close friends and loved ones "people are less likely to become embarrassed around loved ones because they are more certain of their continued high regard" (Tangney et al., 1996, p. 1266).

The vicarious experience of embarrassment is documented neurologically (Krach et al., 2011) and fits in with what is known about emotional synchrony (Prochazkova & Kret, 2017) and the contagious nature of humor (Attardo, 2019). Mayer et al. (2021) claim that "When watching a TV series or stand-up comedy capitalizing on cringe humor, we often experience this immediate affective and physiological response [= embarrassment] in our own bodies. Importantly, we experience this discomfort not because of our own mishaps, but vicariously due to the misbehavior of the protagonist (i.e., the target) (Krach et al., 2011)." (Mayer et al., 2021, p. 3)

What is crucial here is the embodied nature of the reaction. We are not talking of embodiment in an abstract sense (as when Lakoff & Johnson, 1980, p. 16 point out that "GOOD IS UP") but in a very physically concrete

---

[1] This view is not necessarily antagonistic to a different approach in which laughing at the person who has committed a social faux pas is part of the source of embarrassment in the victim (Billig, 2001). This is close to the social corrective view of humor, seen in Chapter 3.

sense: something happens in the symbolic realm (someone says something or behaves in a certain way) and there is a physical reaction in your body.

In short, cringe humor is the comedic equivalent of rubbernecking at an accident (see the first half title of Schwind, 2015: "watching a motorway crash"). It is a mixed emotion: we experience mirth and embarrassment. Much like rubbernecking: we experience compassion or dread for the accident and curiosity.

One of the interesting aspects of embarrassment is that it is socially expected:

> Not showing signs of embarrassment at all after a normative transgression also leads to unfavorable judgments by the audience. For example, in one study, targets who showed only minimal signs of embarrassment after a transgression were rated as more antisocial (i.e., selfish, manipulative, and likely to cheat) and less prosocial (i.e., generous, trustworthy, and cooperative) than targets who displayed clear signs of embarrassment (Mayer et al. 2021, p. 9)

This may account for the uncomfortable nature of cringe humor: neither Silverman nor Leggero in our initial examples shows any sign of embarrassment. This may help explain why the reaction to some of Silverman's humor has been so negative (cf. Shouse & Oppliger, 2012). We will now discuss more in depth the reactions of viewers to cringe humor.

In 2022, I was invited to be part of a conference in cringe humor. When I read the call for papers, a few weeks later, I was surprised by how broad the definition of cringe they proposed was, encompassing sitcoms, films, internet meme collections, such as awkward family photos, people of Walmart), the *Onion*, roasts, etc. The one thing the seemingly endless list of cringe genres had in common is that the vast majority of examples ranged from the 1990s to the present. My daughter (and independently several other people) recommended Scott's Tots (an episode of the American version of *The Office*) as a prototype of cringe humor. So I decided to watch it. https://www.youtube.com/watch?v=x0N2ZxQJYTw (*The Office*'s official website is https://www.nbc.com/the-office/about)

When I first watched it, I could barely stand to do so and I thought it was amazing that this was produced and aired as the episode addresses so many delicate topics (race, white guilt and beneficence). The basic idea of the subplot is that Michael Scott, 10 years before, promised a class of third graders that if they completed high school he'd pay for their college. The students are now graduating and expect to receive tuition grants but Michael does not even remotely have the money to pay up. He now has to go to the school and inform the students, teachers, etc., that he made an empty promise. When he arrives at the school, the students have prepared a whole show to express their gratitude and admiration for their presumed benefactor. In the end, Michael tells them that he cannot uphold his promise and gives them a back-up battery for their laptops (a cheap piece of swag).

The cringe effect is carefully managed. For example, the character of Stanley Hudson (played by Leslie David Baker) provides the necessary background for the story by displaying a newspaper clip from 10 years before, when Michael Scott set up *Scott's Tots*. He does so laughing uproariously and he is shown laughing again a little later. It is clearly not a coincidence that the character is African-American, as most of the children are as well and if the perception were to be that the show is laughing at the children, the effect would no longer be cringe but outright nastiness (the story would be punching down). By stressing that the story is laughing at Michael Scott and by emphasizing that what he did, "This is a terrible, terrible thing you've done. It's terrible. Just terrible." as Pam Beesly (Jenna Fischer) puts it, the story artfully directs the negativity toward Michael, an acceptable target.

## Empirical Tests

Here we need to step back a little and test empirically the claims that this video is perceived as both cringeworthy and humorous. In order to test empirically that indeed the audience finds the segment cringeworthy, I downloaded all the available comments to the YouTube video "Scott's Tots (The Michael Scott Foundation)" on July 12, 2022 (https://www.youtube.com/watch?v=x0N2ZxQJYTw). This resulted in 3,902 comments. I then searched for the word "cringe," "cringing," "cringeworthy," "embarrassment," "embarrassing," "hard to watch," etc. See Table 19.1 below.

**Table 19.1** Results of searches for significant strings (cringe).

cringe: 361
cringy: 54
cringey: 48
cringing: 32
cringeworthy: 16
embarrassment: 23
embarrassing: 11
hard to watch: 79
impossible to watch: 5
awkward: 36
painful: 158
torture: 24

I think that intuitively we can agree that cringe and embarrassment are among the sentiments evoked by this video. Obviously, I needed to test that the segments are also perceived as humorous. Aside from the reputation of the series as very funny, and the presence of a very large number of laughing emojis, I performed the same kind of searches. Table 19.2 confirms that the comments see the segment as funny.

In order to get a more objective feel for the emotional reaction of the viewers, I ran all the comments through LIWC-22 (Pennebaker et al., 2022). LIWC is a common software for sentiment analysis (i.e., the emotional tone of the text). Cohn et al. (2004) and Monzani et al. (2021) define a metric, the emotional-positivity index or emotional tone, as the difference between positive tone and negative tone (in other words, the positive tone score minus the negative score). Higher number indicate a more positive tone of the text. *Scott's Tots* YouTube comments emotional score was -.65. Contrast this with the emotional tone scores that can be extrapolated from LIWC-07 (Pennebaker et al., 2007) and LIWC-15 (Pennebaker et al., 2015) baselines: 1.83 and 1.92, respectively. There is no question then that the comments of Scott's Tots reflect the presence of a strong negative emotional response (i.e., the embarrassment). Note that the comments are interspersed with laughing emojis, LOL and other laughter markers. So it's not the case that the viewers just hated the sitcom.

Finally, I compared the Office comments to the comments of a compilation of Friends clips. https://www.youtube.com/watch?v=EbRHq4bdxl0. The results are drastically different: Friends' emotional score is 2.34.

**Table 19.2** Results of searches for significant strings (humor).

LOL/lol: 205
funny: 130
laugh: 90
laughing: 54
hilarious: 89
haha: 20
LMAO: 17

**Table 19.3** *The Office* vs. *Friends* LIWC analyses.

|  | Positive | Negative |
| --- | --- | --- |
| Office | 1.3 | 1.95 |
| Friends | 2.93 | 0.59 |

So, we can conclude, at least as a preliminary finding, that the claim that viewers perceive the Office episode with a mixture of embarrassment and mirth, unlike for a Friends clip, which evokes only mirth. So, what are we to make of these findings from the standpoint of humor theory?

## Cringe and Emotion

Bergson (1901, p. 16) claimed that humor requires an intellectual perspective, rather than an emotional one. He is very clear about this: he speaks of the "insensibility" or "indifference" accompanying laughter. Finally he states: "Laughter's worst enemy is emotion." That is as clear a statement as we could want. This means that by the definitions of "cringe humor" (see above), Bergson is here flat out wrong.

de Jongste's (2020) claim that viewers of embarrassment comedy, such as the Office, do not actually feel embarrassment because they differentiate between the fictional performer's level and reality, or because they are in a play mode is clearly refuted by the reactions of actual viewers on YouTube, as seen above. Viewers experience real physical embarrassment and actual mirth—and are loquacious about it.

Benign violation theory (BVT; McGraw & Warren, 2010) does not fare much better. Among the ways that a violation can be seen as benign, McGraw and Warren quote: "A violation can seem benign if (a) a salient norm suggests that something is wrong but another salient norm suggests that it is acceptable, (b) one is only weakly committed to the violated norm, or (c) the violation is psychologically distant." (p. 1142) Again, by the basic definition of cringe, psychological distance is out of the question. Where McGraw and Warren are on firmer foundation, vis-à-vis cringe humor is the idea, going back to Plato, that humor derives from a mixture of emotions. Cringe humor seems to be precisely a mixture of mirth and embarrassment, but, contra the BVT, the violation is neither distant, acceptable, nor weakly held (consider again Pam's comment in the script of the *Scott's Tots* episode). Obviously, we cannot equate the scripted reaction of a character in the text with that of the viewers of the show, but in this case, as I argued above, the reactions of the characters are meant to "direct" or model the appropriate reaction of the audience by keying the situation to humor.

It is precisely in these blatant failures of Bergson's theory and the BVT that we can find an explanation of what has happened. It has been remarked that humor theorists observe the humor that occurs around them and elaborate a theory based on it and call it universal. Aristotle's examples come from plays, Cicero's from speeches in the Forum, Bergson's from classical French comedy and vaudeville theater. The risk of so doing is that such definitions are bound to reflect the ideology of the society in which the theory is elaborated. In Aristotle's time discussing one's menstruation cycle on stage was unthinkable (it was however OK to display erect phalluses—go figure). In Bergson's time, violations of the social order had to be reintegrated immediately (either by reinstating the order or by expelling the individual who had violated it from the boundaries of proper society). In the 1990s, what is acceptable as a subject of humor changed. Thus it is now acceptable to laugh at cringeworthy subjects. Plato was right, humor is a mixture of emotions, but what goes into the mix changes.

This is why the conference call for papers appears overly broad: it does not describe a genre of humor. It describes an era, the one we happen to be living in.

## Is Cringe Humor Schadenfreude?

Van Dijk et al. (2012) put forth the theory that enjoyment of embarrassment at poor performance in reality shows (such as *America's Got Talent*) is an expression of Schadenfreude. They list four features that enable Schadenfreude: (1) dislike or negative orientation toward the victim (target); (2) whether the misfortune that befall the victim/target is deserved; (3) envy toward the victim/target; and (4) an assessment that the group with which the perceiver of the Schadenfreude identifies stands to gain from the misfortune of the other group (to whom the target belongs).

It is obvious that the two concepts are closely related: disposition theory (a variant of superiority theories of humor, as seen in Chapter 3) tells us that we appreciate more humor that targets people/groups we are negatively disposed toward. It's clear that Michael Scott deserves to be humiliated and embarrassed, in our Office example, and one could argue that the "people of Walmart" or who take awkward family pictures, etc., "deserve" to be ridiculed because they were in control of their attire and/or poses for the pictures. The case of the last two factors (envy and group assessment) are less relevant to sitcoms and meme appreciation/perception, but we could argue that the categories apply nonetheless, and for example Michael stands metonymically for all "bosses who are jerks" and that so workers envy their bosses (who make more money and tell them what to do), or some other such argument.

Should we then identify Schadenfreude and cringe humor? I think that the two concepts are different enough that we should not. By definition, cringe humor involves vicarious embarrassment. Schadenfreude does not allow for the identification with the victim/target of the humor. So, Schadenfreude is different from cringe because it lacks the crucial aspect of vicariously feeling embarrassment. Schadenfreude is classical superiority (we feel mirth), whereas cringe is a mixed emotion: we feel embarrassment and mirth.

In particular, let's consider again Sarah Silverman's self-directed cringe and Leggero's persona in the skits quoted above: as viewers or readers of the joke we could possibly feel superior to Silverman or feel that she deserved to be raped by her doctor; as viewers of the Notaro-Leggero skit, we may feel that Notaro had it coming or that Leggero is justified in her (fictional) actions. However, that would put us in a morally very difficult situation, that is, someone who condones rape and exploiting cancer survivors for petty reasons. For this reason, cringe is best not explained by Schadenfreude, but rather by its opposite: sympathetic or vicarious embarrassment.

# Chapter 20

# HUMOR VIDEOS

I think it is fair to say that the short form video is one of the main innovations, humor-wise, of the internet. It is very clear that without ubiquitous camera-equipped smartphones the low-fi, video-selfie or video capture would not exist. This is a great example of how the affordances of the technology determine what is feasible. It is not a coincidence that the release of the iPhone 6 featured an ad campaign "shot on iPhone" (which of course has its own satirical memes: https://knowyourmeme.com/memes/shot-on-iphone).

The smartphone videos are essentially the realization of the prophetic vision of the caméra stylo ("videocamera pen") articulated by French film critic Alexandre Astruc (1948) and taken up by the French Nouvelle Vague (e.g., Truffault, Godard) in the form of handheld 16mm cameras and minimal or ambient lighting. Exactly as Astruc had claimed, the filmographer "writes" their personal experience through the camera as if it were a pen. The effect of immediacy and authenticity is striking. Of course, none of this is in the mind of teenagers filming themselves drinking bubble tea or playing video games; quite simply, the tool does what it's supposed to do, using autofocus, stabilization, etc., to produce passable video. The phone even finds people's faces for you.

People have been shooting video of themselves and their friends and families since 16mm and 8mm cameras have been available. Once more, the contribution of the internet and of services like Vimeo and YouTube has been to allow for easy and vitally cost-free distribution, without passing by a broadcast medium (such as America's Funniest Home Videos see Chapter 5).

### Say Hello to My Little Friend: Vine's 6-second Videos

Vine was a video sharing app, acquired and launched by Twitter in 2012–2013 to immediate success. It let users share easily 6-second video clips ("vines"). The clips were recorded directly into the app and could be uploaded very easily. A feature of the vines is that they looped, which allows one to watch it repeatedly. Aside from music and dancing videos, one of the most successful genres were funny videos (Holt, 2013). Vine was discontinued by Twitter, in 2016, but the videos are still available online; for example, search for "best of vines" on YouTube, Google or Facebook. For more technical detail on how Vine operated, see Zhang et al. (2014).

What do vines look like? Predictably, there is a lot of physical comedy, people falling down, falling off things, crashing though ceilings, singing poorly or generally looking weird. Children and animals figure prominently (dogs, primarily, but also an otter plays the saxophone), including rubber chickens (so much for new humor...). In a few cases the vineographer manages to actually produce a recognizable joke: a male voice off screen asks a young woman: "Has anybody ever told you you look like Beyonce?" "No, they usually tell me I look like Shalissa." "Who the f— is that?" "Me." An older woman shouts: "Get the F— out of my yard." Pan to a large F letter being carried by a running man. Weather forecast: "We are told to stay off roadways unless absolutely positively necessary." Woman outside a convenience store: "I want a donut." A young man playing two recorders with his nose. Another one getting punched in the face by someone off screen. A female voice telling a young male teen: "Hey, I am a lesbian." Teen: "I thought you were an American." In short, nothing that would revolutionize humor.

An exception is a video that manages to inject political commentary: at a Ted Cruz news conference someone holds up a large sign asking if Ted Cruz and Kevin Malone, from the *Office* cast (played by Brian Baumgartner) are the same person (Figure 20.1) and shouts "we want answers." Ted Cruz is shown looking dejected (Figure 20.2).

That it may be possible to mock Cruz in under 6 seconds is obviously a reflection of his notoriety as "the most hated man in Washington" (Ball, 2016) and of the recognizability of the Office cast. In general, the shortness of vines forces authors to use stereotypes (Calhoun, 2019, p. 36), much like in short spoken jokes.

There have been a few academic studies of humor in vines. Marone (2016) provides a multimodal analysis. He finds that in a small corpus of vines focused on prejudice, the speakers perform characters and that there is a sort of punch line at the end of the text. Many of the videos are recorded in "selfie" mode (i.e., holding the camera in one hand) which limits the amount of gestures. Of particular interest is the use of hashtags, which can create a connection to other vines.

Calhoun (2019) examines the vines of Andrew Bachelor (Figure 20.3), a Canadian-American comedian, who had 16.2 million followers on Vine and was the most followed person on the platform. Since then, Bachelor has appeared in several films and other shows (https://en.wikipedia.org/wiki/King_Bach). Calhoun shows how Bachelor manages to engage and reverse

**Figure 20.1** The sign comparing Cruz and Malone.

**Figure 20.2** Cruz' reaction.

**Figure 20.3** Andrew Bachelor.

stereotypes about African-Americans, despite the limit of the 6-second loop. Both of the examples she describes involve African-American characters behaving non-stereotypically and taking advantage of the stereotypical expectations of the white characters to get ahead or effectively "turns the table on reality" presenting the opposite of what the audience knows would happen and thus challenging the expectations of the audience. Yarosh et al. (2016) show that a much larger percentage of Vine videos were authored by teens, compared to YouTube and that teens used Vine as a place to stage self performances, whereas adults used social media more in an archival manner, that is, to preserve memories (like a photo album, essentially).

Another, longer, genre that is uniquely tied to the internet are mashups of rants and musicians.

## Remixing Rants into Music

The practice to attach a soundtrack to someone ranting or to play one or more instruments as an accompaniment to someone ranting is seen as a multimodal parody. We need to define more carefully parody. So far, we have used "parody" as reproduction of some of the features of the original text, with an added script position which is responsible for the humor (Chapter 17). This is in line with most current definitions, for example, Vásquez (2017, p. 219) who considers parody as "a textual imitation, which usually combines humor and critique." However, a broader perspective, such as Rose (2014), which incorporates music and visual arts, accepts that parody may be a "noncomic imitation" and "may not necessarily involve mockery" (p. 553). For example, Wikipedia (https://en.wikipedia.org/wiki/Who%27s_on_First%3F) lists over 30 parodies of the Abbott and Costello famous routine "Who's on first?" Let's focus on a very inventive one "The October 19, 2014 strip of the comic *Pearls Before Swine* sees Rat ask Goat 'Whose drummer was Keith Moon?' Goat responds that he is correct (...)" (Wikipedia). There is no sense in the strip that it is mocking the Abbott and Costello routine. It reads more as a virtuoso homage. Obviously, in most cases, the parody includes enough incongruities that the reader (or viewer/listener) will perceive a critical humorous element.

One version of the rant-to-music meme involves the use of autotune. The concept is fairly simple: take any video of a discussion among pundits or video from *Star Wars* and remix the dialogue, using autotune, to turn it into a song. The following example does this https://www.youtube.com/watch?v=DhkgohG9lTM. The obvious script opposition which triggers the incongruity is between the original dramatic or serious content of the original video and the musical remix, which inevitably distorts the original. In this case the repetition of "Tosche Station" as the chorus of the song creates an incongruity. The distortion of the original dialogue (pitch-wise) to fit the melody of the song introduces another incongruity. The situation is obviously the original video (the *Star Wars* movie in this case).

The remixed video can be seen as gently mocking the original work (which would then be the target) or simply as an homage, which would mean that there is no critical parodic element. Another example is schmoyoho (https://www.youtube.com/c/songify) who boasts 3.4 million subscribers.

All these examples show the same parallelism logical mechanism inherent in parody: a photoshopped image inherently invites a comparison between the original and the modified image (there must be enough of the original image left in the modified image to be able to identify the original).

The other genre is to take rants, usually emotional outbursts, and put them to music. A subgenre is Karen metal (i.e., taking a "Karen" rant and turning it into a heavy metal "song") https://www.youtube.com/watch?v=o8hYrNsRoTs

In our next example, a rant to music video by Andre Antunes is remixed. The original video is Kenneth Copeland, a charismatic televangelist, based in Texas, apparently casting out demons causing Covid-19. Judgement on COVID-19 goes HEAVY METAL [Kenneth Copeland remix] - Andre Antunes (Guitar cover) https://www.youtube.com/watch?v=FtkNN_QX5xc. Obviously, by adding heavy metal music to the religious ceremony, the effect is to ridicule it. Antunes, a guitarist from Portugal, has produced an entire album *Goes Metal* of these remixes (https://music.apple.com/us/album/goes-metal/1618068129).

Finally, we turn to another parodic genre: the Lego remake of videos.

## Lego Rammstein

Imagine you are browsing the internet, idly clicking on this or that video on YouTube, when you come across a video with the words "Lego Rammstein" and the clearly recognizable silhouette of a Lego figurine. Perhaps you are just curious, perhaps you guess this may be funny. You click on the video. You start smiling. Then you think: "This is really clever." Then if you are a humor scholar, you think: "How does that fit in with the theories of humor?" Quite nicely, actually.

### *Who Are Rammstein?*

Rammstein is a heavy metal band, centrally associated with the Neue Deutsche Härte (NDH) style ("new German hardness"). "NDH imagery is often strongly masculine and militaristic." (Wikipedia, https://en.wikipedia.org/wiki/Neue_Deutsche_Härte). Burns (2008) states that Rammstein's music is associated with "the extreme metal style with its connections to dark metal and thrash metal," and with "'industrial metal,' a sub-genre of heavy metal that she describes as a combination of punk-influenced 'thrash' metal" (Burns, 2008, p. 460).

Heavy metal as a genre is quite fond in general of BDSM imagery (black leather, metal spikes, etc.). This is very much the case for Rammstein: "Rammstein's incessantly emphasized militaristic hyper-physicality represents a problematic patriarchal machismo, linking masculinity to violence. However, frequent references to Bondage, Discipline/Domination, Submission/Sadism, and Masochism (BDSM), black leather and gender play, as well as the explicit depiction of homosexuality, also lend themselves for a queer reading" (Schiller, 2020, p. 275). We will return to the queer reading of hypermasculinity.

Another, controversial, aspect of Rammstein imagery are the visuals. Burns comments that "the band's visual presentation, however, that particularly demonstrates performance elements that might support" (2008, p. 461) the accusation of links to National Socialism (i.e., Nazism). Let us note that the band has repeatedly denied such connections and in today's world that counts for something, since there are plenty of people happy to make that kind of connection explicitly. My point here is simply that Nazi imagery was

**Figure 20.4** A still from the Rammstein video, Feuer Frei (https://www.youtube.com/watch?v=ZkW-K5RQdzo).

itself hypermasculine and so a link, perhaps involuntary, is easy enough to find.

## *The Lego Rammstein video*

As we anticipated the video is a mashup between Lego blocks and one of Rammstein's most popular videos/songs, Feuer Frei ("fire at will"). Obviously, even from the title we have militaristic imagery being evoked. The extensive use of pyrotechnics, likewise, evokes war-like or hellish imagery. As we will see in Chapter 20, this is an aspect of the video that clearly catches the imagination of the audience. The Lego version follows very closely, almost frame by frame, the original while leaving the soundtrack entirely unchanged. This is similar to the Hitler's rants (or Downfall parodies) which leave the film unchanged but add new subtitles. Here the audio is unchanged but the visuals are completely replaced by Lego blocks and figurines. Contrast Figures 20.4 and 20.5, which show a frame from both videos.[1]

A GTVH analysis of the Lego Rammstein Feuer Frei video is relatively simple: The script opposition is between actual (i.e., the actual video as originally produced) vs. not-actual (i.e., the parody version). There are further more specific oppositions: toys vs. people; adult vs. child; hard vs. soft; cute vs.

---

1 The Lego version of Feuer Frei video was removed from YouTube, presumably due to copyright reasons, but was still available on Vimeo at the time of writing. This video should not be confused with another parody of Feuer Frei (https://www.youtube.com/watch?v=g0gLkQow3Sc) which is not as effective, as it lacks the parallelism with the original video. The original YouTube video was re-uploaded minus the soundtrack (https://www.youtube.com/watch?v=bU_vL24Z5rw).

**Figure 20.5** An image from the Rammstein Lego video, Feuer Frei (https://vimeo.com/314441522).

threatening. The Logical mechanism is simply the parallelism of the original video and of the parody Lego version (which as we discussed, matches the original very closely). The narrative strategy (or genre) is here the fairly well-codified music video. In the original GTVH the term "Language" was used for what we now refer to as the semiotic strategy, which in this case is the visual match between the "Lego flames" and the actual flames in the original video, for example. In short, the visual mechanics of matching the visuals is the semiotic strategy. The situation is set by the Feuer Frei video.

Of more interest is who the target of the parody is. Obviously, by not taking seriously the video's imagery, the parodist ridicules the band (Rammstein) and their fans, who presumably take the video seriously. However, the careful reproduction and painstaking labor required to produce the visual parody reveal that at some level the parodist must enjoy the material or at least find it worthwhile.

Legos are toys and as such they are associated with children. However, they are also associated with some of the features of "cuteness" which, as we saw in Chapter 13, include a large head, round body, small nose and mouth.

In these respects then the opposition between the childish, cute Legos and the adult, hard, threatening, hypermasculine imagery of Rammstein could not be any more extreme. This is not just a simple script opposition, but an oppositional cluster, in which each related opposition reinforces the others to create a mutually supporting effect. This is one of the reasons why the video gives the impression of being extremely clever. The other reason is the accuracy of the reproduction of the visuals with Lego blocks.

The video is a remix of the original music video. There are many Lego remixes and parodies of current movies, such as the Marvel super hero movies. So this is obviously a well-established source of humor.[2] Let us turn now to a more detailed discussion of the idea of hypermasculinity and its links to Nazi imagery/ideology.

## *Hypermasculinity*

Hypermasculinity, not to be confused with toxic masculinity, is an exaggerated form of masculinity. The three characteristics associated by scholars with hypermasculinity are (1) viewing violence as manly; (2) viewing danger as exciting; (3) viewing women and the display of emotions as inferior to men, who do not display emotions. Toxic masculinity essentially consists of concrete behaviors that take hypermasculine traits and turn them into assault and violence (misogyny homophobia, rape, domestic violence, etc.). For an example of a study of hypermasculine traits, see Oppliger (2003) who studies pro wrestling. For an application of the idea of hypermasculinity to Rammstein, specifically, see Herbst (2021).

Rammstein unquestionably projects a masculine image. In fact, as we saw, it has been argued that it is such that it ends up harking back to Nazi Germany: "Rammstein's performance of masculinity, for instance, often appears reminiscent of the Nazis' idealized broad-shouldered and naked German male image" (Schiller, 2020, p. 266). The link between Nazi Germany and hypermasculinity is well established. For example, Westermann (2018, p. 369) explicitly argues that "the glorification of martial virtues and violence emerged as defining characteristics of the National Socialist ideal of hypermasculinity, especially in the SS and the police." Schiller (2020) argues that Rammstein's use of Nazi imagery and themes is in fact "over-the-top spectacle, exaggerated [performance] that suggest a self-critical and self-conscious ironic strategy" (p. 268). While Schiller's interpretation is plausible and perhaps even probable, we need not establish whether Rammstein's act is ironical or genuine. As we saw, the band denies the charges of fostering a Nazi

---

2 I am grateful to one of the anonymous readers who introduced me to the "Brick Bible" or "Brick Testament," i.e., a retelling of the Bible using images of Lego figurines (https://en.wikipedia.org/wiki/The_Brick_Testament). The images are available here: https://thebrickbible.com

imagery, despite the fact that some of their fans obviously take it to be so. My point here is simply to establish the link between Rammstein's imagery and hypermasculinity.

Of course another group that cherishes hypermasculine behavior is gay men (Nordling et al., 2006). Nordling et al. find significantly more hypermasculine behavior in gay men compared to straight men. This is probably why there is always a homosexual undertone to all hypermasculine displays. "Leather" is the term used in the gay community to refer to BDSM practices. We will see that hypermasculinity easily crosses the boundary into toxic masculinity and is one of the defining features of the alt-right use of humor in Part 4 of the book.

# Chapter 21

# REACTION VIDEOS

The reaction video is another genre unique to digital humor. According to Wikipedia, reaction videos go back to the 1970s in Japan (https://en.wikipedia.org/wiki/Reaction_video). The basic idea is that one shows a video of someone reacting to something, usually another video. There is a general consensus that one of the first set of viral reaction videos were the reactions to the infamous "2 girls 1 cup" pornographic video (which features coprofagia—the eating of excrement—and worse; Bliss, 2022). This is in line with the old observation that whenever there is a technological advance in the field of communication, pornography is among the first uses. Bliss (2022) maintains that a lot of reaction videos still revolve around pornography. In this sort of reaction video, the amusement or pleasure we draw is from watching the disgust of the viewers or their amusement, embarrassment or other emotional reaction, alone. In particular, Warren-Crow (2016) focuses on screaming "like a girl." Indeed, according to Anderson (2011), the point of this sort of reaction video is that it allows the experience of a vicarious thrill without having to actually experience watching coprofagia, for example.

There are other, different kinds of reaction videos. In the genre that concerns us here, the screen is divided into two parts, either side by side, or one above the other, or in some cases the reaction is an inset video. The significant fact is that there are two different videos, and there is a contrast (incongruity) between the two videos. For ease of reference we will refer to the video that is being reacted to as the "target video."

This is different from another genre of reaction video, in which a video which is not necessarily shown to the viewers is played for an audience in the video and the reactions are the subject of the video. There is debate as to what the first reaction video was. Warren-Crow (2016) claims that the first reaction video was "Nintendo Sixty-FOOOOOOOOOUR" a video of a young boy and his sister who get very excited unpacking their Christmas present (https://www.youtube.com/watch?v=pFlcqWQVVuU). The video dates back to 2006 and is an unboxing video. The claim that this is the first unboxing video is challenged by Know Your Meme (https://knowyourmeme

.com/memes/unboxing). In any case, since both videos date back to 2006, this took place immediately after YouTube got started. Unboxing videos are videos, in which someone videos themselves or others opening a package containing a purchase, usually tech gadgets (e.g., a new iPhone or video games), but also clothing or tools (https://knowyourmeme.com/memes/unboxing). Obviously, here the desirability of the object being unboxed is a crucial aspect of the appeal of the video, as is the vicarious experience of joy, surprise, excitement or other emotion displayed by the "unboxers." The videographer then enjoys the social prestige that comes from owning the object ("conspicuous consumption" Veblen, 1889). However, we should not discount merely broadcasting one's everyday experience as a source of interest, as evidenced by the existence of streaming game play, in which people broadcast themselves playing a video game, on platforms such as Twitch. I confess having a hard time understanding the appeal of watching someone play a video game, aside from the voyeuristic pleasure one can derive from watching strangers, which was the appeal of the early webcams experiments with "lifecasting" (e.g., JennyCam: https://en.wikipedia.org/wiki/Jennifer_Ringley). However, the success of platforms such as Twitch (https://en.wikipedia.org/wiki/Twitch_(service)), which as of February 2020 had 15 million daily users, clearly shows that other people, including my grandson, find plenty of interest in that sort of video.

All these types of reaction videos, and there are plenty more, such as music reaction videos, in which a musician listens (allegedly) for the first time to a given piece of music (Rodgers, 2020; McDaniel, 2021), share the feature that they are once removed from the direct experience. The viewer is watching someone else watch (or unpack, or play, etc.) a video. As Anderson (2011) notes, there is potential for infinite regression here: one could easily video themselves watching a video of someone watching a video, etc. In fact, it's been done, in the following 2004 video: https://www.youtube.com/watch?v=gNS04P8djk4&t=31s featuring Tyler Oakley reacting to teenagers reacting to Tyler Oakley videos. (Figure 21.1) The video has received 11 million views. Oakley is a web celebrity, of course, having 5.6 million followers both in Instagram and Twitter, and his videos having been viewed more than 680 million times. So, part of the interest comes from seeing a celebrity interacting with their fans. Nonetheless, the recursive nature of this phenomenon remains to be explored fully.

From the standpoint of humor we will observe that the duality of perspectives between the author of the target video and that of the author of the reaction video is the mechanism whereby an incongruity is most likely to be introduced. In other words, reaction videos have a built-in incongruity and resolution: if the author of the reaction video is mocking or ridiculing the

**Figure 21.1** Tyler Oakley reacting to a teenager watching a video of himself (2004).

author of the target video, that in itself is enough to generate and explain humor. In the case of reaction videos in which the emotional load overwhelms the subject and causes them to "flood out" (Goffman, 1974, p. 351) that is, "let out" the emotion, there is also a sense of superiority over the person who is incapable of controlling their emotions. That can cause a perception of humor.

## Reacting to Stupidity

Middleton (2014) identifies the "reaction video" as one of the core genres of cringe/embarrassment comedy. Here we will consider the reaction videos of Khabane "Khaby" Lame, a TikToker whose reaction videos to supposedly clever "hacks" have garnered over 2.4 billion likes, as of August 24, 2022 (https://www.tiktok.com/@khaby.lame?lang=en).

Khaby's story is quite interesting. In June 2022 he became the most followed TikTok account with 148+ million followers. A Senegalese immigrant to Italy, who only recently received citizenship, his rags-to-riches story has helped his popularity (at least in Italy). He is known worldwide for his silent reaction videos. His specialty is reacting to needlessly complicated ways of doing relatively simple tasks (such as peeling a cucumber or putting a liner in a trash can). His videos are usually completely silent: they have a music soundtrack, but no dialog, which of course helps his transnational success. In some cases, he has produced some non-reaction videos with dialogue. The videos usually start the clip and are followed by the reaction, but in some cases the two are presented side by side. There is always a title (in Italian and English), but, in the reaction videos, the real source of the incongruous opposition between scripts is the simplicity of the activity as performed by Khaby contrasted with the needlessly complex or improbable way of doing it displayed in the video he is reacting to.

Khaby relies on the implicit knowledge of the situation script (e.g., putting a liner in a trash can) which comes with a standard way of performing the activity (insert the bag in the trash can, fold the edges of the bag over the sides of the can) and having displayed the needlessly complex way of doing it in the video he is reacting to, he then reasserts the standard way of doing things (Figure 21.2). This in itself has the ingredients of humor (incongruity, situation, target, etc.) but Khaby adds two ingredients (his "secret sauce," so to speak): a non-plussed expression usually displayed by wide-open eyes and an incredulous look and a certain degree of exasperation directed at the author of the video he is reacting to. This meta-commentary is crucial: by directing a small degree of criticism toward the author of the target video, Khaby channels the annoyance at influencers who bombard their audience with unnecessary and unrealistic "information" but does so in a mild, "benign" way (unlike, say, trolling them). Furthermore, by looking non-plussed, Khaby subtly established a us vs. them dynamic, in which the viewer of his videos identifies with him, against the would-be influencer.

**Figure 21.2** Khaby Lame and the trash can liner.

**Figure 21.3** Khaby Lame and the pot. https://www.tiktok.com/@khaby.lame/video/6939490109800729862

In this video, Khaby reacts to a video suggesting that to save space one remove the handle of a pot, while obviously it is easier to just flip the lid and store it with the handle inside the pot. Note how the entire video (target and reaction) lasts 12 seconds, overall! This video has been liked 13.6 million times, has had almost 50,000 comments and has been forwarded more than 95,000 times. (see Figure 21.3)

## Counter-trolling

Another set of interesting reaction videos are counter-trolling. Drew Afualo on TikTok has established a large following by producing reaction videos to misogynistic trolls in which she mocks them mercilessly and laughs at them (Barinka, 2022). Afualo has a remarkable 7.7 million followers (https://www.tiktok.com/@drewafualo?lang=en) and has garnered 253 million likes (figures as of August 11, 2022).

Afualo intermixes parts of the original video, still from the poster's account, and deliberately amateurish video, as can be seen from the screen capture in Figure 21.4.

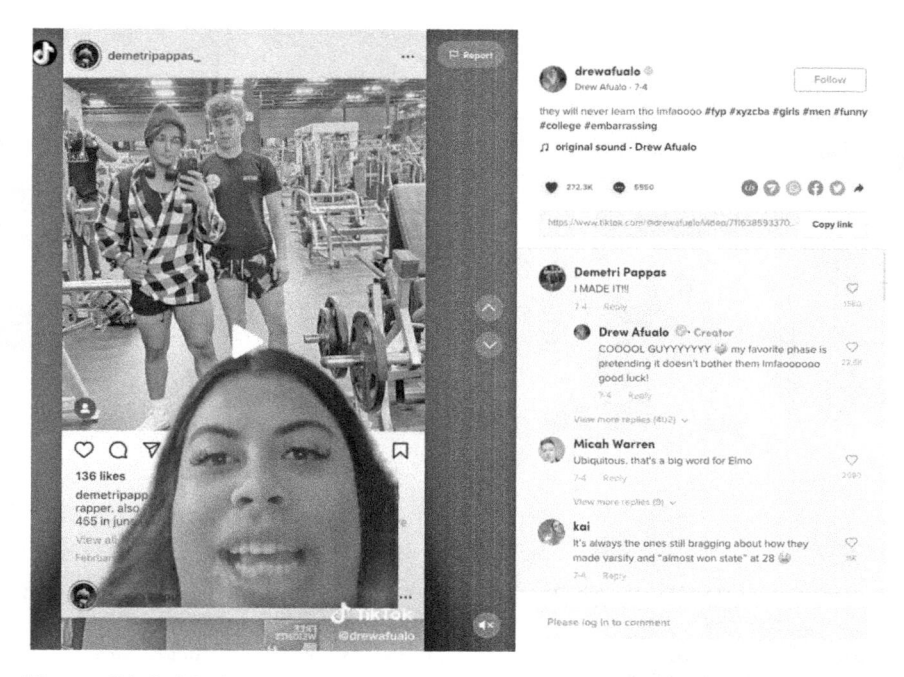

**Figure 21.4** Afualo counter-trolling the young man wearing a hat.

Her tone is relentless. Not only she mocks the troll (who in this case posted a video against fat people) but she mocks his (rather pathetic, to be sure) attempt at pretending that he is happy that Afualo has covered him (on the right his comment saying "I made it" in all caps can be seen). Her biting sarcasm (she addresses the troll as "cool guy") and her signature laughter make the video quite entertaining, but we should note that she is quite vicious: Afualo literally mocks him for his clothes and for being short. In other words, she counter-trolls.

## Tribal People React

We turn now to a series of video that feature "tribal Pakistani people" reacting to various items, including cheesecake, Texas barbecue, and various videos, primarily musical. There are a couple of YouTube channels dedicated to this sort of video: Reactistan (426,000 subscribers) and Trybals (190,000 subscribers). Subscribers data are as of December, 2022.

In particular we will focus on the video "Tribal People React to Rammstein - Du Hast Live Reaction" https://www.youtube.com/watch?v=oAb26NkUz2c

The rhetorical trope is again the person from another culture (outsider) looking in on Western culture. As we saw in Chapter 7 "Stuff White People Like" that is a well-known stance that has been used repeatedly to generate humor. Here too we have a default script opposition between the tribal people and Western culture.

The YouTube channel "Trybals" does not provide a lot of information as to who these "tribal" people are, aside from stating that they come from the Sindh province of Pakistan. In fact, they come from different tribes in Sindh and speak Sindhi, Urdu and Balochi. The interpreter switches into each language. The Twitter and Facebook accounts linked to the YouTube channel describe the content as "Tribal people trying outside world," hence presumably they must live in an isolated, remote part of Sindh, since Karachi, the capital of Pakistan, is in the Sindh province and is a rather large metropolis of roughly 22 million inhabitants.

The choice of exposing Pakistani "tribal" people to Rammstein is perhaps somewhat of a cheap shot, since Rammstein, a German heavy metal band we discussed in Chapter 19, is rather extreme, even within Western culture, and so we could expect the tribal people to be shocked. However, in fact Rammstein is probably not that extreme within the heavy metal community, which include subgenres as "blackened death metal," "brutal death metal," "death grind" and "melodic death metal." To be fair, I had the feeling Wikipedia was pulling my leg about these names, but a few quick spot checks convinced me that these genres exist.

The setup of the video is very simple: a tribal person watches a video on a laptop and an inset show us what they are seeing. A person off screen explains what Rammstein is, and provides the title of the piece ("Du Hast"). The tribal viewers can stop the video, ask for explanations and freely provide feedback. The result is quite funny. One person asks: "Do they perform at weddings?" Another comments that they find the music "soothing and relaxing." They are all fascinated by the fact that one of the Rammstein musicians is on a treadmill and one of the viewers wishes he had a treadmill so he could lose some weight. He is clearly taken by the musician and comments "this guy is having the most fun job." Once the song gets going, they follow the beat and clearly enjoy it. They ask questions about the lyrics. The pyrotechnic effects raise some serious concerns for the safety of the audience ("What if that place caught fire? it was packed with thousands of people") and of the performers. One of the viewers expresses envy for their stockpile of natural gas, which he compares positively to the situation in his region, where he says "there is a shortage of natural gas." They are impressed at the size of the crowd (the video is a live performance) and that the crowd is mixed: "Both men and women are together?" At the end they give general comments: "they are very skilled musicians," "great song," "very energetic."

In short, the tribal people completely miss the broad connotations of the music and imagery (dark, brooding and dangerous), let alone the specific German and national socialist ones, discussed in Chapter 19, and instead relate it to their experiences. For example, the discussion of the use of pyrotechnics at a show is a textbook case of cross-cultural diversity: rather than marveling at the impressive nature of the pyrotechnics, the viewer marvels at the availability of natural gas, comments on the unavailability of gas in his area and concludes that it's "expensive."

Is this video paternalistic and reinforcing neo-colonial views through stereotypes? Is the Pope catholic? If you place people who are unaware of rock music, let alone heavy metal and related genres, in the position of watching a video of a rather extreme performance (from a Western standpoint) they are bound to miss the point, much like if we asked random people from Gary, Indiana, to comment on a Kabuki performance. Of course, the point of the video is not to be fair, or to provide an anthropologically sound study of cross-cultural comprehension, but to elicit a feeling of mild superiority over the misunderstanding of the tribal viewers of the cultural artifact. Thus the tribal viewers are the targets of the joke. The built-in script opposition Western vs. tribal Pakistani is clearly working. Interestingly, the situation, usually not very relevant in humor, is here fully in play: the biggest problem that the tribal viewers have is that of not being able to identify the background frame (the situation) which the video depicts (i.e., a rock concert).

In conclusion, this video at a deep level reveals that Pakistani tribal people, Europeans, Americans, all humanity, are alike: faced with an unresolvable incongruity, we all ask the very same question "Why is the keyboardist on a treadmill?" Why, indeed?

## Are Reaction Videos Authentic?

Finally, we need to address whether these reaction videos are authentic. Commonsense tells us that no young child is that good of an actor as to be able to convincingly fake the Nintendo 64 reaction video. Conversely, it is clear that Khaby Lame is performing for his audience. There is a whole industry of TikTok and YouTube videos where people pretend to be surprised, pranked and so on. In fact, there are plenty of video "scams" in which amazing feats, such as the construction of a swimming pool in the jungle, by one or two crafty people, are completely faked. See for example the video "How primitive building videos are faked" (https://www.youtube.com/watch?v=Hvk63LADbFc).

When it comes to the Pakistani tribal videos, for all we know, these people could be actors living in downtown New York City. This would explain how they have access to cheesecake and Texas barbecue. Conversely, perhaps Karachi has vast stores of cheesecake, Texas BBQ and Nutella. Yes, in one video (https://www.youtube.com/watch?v=djMmFopOmx0) they try Nutella. They like it (unsurprisingly, come on now...). For what it's worth, to this viewer, the participants look authentically bemused by these Western foods, videos and songs. Both Saleem (2020) and Mohammed and Mohammed (2021) treat them as authentic. Ultimately the authenticity of the videos does not really matter: they are presented as such and as sources of mild-mannered amusement they work. If these people are actors, they are extremely good.

# Part 4

# THE DARK SIDE OF INTERNET HUMOR

This final part of the book attempts to cast some light on some of the darkest, most disturbing corners of the internet.

The first chapter of this part, "The use of humor by the alt.right," considers its strategy used to recruit new followers to present their propaganda under the guise of humor, taking advantage of the retractability of humor ("I was just kidding").

The second chapter considers some of the humor on 4chan, a website that allows anonymous posting. In particular, we examine the practice of trolling that is, the posting of deliberately inflammatory posts to elicit outrage, and lulz, the laughing at the victim of a trolling incident.

The last chapter considers the adoption of cartoon mascots by right wing groups.

In many ways, these were the hardest chapters to write. One of the nice perks of studying humor is that one's data tend to be fun, amusing and entertaining. The humor we will consider in this section is rarely so wholesome. In fact, short of snuff movies, it comprises some of the vilest, most disgusting, most depressing material in circulation. Yet it is crucial that it be examined and brought out into the light.

Nietzsche said: "Beware that, when fighting monsters, you yourself do not become a monster ... for when you gaze long into the abyss. The abyss gazes also into you." As I delved into the cesspool of the alt-right humor, I found myself fondly remembering the "asteroid for president" memes I had seen in 2020 (Figure P4.1). Perhaps humanity is not worth saving, if we go by these specimens.

**Figure P4.1** The Giant Meteor 2020 parody of electoral sticker.

It is very difficult to maintain a detached, objective, dare I say, scientific stance when dealing with this sort of material. I tried my best to do so, because to simply reject trolling or racist humor as not funny means forgoing the possibility of understanding the phenomenon and/or understanding why some people find it funny, let alone what they do with it. Having said this, I will issue a blanket disclaimer: I do not endorse, approve or even find funny any of the humor discussed in this part. So, holding our noses pinched firmly shut, let's dive in.

# Chapter 22

# THE USE OF HUMOR BY THE ALT-RIGHT

In this chapter, we will consider how the alt-right (see Chapter 1) uses humor to recruit new followers by presenting their propaganda under the guise of humor/satire/irony and tries to take advantage of the retractability of humor ("I was just kidding").

### Is the Right Even Funny?

The title of this section may seem peculiar, after all, why wouldn't the right be funny? Admittedly, the Nazis were not particularly known for their sense of humor, but surely we would expect less extreme forms of right wing groups to have humor. However, there is a general sense in the academic community of humor researchers that right wingers are just unfunny. In fact, Young (2020) is a book dedicated to explaining why conservatives prefer outrage to irony and satire. The problem is that indeed a lot of right-wing humor will be absolutely unfunny to the average reader because of the problems we discussed in Chapter 3 that is, the unavailability of the scripts required to understand the joke.

However, Sienkiewicz and Marx (2022) provide evidence, based on viewership data, that not only is the right producing humor and satire, but that it is quite successful (for example, *Gutfeld!* had excellent ratings of over two million viewers, beating all other late night satirical news shows, in 2021).

### The Alt-Right Propaganda Machine

Having established that the right does produce successful humor and satire, Sienkiewicz and Marx argue that the right is using them to recruit and radicalize supporters. The idea, well developed in Sienkiewicz and Marx (2022; see also Greene, 2019), is that mainstream shows such as *Gutfeld!* or publications such as *Babylon Bee*, or podcasts such as *The Joe Rogan Experience*, through a complex network of promotions, recommendations and advertisement funnel an audience toward increasingly radical material that culminates in explicit white suprematism, Nazi propaganda and recruitment. For a more detailed discussion of Sienkiewicz and Marx (2022), see Attardo (2023).

This is not just speculation. Bowman-Grieve (2013) shows that "whites only" dating sites promote discussion, interaction and the formation of interpersonal bonds and relationships among white supremacists and therefore contribute to the recruitment and radicalization of the recruits in terrorist groups. Indeed, this sort of recruiting for right-wing groups in the United States is attested as early as 2001: Ray & Marsh (2001) document the presence and effectiveness of recruiting in extremists right-wing groups targeting young people via computer games, music videos and cartoon characters. Quantitative studies confirm the connections and the pathways of recruits from mainstream to radicalization. Horta Ribeiro et al. (2020) analyze the traffic and recommendations between mainstream right, "alt-light" and "alt-right." Mamiè et al. (2021) study the connections between anti-feminist and "alt-right" sites. Granted, these studies are not specific to humorous content, but there seems to be no reason to believe that the mechanisms at play (mutual endorsement, algorithmic recommendations, links, etc.) have a different effect in the case of comedic content. Specifically, Horta Ribeiro et al. (2020) find "strong evidence" of radicalization on YouTube. About half of the users who watch mainstream right content also comment on Alt-Right content. "A significant fraction" of users who start out commenting only on the mainstream right content end up commenting on the alt-right content (i.e., they become radicalized). (p. 2).

It may appear incredible that such mainstream companies as Facebook (Meta), Twitter, Reddit, etc., tolerate such content, but they do. In fact, they are far more tolerant of right-wing terrorist than Islamic ones (Meier, 2019). Only when they are caught "red handed" they take action. According to Wikipedia,

> Facebook was found to be offering advertisements targeted to 168,000 users in a white genocide conspiracy theory category, which they removed shortly after being contacted by journalists in the wake of the 2018 Pittsburgh synagogue shooting. [...] After the March 15, 2019 Christchurch mosque shootings, Facebook announced that they have banned white nationalist and white separatist content along with white supremacy. [...] (Wikipedia: https://en.wikipedia.org/wiki/Radicalization#Right-wing)

Million Dollar Extreme, a comedy group with ties to white suprematism, was banned on YouTube and Reddit in 2018. Their series *World Peace* on Adult

Swim was canceled after three weeks. (https://en.wikipedia.org/wiki/Million_Dollar_Extreme). The effectiveness of "deplatforming" (i.e., the forcible removal of controversial accounts on YouTube, Twitter, etc., has been questioned (e.g., Horta Ribeiro, 2022) since the agitators move to other platforms, which do have a smaller reach, but allow more radical content. However, generally speaking, the research community agrees that the algorithms of Facebook, and other social media, deliberately facilitate radicalization.

## An Example of Alt-Right Comedy: Murdoch Murdoch

It is tempting to dismiss the argument so far as exaggeration. After all, it seems absurd that one may be able to find overt Nazi propaganda on the internet. Perhaps on the dark net, one would think, but surely not a click away. Think again. We will examine *Murdoch, Murdoch* "the Alt-Right's very own sitcom" as Robertson (2019) puts it. All you really need to know about it is that "Murdoch Murdoch is Nazi propaganda" (Robertson, 2019). If you really want to know more, a listing of the episodes is available here: https://www.imdb.com/title/tt8258924/

I watched Episode 1: The reddit cuck discovers pol. https://www.murdochmurdoch.net/murdoch/episode-1-the-reddit-cuck-discovers-pol/ It involves images of Hitler and other Nazi manifestations, interspersed with racist, anti-muslim and misogynist propaganda, Pepe imagery, and a vaguely pornographic cuckolding theme (with the word "cuck" repeated obsessively; on the "cuck" meme, see Chapter 23). The video lasts about 100 seconds and is otherwise incoherent. The propaganda pieces are flashed on screen and can be read only by freeze-framing the video. Any hints at humor are in the introductory part in which the "cuck" leaves his girlfriend in the hands of a black "bull"[1] and is accused of "triggering" (a swipe at PC terminology) him because he dares give him instructions.

## The "Just Joking" Argument

As Daviess (2019) remarks,

> ... in part because anything can be chocked up as "for the lulz," alt-right communities provide space to air and thereby normalize extremist views (p. 13)

---

1 Per *Urban Dictionary* a "bull" is "a sexually dominant male who (…) cuckolds and humiliates husbands while servicing their wives."

> Irony and parody allow meme makers to disclaim their own seriousness. (...) the particular vernacular in which discourse occurs means mememakers can always claim that "normies" don't "get it." (...) (p. 14)

The defense of "joking" or in this case "playing a comedic character" is still being used at the time this writing: see Paul (2022) reporting an interview of Andrew Tate, a troll who was banned from Twitter, Instagram and Facebook for misogynistic posts. Daviess (2019) states that the alt-right "views itself as invulnerable to attack" (p. 14) because of anonymity and the defense that one was joking: "The alt-right disclaims its own seriousness, and claims to use extreme memes only in the name of irony, parody, or triggering the libs." (p. 14) However, as Daviess notes: "the speech the alt-right engages in still has meaning, and has the effect of disguising and normalizing extremist content." (p. 14)

Ultimately, though the "I was joking" defense or the question of "freedom of speech" (should one be allowed to joke about anything?) is irrelevant. Regardless of whether one is joking or not one is not free to shout "fire!" in a crowded theatre. Outside of metaphor, there are practical consequences to what one says.

First, as we saw in Chapter 2, in our discussion of memetic virality, forwarding a meme implies endorsing the content and the credibility of the source from where we received the meme (Harvey et al., 2011). If I forward you a meme of a funny kitten, I am endorsing the content (in the sense that I think it is funny, not that it's a cat...) and therefore I am endorsing the credibility of the source as a provider of humorous content.

Because of enregisterment (see Chapter 2) if one jokes about a topic or if one exercises their freedom of speech to talk about a topic, one becomes associated with the kind of people that do those things, applaud them and agree with them, and the circumstances in which they do so. In other words, if fascists, white suprematists or misogynists are your audience, they agree with what you say, and you move in their milieu, then you are a fascist, white suprematist, misogynist, etc., regardless of what your stated intentions may have been. If it walks like a duck and quacks like duck...

It should be noted that the strength of the enregisterment argument comes from the repetition aspect. Any statement taken in isolation is undecidable as to its ironical or humorous status. Suppose I say: "I think Evaristo Baschenis's paintings are wonderful." You have no way of deciding whether I mean this sentence literally or whether I am joking or being ironical. If you knew that I collect baroque paintings, the fact that I obviously invested significant time and money in acquiring paintings similar to Baschenis's oeuvre would be a clue I am sincere (note the repeated nature of the action). If you happen to know I have numerous reproductions of Baschenis's paintings on my walls, again, you would conclude I am sincere. Note how having a single painting does not imply this. I used to have a reproduction of *A Friend in Need*,[2] by Cassius Marcellus Coolidge, hanging in my office, ironically.

Let us note also that practically the "just kidding" defense seems to have failed: in one form or another, retribution has come: Palmer Luckey was fired from Facebook in 2017; Alex Jones was sentenced to a $49 M fine and declared bankruptcy; Andrew Tate was banned from various platforms (Paul, 2022), and is currently in jail.

Finally, one might argue (e.g., Spitzberg, 2014, p. 317) that a meme successfully spreading to a population shows that the meme exhibits greater fitness (i.e., it is a meme better adapted at spreading) the fact that alt-right memes have spread as widely as they have, within the United States, could be considered proof that these ideas are "better" or more "viable" than others. This is a fallacy already refuted in Henrich et al. (2008). One simply cannot deduce from the fact that a meme has spread to a population that that meme was particularly fit in general (i.e., it had some valuable aspects), nor even just particularly fit to spread to that population. Consider the spread of the Western business suit, for example in Japan, Africa or the Arab world. Obviously, you cannot deduce that the suit-and-tie attire is "better" in any sense (a suit is not better clothing than the traditional local garb—it may in fact be much worse, for example, in a very hot climate—or better at spreading among business people). The reason the Western business suit has spread outside of its original population is simply that it is associated with the undeniable success of Western economic and military might. So, from the spread of alt-right memes we cannot conclude anything about the memes themselves.

---

2 The painting is known as "Dogs playing poker."

# Chapter 23

# 4CHAN, TROLLS AND LULZ: FASCISTS AT PLAY

What is 4chan (Figure 23.1)? As the website helpfully informs us, it is an "image-based bulletin board where anyone can post comments and share images. There are boards dedicated to a variety of topics." Topics include anime and manga, video games, sports, origami, do it yourself, advice, food and cooking, and of course pornography. It should be noted that this is the original 4chan.org; a new, "safe for work" version can be found at 4channel.org; the latter does not have the NSFW (not safe for work) boards indicated in red. So, why is it widely considered to be one of the principal gathering spaces of trolls and hackers, the source of many extremely popular memes, the birthplace of Anonymous and one of the bases of the alt-right? It all comes down to the fact that 4chan allows anonymous posting. In fact, most posts are credited to "Anonymous." This also explains why the hackivist collective was also called Anonymous.

4chan was started in 2003 by a Christopher "moot" Poole, who was part of the endearingly named "Anime Death Tentacle Rape Whorehouse" a part of the "Something Awful" forums. The details are essentially irrelevant. Poole stepped down in 2015 as part of the backlash on the "Gamergate" controversy, and it was announced that Hiroyuki Nishimura had purchased the website. (Wikipedia: https://en.wikipedia.org/wiki/4chan)

As we mentioned, 4chan is known for being the gathering place of the alt-right. Obviously, this is unrelated to origami enthusiasts. The board known as /pol/ (short for "Politically Incorrect") is your go-to place if you are looking for racist, misogynist or openly fascist images and discussions. When I visited to check out that the place was as bad as reported, I found within seconds memes openly praising Hitler, racist posts freely using the N-word, bestiality, attacks on Freemasonry, anti-Covid vaccine propaganda and of course anti-semitic conspiracy theories. Figure 23.2 shows the first page of /pol/.

In this chapter we will consider 4chan as the historical epicenter of some of the phenomena of the most fringe and radical alt-right but also as the cultural

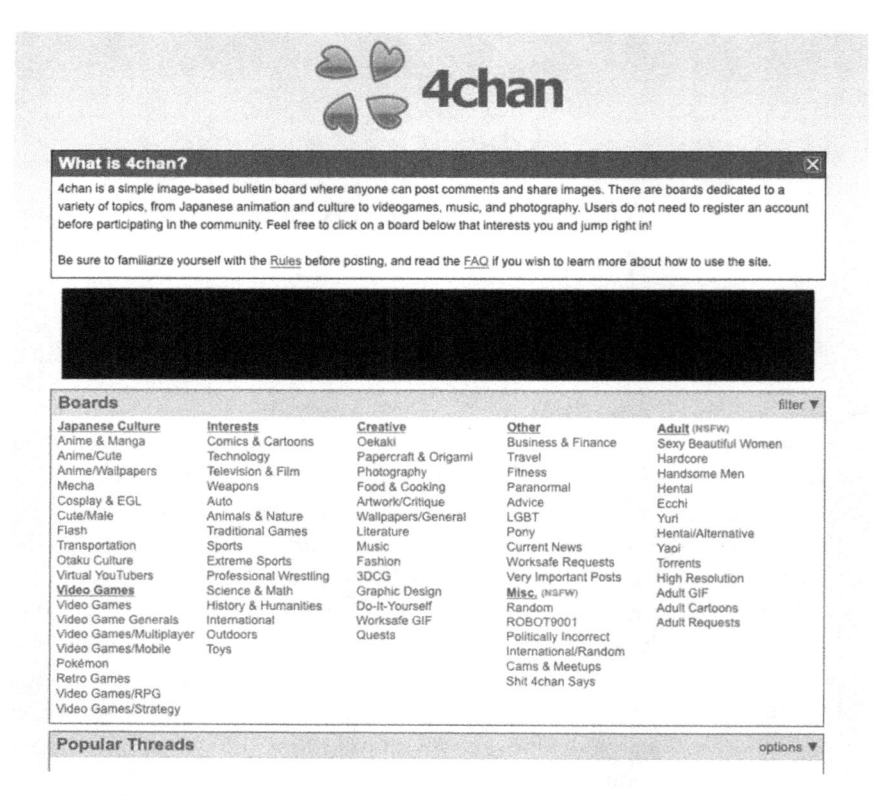

**Figure 23.1** The 4chan website.

background in which a general attitude of aggressive behavior/humor has emerged, known as trolling. From a strict humor-centric standpoint, there is nothing new here. Aggressive, ridiculing and derisive humor has been used to build in-group solidarity and conversely to "other" an out-group since the earliest records of humor. What is new and significant is how these groups have managed to mainstream discourse that was radically outside the bounds of socially acceptable discourse.

Defining trolling is difficult for a number of reasons; the primary one is that there does not seem to be an agreement on what exactly "trolling" means. Let me quote here a prototypical example of trolling, of which I became aware in the mid-1990s, so very early on in Internet history. In Usenet there were newsgroups (discussion board) dedicated to various topics, such as computers, literature, etc. Of course there were groups dedicated to cats, such as rec.pets.cats. In 1993, trolls from the alt.tasteless newsgroup, led by a user who went by the handle of Trashcan Man, started posting in rec.pets.cats, ostensibly

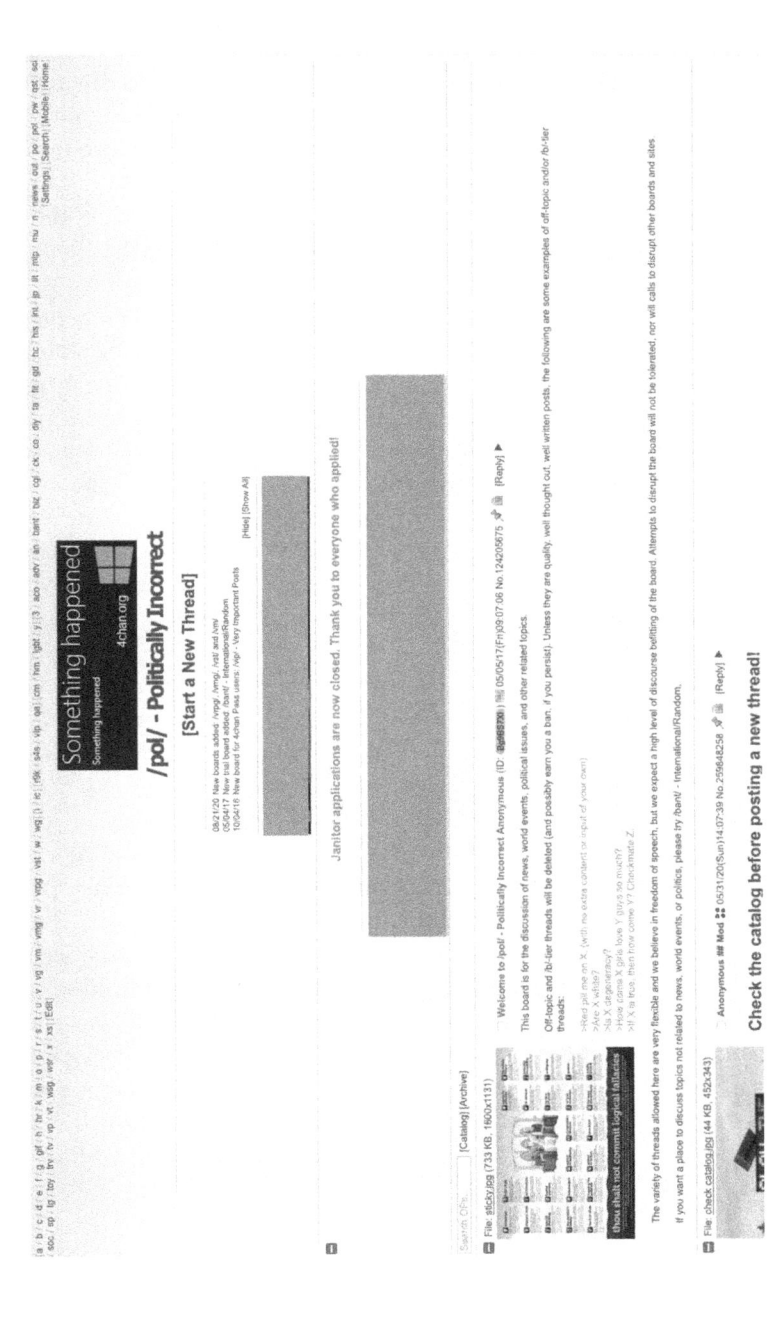

**Figure 23.2** Front page of /pol/ the politically incorrect broad of 4chan; I have greyed out advertisements.

asking for advice about dealing with difficult cats, but in fact just suggesting gruesome ways of killing cats. This predictably caused distress and aggravation. For an account of the details, see Quittner, (1994).[1] Here we see the typical features of trolling: repeated posting, deception, intention to disrupt and harass the members of the group, punching down, and no direct connection between the trolls and their targets. Other definitions are more restrictive. For example Herring et al. (2002) add the requirement that the troll "appear outwardly sincere." The difficulty of defining trolling is attested by the different definitions listed by Fichman and Sanfilippo (2016, p. 8). The general consensus is that trolling is disruptive, deliberate and antagonizing. The deliberately disruptive, misogynistic nature of trolling is well-documented in Herring et al. (2002). Fichman and Sanfilippo (2016, p. 13) stress the repetitive nature of trolling, which differentiates it in their eyes from flaming (a single direct attack). The motives range from entertainment ("lulz") to ideologically motivated attacks intending to disrupt a website's purpose or show opposition to a politician. Trolling is distinct from cyberbullying insofar as the latter usually takes place among people who know each other, whereas trolling is usually anonymous or directed at an unknown audience (Fichman & Sanfilippo, 2016, p. 10). Trolls may act alone or in coordinated groups. Many groups of trolls coordinate their actions on boards such as 4Chan (https://en.wikipedia.org/wiki/Internet_troll#Troll_sites).

Trolls do not attack only random internet users. There are reports of trolling attacks against corporations such as McDonalds or Coca-Cola or organizations such as Scientology, famously attacked by Anonymous, or against right-wing politicians (e.g., Fichman & Sanfilippo, 2016, pp. 11–14). The punching up or down distinction is also relevant here: when trolls target the grieving relatives of suicide victims, they are clearly punching down, whereas when Anonymous attacked Scientology they were punching up (and paid a price for it). When trolling punches up it borders hacktivism, the use of hacking techniques as civil disobedience (e.g., Wikileaks and the already quoted Anonymous). While trolling that punches up shows that trolling is not necessarily a right-wing practice, it seems clear that there is a much stronger affinity and connection between the trolling subculture and the alt-right. I will review some of the evidence of this claim in what follows, but the primary source is Phillips (2015) which has a very nuanced stance toward the trolling subculture, at times approaching supporting it. That is to say, I have not

---

[1] The last sentence of the article is prophetic: "I have political aspirations," Trashcan Man said. "I'm a member of the Republican Party on campus. I have often proclaimed that I am the future of the Republican Party" (Quittner, 1994).

chosen an antagonistic account of trolls; rather, even a sympathetic account of the trolling subculture reveals its links to the alt-right misogynistic, racist, entitled culture.

In conclusion, it seems fair to characterize the trolling milieu as including a broad continuum of behaviors and groups, ranging from the purely playful to the utilitarian (where trolling is a means-to-an-end) and ranging from the progressive to the extreme-right wing. Attempts to "ennoble" or justify trolling (e.g., Phillips, 2015; Nagle, 2017) by comparing it to Situationism, or Surrealism, or Schopenhauer ultimately fail, not just because they are prima facie silly (Bréton, Debord or Schopenhauer would have been horrified to be mentioned in the same breath as people who openly advocate for white supremacy and mock the families of teen suicides) but also because the trolling milieu is not a unified, or even coherent system, but is best understood as a loose aggregate of groups and factions that bear some "family resemblance" to one or another but by no means to all or that share some cultural/rhetorical tools (e.g., memes). After all, we would not put Leni Riefenstahl, Luis Buñuel and Ingmar Bergman under the same banner just because they all directed movies.

## 4Chan and Other Unmoderated Boards

Thorleifsson (2021) states that "the combination of anonymity with a lack of moderation has made such chan [sic] platforms gathering places for an uneasy community of far-right nationalists and white supremacists who rapidly and anonymously produce and spread fascist content online" (p. 287) Daviess (2019) stresses the importance of anonymity to ensure impunity: "The emphasis on maintaining anonymity at all costs prevents 'real world' offline consequences from affecting meme-makers." Phillips (2015) stresses the anonymity and relative impunity of US-based trolls, contrasted with other countries, where the police do prosecute trolls (p. 76). Anonymity had been identified as one of the main affordances of much online communication in Herring (2007), although to be fair not all internet communication is anonymous. Most of 4chan postings in the /pol/ area are anonymous.

One of the most striking features of 4chan and such websites is the extreme use of jargon and specialized memes. For example, the use of triple parentheses around a name (((bob))) is an anti-semitic marker. Another such marker is the use of the Pepe character (see Chapter 24. The use of specialized jargon automatically creates an in-group vs. out-group dynamic. Outsiders who need to ask what, say, "Tits or GTFO" means are ridiculed (Ludemann, 2021, p. 9). Conversely, fluency in the jargon creates a sense of community and shared purpose.

The other feature of 4Chan that originates completely accidentally from the affordances of the software platform which originally supported the website and lacked appropriate storage is that posts are not archived and in fact disappear rather quickly if they are not responded to. We return to 4chan below.

## Are They Really Fascists?

The first issue to clarify is what does Thorleifsson, and for that matter the title of this chapter, mean by "fascism"? After all, wasn't fascism defeated in 1945 and both Fascism and Nazism ended *manu militari*? Most definitely, Italian fascism and German Nazism were defeated by the Allied forces, but those are only historical manifestations of a more abstract ideology, which Umberto Eco (1995) calls "Ur-fascism" (or in Italian "eternal fascism") and Roger Griffin (1993) calls "generic fascism." So, while fascism made it to an official regime in Italy, Germany, Portugal and Spain it appears as a political force in many more countries (see a list in https://en.wikipedia.org/wiki/List_of_fascist_movements) and as Griffin puts it, "Fascism continues to inspire both theorists and activist to the present day (...) as a political ideology capable of spawning new movement it should be treated as a permanent feature of modern political culture" (1993, p. xii).

> [T]he cyberfascism produced at /pol/ lends itself to calls for violent action against minority communities, including terrorism. The dynamics of the /pol/ platform, where fascist fantasies of white supremacy are spread fast and anonymously in a transnational network through *transgressive play frames*, is particularly powerful for the amplification of the logic of an endangered ultra-nation that needs urgent violent defence to obtain racial palingenesis. [my emphasis, SA] Thorleifsson (2021)

There is a lot to unpack here: "palingenesis" refers to Roger Griffin's work on the core ideas of fascism. Palingenesis is the "rebirth" of a nation, as for example Mussolini's Italian fascism involved the rebirth of the Roman Empire. Palingenesis corresponds to Umberto Eco's "traditionalism," the first of the list of components of "Ur-fascism" (Eco, 1995). Racism[2] is another of the core components of Ur-fascism: "Ur-Fascism is racist by definition" (Eco, 1995). The paranoid sense of endangerment mentioned by Thorleifsson in the quote above also appears in Eco's list, for whom fascism appeals "to a frustrated

---

2 On racism as part of the right wing political landscape, see Pérez (2022).

middle class, a class suffering from an economic crisis or feelings of political humiliation, and frightened by the pressure of lower social groups" (Eco, 1995, p. 6).

Another component which Eco had identified before it became rather obvious was the predilection in Ur-fascism of conspiracy theories: "At the root of the Ur-Fascist psychology there is the obsession with a plot, possibly an international one. The followers must feel besieged. The easiest way to solve the plot is the appeal to xenophobia. But the plot must also come from the inside: Jews are usually the best target because they have the advantage of being at the same time inside and outside" (Eco, 1995, p. 10).[3]

Yet another component is syncretism (Eco, 1995), the merging of different cultural themes (or memes in the original Dawkinian sense): Holmes (2019) argues that fascism

> can colonize just about every expression of identity and attachment, every aspect of truth, beauty, virtue, and depravity. From the motifs and metaphors of diverse folkloric traditions to the countless genres of popular culture, fascism acquires and assimilates new meanings and affective predispositions foregrounding fascism's capacities to merge, fuse, and synthesize what would otherwise be considered incompatible elements not merely those drawn from the Right and the Left. (p. 83)

Therefore it is not surprising that fascist discourse has subsumed images, memes, genres and even modes of communication, such as irony and play.

One final clarification: there has been an unfortunate tendency, especially within the left, to use fascist as a sort of generic insult. So, for example, Traub (2003) already 20 years ago remarked on a tendency to define as "fascist" things are not necessarily actually displays of fascism. Indeed, the alt-right exploits this. The following is a quote from the Cuckistan entry in the Republic of Kekistan Wiki (https://kekistanreborn.fandom.com/wiki/

---

3 Nor are these definitions at the fringe of scholarship. For example, another definition, from Paxton (2004, p. 218) is "a form of political behaviour marked by obsessive preoccupation with community decline, humiliation, or victimhood and by compensatory cults of unity, energy and purity in which committed nationalist militants abandons democratic liberties and pursues with redemptive violence and without ethical or legal restraints goals of internal cleaning and external expansion." There is a current of thought that distinguishes fascism from populism (e.g., Finchelstein, 2017) but it would take us too far afield to discuss the differences between the two. In a nutshell, fascism is populist, but not all populisms are fascist. For example, the Spanish party Podemos has been described as left-wing populist.

Cuckistan). Cucks (short for Cuckolds), in the alt-right lingo, are people who are not members of the alt-right.

> Cucks tend to immediately dismiss ideas and ideologies different to their own, labelling them as hate speech or simply as racist (Other terms can include, but are certainly not limited to: homophobic, Islamophobic, bigoted, anti-LGBT, Trump-supporting, Nazi, alt-right, sexist, misogynistic, etc.). These terms can (and if needed, will) be applied to anybody who disagrees with them, particularly on issues concerning Trump, Islam, cultural marxism, and other controversial issues.

Let me be very clear that I am using the term "fascist" and "fascism" in a literal, non-metaphorical sense, as defined above, by Eco and Griffin. The big difference between Eco's and Griffin's definitions of fascism and "internet fascism" in Thorleifsson's definition is the play element, which I highlighted in the Thorleifsson quote above and that difference brings us right back to our topic: the use of humor by the fascist right on the internet.

4chan is where LOLCats, Rickrolling and many other amusing memes have originated, but, and it is not a coincidence, that it is also where fascism has seeded one of its most profound roots, because fascism uses humor and irony to cover up their propaganda, as Sienkiewicz and Marx (2022) showed (see Chapter 22).

Let us be clear: I am not claiming that anyone who logs onto 4Chan is ipso facto a fascist. That would be silly. The point is that 4Chan hosts online forums in which fascists congregate, radicalize and proselytize. As Holmes (2019, p. 83) puts it, what exists today is a

> recursive, screen-mediated fascism that orchestrates—with the aid of bots and trolls—the ways of thinking, feeling, and experiencing of shadow publics networked in cyberspace (…) Via a ubiquitous technology, (…) fascism is being produced and reproduced (…) attaining the features of mass movements capable of getting in the heads of a broad swath of the European public. (p. 83)

There is no reason to believe that Holmes' analysis, based on European data, cannot be extended to the US situation and to other cases.

## Shitposting

The term "shitposting" was used by the Christchurch shooter and was apparently very popular in alt-right circles. It certainly gained notoriety in 2016,

**Figure 23.3** The Twilight shitposting page on Facebook.

when it was revealed that Palmer Luckey, one of the founders of Oculus and a Facebook exec, had been funding a group of trolls intent of shitposting against Hillary Clinton. (Bogost, 2016; see also the Wikipedia page on the subject https://en.wikipedia.org/wiki/Shitposting).

A more recent development (or change in meaning) of shitposting is exemplified by the Twilight Shitposting Group on Facebook (see Figure 23.3 )

This group organizes "watch parties" (of the Twilight movies), book clubs, has a merch shop, and is present on Twitter, Instagram and Discord. Discord is an anonymous voice chat software, that can be used in conjunction to video gaming.[4]

This sort of meta-commentary shitposting is reminiscent of the granddaddy of all reaction videos, MST3K, a.k.a., Mystery Science Theater 3000 (1988–1999). MST3K's premise is that a group of mad scientists has imprisoned a human subject and is trying to drive him mad by forcing him to watch bad movies. The human constructs a couple of robots and they watch the movies together commenting humorously on them. In its present version one

---

[4] While presumably the Twilight shitposting group has no such connections, Discord is the medium that the users of the banned r/The_Donald subreddit used to reconvene after its ban. The group was then banned from Discord as well. Discord has been linked to several alt-right groups, including the one involved in the planning of the Unite the Right rally in Charlottesville, Virginia, in 2017, which resulted in one homicide and numerous injuries, the one planning the Capitol coup attempt of January 6, 2021, and the mass shooting in Buffalo in 2022 (10 dead).

can download audio-tracks that can be synched to famous movies (such as *Star Wars*). https://www.rifftrax.com/howto

Hate-watching (Cohen et al., 2021) is related to shitposting in the sense that it is a preliminary step: essentially it consists of watching a TV show, but this can be expanded to any medium (books, videos, etc.) for the explicit purpose of shitposting about it. This may sound completely counterintuitive, as one who hated, say, *Game of Thrones* would have to subject themselves to watching it, just to make fun of it on Twitter or other discussion boards. However, if we consider the personality types of those who are willing to shitpost or troll (see below), we can explain this simply as the fact that the enjoyment that they get from shitposting or trolling about it is greater than the displeasure they must suffer in order to be able to shitpost about it accurately. One of the easiest rebuttals of the criticism of a show, book, etc., is that the critical person has simply not understood or appreciated it and evidence for this can be drawn from incorrect references to it. Hence, in order to shitpost effectively, one has to be informed about the topic. Hate watching is also related to anti-fandom (Click, 2019).

We will turn next to the differences between shitposting and trolling. The two things are obviously closely related, in that their aim is to disrupt the normal activity of a forum, but according to Ludemann (2021) shitposting is more humor-oriented than trolling, which is more antagonistic.

## Trolling

There are many definitions of the terms "trolling" and "trolls." The definitions are roughly concordant, but differ in significant details. Most scholars agree that the term "troll" is a reference to demons in Norse mythology. Norse trolls live in isolated spots (mountains, caves, etc.). The popular idea that trolls live under bridges comes from a translation of Norse tales (*Popular tales from the Norse*, translated by Sir George Webbe Dasent, in 1859) which includes the tale "The Three Billy-Goats Gruff" which features a large troll that lives under a bridge (see James, 2014). There may be also a reference to fishing by trolling or trawling (the difference between the two methods is that trawling is done using a net, whereas fishing by trolling is done with a rod) which involve pulling a net or lure through water.

There are generic uses of trolling, in which it means more or less "playing a practical joke on someone." For example, Monroe (2018) uses it in the title of an article reporting that the band Weezer released a cover of the song *Rosanna*, by Toto, and tweeted it to the twitter account @WeezerAfrica set up by fans agitating for the band to cover the mega hit *Africa*, also by Toto. The "trolling" aspect of course consists in the band releasing a cover of the wrong song, from the standpoint of the fans asking for the *Africa* cover. Aside from the remarkable amount of effort expended by Weezer to play the prank on their fans, what is relevant here is that a few days later they released a cover of *Africa*, which was the single of their "teal" album. In other words, they ultimately did what the fans wanted them to do. This makes the prank very benign.

However, many and perhaps most examples of trolling are not this kind of kind-hearted prank.

Phillips, who did an ethnographic study of trolls, characterizes them as anglophone, economically privileged (at least able to afford a computer, an internet connection, vast amount of leisure time and some degree of privacy—it is hard to troll on 4chan from your local public library…), young (under 30), white, male and with homosexual tendencies (for example, the posting of the picture of one's penis asking other users to "rate it"; 2015, pp. 53–55). Obviously, the demographic described by Phillips is just a general tendency; there may be or have been black, poor, middle-aged, women trolls, for all we know. However, in my mind, the crucial aspect of the troll is the anonymity which afford "no repercussions" for posing "racist, sexist, homophobic, or exploitative text and/or images (…) including child pornography" and other illegal content (Phillips, 2015. p. 55).

In order to properly understand trolling, and in particular the motivations behind it, we need to introduce a technical term: "asshole" (James, 2014). James, who is an ethics professor and chair of the department of philosophy at UC Irvine, defines "asshole" as follows: "A person counts as an asshole when, and only when, he systematically allows himself to enjoy special advantages in social relations out of an entrenched sense of entitlement that immunizes him against the complaints of other people" (pp. 2-3). When viewed through this interpretive lens, trolling and the personality of trolls are immediately understandable: trolls are assholes, who enjoy trolling because of their sense of entitlement and false superiority. This also explains why trolls are predominantly male (note that the definition of asshole uses—deliberately, one assumes—a male pronoun). Needless to say, trolling is by definition, not benign but a clear violation of pretty much any standards or rules of interpersonal behavior.

It may be interesting to examine the personality of trolls. Dionigi et al. (2022) connect the "dark triad" of personality traits (narcissism, Machiavellianism and psychopathy) to irony, sarcasm and cynicism. Narcissism is characterized by an exaggerated sense of self-worth, Machiavellianism by indifference to morality and manipulativeness and psychopathy by "lack of empathy and antisocial behavior" (p. 1). If that seems to you like a description of trolling behavior, you are correct.

Trolls are the ultimate eristic opponent in a debate. Named after Eris, the Greek goddess of discord and strife, the eristic mode of argumentation was introduced by the sophists. Essentially, it is arguing not to find the truth, but rather merely to defeat one's opponent. While the Sophists used it in ways reminiscent of today's lawyers in court (where the parties argue not to find out the truth but to secure a favorable verdict to their side), in its modern assumption (e.g., Wodak, 2017) the assumption is not only that the eristic rhetor is merely interested in winning the argument but they use tactics such as interrupting frequently, ad hominem fallacies (personal attacks), unsubstantiated accusations and outright falsehoods. Phillips (2015) explicitly links trolling to eristic behavior (she does not use the term, but it's clear that it's what she means). The only way to fight an eristic opponent is to out-eristic them: if someone interrupts you, interrupt them; if they slander you, slander them worse; if they lie, lie even more, etc. Of course this has the unwitting side effect of turning both opponents into eristic argumentators. An alternative strategy is just to ignore them and their arguments entirely, but that effectively concedes the space to the trolls. The only way to actually confront a troll is by out-trolling them. This is the strategy chosen by Drew Afualo, which we considered in Chapter 21: fighting trolls with trolling.

This strategy is successful insofar, as Phillips (2015) claims, the purpose of the troll is to elicit anger. Being counter-trolled not only denies the troll his prize, but exposes his personal weaknesses, whereas the troll is supposed to be anonymous, detached and above the fray. Here the troll finds himself twice ridiculed, for failing as a troll and as a person.

## Lulz on 4chan

Thorleifsson's analysis of memes on 4Chan /pol/ board leads her to conclude that "the content, even if intended by the users to produce transgressive lulz, reflects a core feature of the fascist phenomena: the perception of an endangered community that need to be reborn through violent means" (2021, p. 290). Thorleifsson finds that memes are used to "cover up" sensitive material; Pepe the Frog was the most popular meme (see Chapter 24).

Thorleifsson finds an apocalyptic ideology, grounded in the conspiracy theories of "the great replacement" and "white genocide" (respectively, the fantasies that white people rare being "replaced" by non-white immigrants and that white people are being eliminated by various means including interracial marriage and genocide; https://en.wikipedia.org/wiki/Great_Replacement and https://en.wikipedia.org/wiki/White_genocide_conspiracy_theory). This provides a justification for a sense of "threat":

An overwhelming part of the eclectic memes at /pol/ contains generalized dehumanizing and racist imaginary, playing on racial stereotypes, themes of racial impurity, and the threat of cultural differences. The users producing fascist content operate a "primordialist" concept of the nation in tandem with scapegoating racial, religious and sexual minorities as existential threat to the purity, survival and superiority of the white ultra-nation. Other despised enemies are liberals, feminists and members of the left. (...) Antisemitism is (...) by far the most prevalent form of online racism (2021, p. 291)

Feminists and women in general are also a target because they are blamed for falling birth rates and male emasculation (see the "incels" phenomenon, i.e., involuntary celibate https://en.wikipedia.org/wiki/Incel).

The ultimate connection between white suprematist terrorism and the alt-right memes come from the glorification and memeization of terrorists, such as the shooter of the Christchurch shooting:

Observing posting behaviour at /pol/ in the months following the Christchurch shooting, [the shooter]'s fascist actions were glorified as a 'living act' carried out by a racial warrior determined to protect and bring about the palingenesis of the ultra-nation imagined as a white civilizational space. Anons would routinely praise [the shooter]'s livestreamed massacre, producing and spreading gamified images of the atrocities. The attack was scored and rated like a video game, pointing to a wider trend emerging from this online milieu: the gamification of fascist propaganda and violence. Reducing victims to numbers and circulating gamified memes of the atrocities become integral to glorification of fascist violence at /pol/. Several post combined glorifications of violence through memetic irony with shitposting language characteristic of the subcultural style of communication. (Thorleifsson, 2021, p. 293)

The shooter was "sanctified" in 4Chan and other white suprematist right wing sites. See for example Dearden (2019). The connection between the alt-right and trolling is also explicitly theorized in Aspray (2019) who claims the alt-right "originated within the proudly antisocial internet subculture of trolling" and by Nagle (2017, p. 19) "What we now call the alt-right (...) [is] a bursting forth or anti-PC cultural politics. The irreverent trolling style associated with 4chan grew in popularity in response to the expanding identity politics."

## Conclusion: Don't Take My Word for It. Take Theirs

Alt-right website The Daily Stormer's style sheet explicitly describes coopting humor to hide the alt-right's true purpose (see Greene, 2019, for discussion). The following is an unedited excerpt from their "style sheet" published in its entirety by *Huffington Post* (Feinberg, 2017):

> Lulz
> The tone of the site should be light.
> Most people are not comfortable with material that comes across as vitriolic, raging, nonironic hatred.
> The unindoctrinated should not be able to tell if we are joking or not. There should also be a conscious awareness of mocking stereotypes of hateful racists. I usually think of this as self-deprecating humor—I am a racist making fun of stereotype of racists, because I don't take myself super-seriously.
> This is obviously a ploy and I actually do want to gas kikes. But that's neither here nor there.

# Chapter 24

# PEPE, KEK AND FRIENDS

This chapter considers the adoption of cartoon mascots by US right-wing groups. This seems to be a phenomenon limited to the US context (McSwiney et al., 2021), although there has been some diffusion of this imagery beyond the United States. For example, Pepe the Frog is a character from the comic *Boy's Club* (2005) by Matt Furie (who has decried the appropriation of his character and even proclaimed him dead, as we will see). While originally there was no connection with right-wing ideas, in 2015, a number of memes associating the alt-right and Pepe were published on 4chan and in October, Donald Trump posted a cartoon of himself as Pepe. Kek is the deity of another satirical religion (The Cult of Kek) associated with the right. Pepe is considered an avatar of Kek.

Originally, right-wing propaganda took the form of "dog whistles" (Bhat & Klein, 2020) that is, references known to the initiated but that maintain a degree of deniability or simply appear nonsensical to the uninitiated. For example, the number 1488 is a white suprematist dog whistle: it consists of the number 14, which stands for "14 words" which is itself a short hand for the slogan "We must secure the existence of our people and a future for white children." The number 88 stands for Heil Hitler, since H is the 8th letter of the alphabet. Thus white suprematist merchandise is often priced at $14.88. (https://www.adl.org/resources/hate-symbol/1488)

With the mainstreaming of Nazi imagery, the motivation for dog whistles seems to have diminished or possibly the amount of openly pro-Nazi, anti-semitic, pro-klan, etc., has increased along with dog whistles.

More recently, the alt-right has switched to using memes to recruit and spread their propaganda. According to Trillò and Shifman (2021, p. 2485), "Memes perform a number of key functions for the far-right, including channeling a dispersed user-base towards far-right movements and fostering in-group belonging among constituents." They also point out that "the far-right's ability to accrue such a following depends on their ability to tap into the audience of commercial social media platforms." (Trillò and Shifman, 2021, p. 2485)

Not only is alt-right propaganda and recruitment active on all social media, but the alt.right has found alternative spaces in which to express its ideology and recruit. For example, the Anti-Defamation League (ADL) states that

> Steam, the largest and most important online store for PC gamers with over $4 Billion in revenue in 2017, has recently gained popularity among white supremacists for being a platform, like Gab and Telegram, where they can openly express their ideology and calls for violence.
>
> The difference between Steam and social media platforms like Telegram or Gab is that while the latter do not share a formal business relationship with the wider social media industry, Steam has direct and lucrative relationships with most major game companies, including 2K, Electronic Arts, Xbox Game Studios, Ubisoft and others. Many of these game companies have made public statements about and dedicated significant resources towards keeping their products safe from the kinds of hateful ideologies espoused by extremists—while continuing to work with Steam. https://www.adl.org/steamextremism#introduction

As mentioned before, Pepe the Frog (Figure 24.1) is a central meme, in the alt-right strategy. It is worth quoting at length the ADL on the use of Pepe:

> The Pepe the Frog character did not originally have racist or anti-Semitic connotations." (…) The majority of uses of Pepe the Frog have been, and continue to be, non-bigoted. (…)
>
> In recent years, with the growth of the "alt right" segment of the white supremacist movement, (…) the number of "alt right" Pepe

**Figure 24.1** Racist Pepe memes.

memes has grown, a tendency exacerbated by the controversial and contentious 2016 presidential election. Though Pepe memes have many defenders, the use of racist and bigoted versions of Pepe memes seems to be increasing, not decreasing.

(...) The mere fact of posting a Pepe meme does not mean that someone is racist or white supremacist. (...) In the fall of 2016, the ADL teamed with Pepe creator Matt Furie to form a #SavePepe campaign to reclaim the symbol from those who use it with hateful intentions. https://www.adl.org/education/references/hate-symbols/pepe-the-frog

(...)

Bigoted humor and irony are hallmarks of the emerging virtual counterculture that promotes radical, extreme and violent views as cool and/or humorous. In that vein, it's not uncommon to find references on Steam to white supremacist memes, common vernacular or other trappings of this white supremacist subculture. A significant number of Steam profiles feature Pepe the Frog, a popular Internet meme that was hijacked by the alt right, in clearly white supremacist contexts. For example, user "Agent Pepe Kekson" writes in his bio: "Kekson—Pepe Kekson, Agent 1488, With a License to Troll."

## A Cast of Characters

Of course, Pepe is not the only cartoonish character. There are several others. We will start with Wojak (Figure 24.2) and related characters.

The Wojak character (a.k.a., "feels guy") is a caricature of a bald man with a sad or wistful expression, "used as a reaction image to represent feelings such as melancholy, regret or loneliness." (Know Your Meme) There exists several variants of the Wojak meme, including Soyjak and NPC Wojak. Soyjak (Figure 24.3) (a.k.a, nu male Woyjak) is a cross between the soy boy

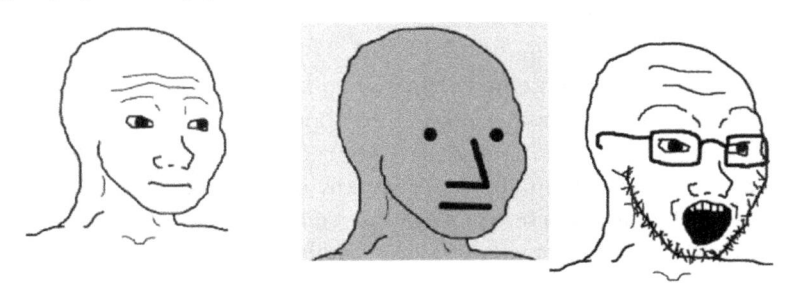

**Figure 24.2** Wojak, NPC-Wojak, and Soyjak.

**Figure 24.3** Chad.

**Figure 24.4** Screenshot from 4chan.

meme (young males represented as open mouthed in fake surprise and delight over a video game or another object). Soy boys are not "real men." Soyjak can be open or close mouthed and of course countless variations exist. A common one is to represent him crying, generally upset at something. He is often opposed to Chad who is a secure, virile (as symbolized by the full beard) man, usually espousing alt-right values (Figure 24.4).

NPC Wojak is interesting because it shows how easily these characters can be politicized. NPC Wojak represents Wojak with "a blank stare and facial expression, named after non-player characters" (NPC) in video games. NPC characters have no autonomy and minimal reactions, if any, in games. So they function as metaphors of soulless individuals. Before attributing profound meaning to what may on the surface look like a metaphor for the "one dimensional man" of Herbert Marcuse (Marcuse, 1964)[1] we need to read some passages from an anonymous post on 4chan (reproduced in its entirety in Figure 2.4).

> the soulless extra flesh [i.e., human NPCs] (...) or ultimate normalfags [another derogatory term for norms, i.e., non-4chan users] (...) follow group think and social trends (...). I call them NPC's because when you talk to them they just say the same shit every time. "TRUMP IS HITLER," "JUST BE YOURSELF," (...) They're the kind of people who make a show of discomfort when you break the status quo like by breaking the normie barrier to invoke a real discussion.

In other words, those who express thoughts critical of Trump or that object to the violation of cultural norms ("breaking the normie barrier") are therefore "soulless" whereas the soulful, fully human, players are pro-Trump.

More Wojak-derived characters are Doomer (a portmanteau-word composed of "doom" and "boomer" short for Baby Boomer, the generation 1946–1964) and Doomer Girl (Figure 24.5). Doomerism is in fact a movement of people who argue that climate change, the depletion of resources and overpopulation will destroy civilization as we know it or worst cause human extinction (https://en.wikipedia.org/wiki/Doomer). Doomer Girl also started on 4chan, as the counterpart of Doomer, who rejects him (because women are evil—remember, this is 4chan, home-of-incels speaking), but was soon adopted by young women who repurposed her character as "a cool girl, dark and sad in a stylish way" (Tiffany, 2020).

## The Rage Comics

We have already mentioned the rage comics, deliberately poorly drawn characters including "Rage guy" (Figure 24.6), Trollface (which we do not reproduce, as it is one of the few memes that is actually copyrighted, since it was

---

1 Marcuse argues that both under capitalism and communism, through advertising and propaganda, false needs eliminate critical thoughts and thus the possibility of a real opposition, i.e., produce a one-dimensional person.

**Figure 24.5** Doomer Girl and young woman cosplaying as the character.

**Figure 24.6** Rage guy (left) and Forever alone (right).

drawn by Carlos Ramirez in 2008), Forever alone (Figure 24.6) and a rarer upbeat image (Figure 24.7).

Most of these images are used as reaction faces to indicate the feelings or attitude of the poster. They can also be incorporated in simple four panel cartoons where usually the last panel is the rage face.

## The Cult of Kek and Kekistan

As we saw in Chapter 14, the cult of Kek is another invented religion. I will compare[2] the cult of Kek and the Kekistan "state" to Pastafarianism. The

---

2 I base this discussion on the webpages https://micronations.wiki/wiki/Republic_of_Kekistan and https://kekistanreborn.fandom.com/wiki/The_Republic_of_Kekistan_Wiki.

**Figure 24.7** A rare upbeat rage comic.

comparison is fair, since they are both invented satirical religions. Fandom, formerly known as Wikia, is a site that hosts wikis about fictional universes, such as Star Wars. It is already troubling a priori that materials that openly proclaim their affiliation with Nazi ideologies are available on a website where one may go to check out the history of Han Solo, for example. The micronations wiki labels the page as "largely non-serious or comical in nature."

There are Facebook pages associated with Kekistan, but they seem inactive and have only a few thousand followers. A Reddit page on Kekistan has 14,000 members but seems, at the time of writing, inactive. Among the most recent posts, I found Figure 24.8. There is no question that the choice of image for Trump makes him look ridiculous, and so does the image of Pepe wearing a Meme war veteran baseball cap and carrying a gun. Trump is also wearing an armband that reads "Meme war veteran" in all caps. The exaggerated smile on Pepe and the smiley face in the shape of a heart on Trump's sleeve are probably meant to create a reassuring and comical incongruity.

The cult of Kek is said to go back to an Egyptian deity (Kek) represented with the head of a frog. This is accurate (https://en.wikipedia.org/wiki/Kek_(mythology). However, the image reproduced in the Micronations wiki is of another frog headed Egyptian goddess (Hequet), associated with Horus. https://www.timelessmyths.com/gods/egyptian/heqet/. "Kek" is also an onomatopoetic term in Korean corresponding to "lol" so it became associated with Pepe the Frog. Pepe and Kek became associated with Donald Trump (see Donovan et al., 2022 for a detailed discussion of the historical process). Trump explicitly endorsed the association. Claims of (dark) magic have also been associated with Kek. In the Kek mythos, Kek is the god, Pepe is the prophet and Donald Trump is the "President / God Emperor"

**Figure 24.8** A recent meme, featuring Donald Trump and Pepe, posted on the Kekistan Reddit.

(https://kekistanreborn.fandom.com/wiki/The_Republic_of_Kekistan_Wiki). The "People's Republic of Kekistan" is populated by "shitposters" who are "currently at war the normies and SJWs [Social Justice Warriors] who have forced many of them out of their land. Some Kekistanis now seek refuge in other countries." Notice the mimicry of the refugee theme and the implicit claim of a status of victimhood, which echoes Nagle's (2017) claim that the alt-right is a reaction to the "callout culture" of the 2010s (see Chapter 22).

Under "Forces of Kek," the page list Pepe and Adolf Hitler (Figure 24.9). In the text, we read that

> Hitler was not actually an anti-semite, the entire holocaust was actually part of Hitler's plan to become a meme god and a prank gone horribly wrong. With the takeover of Germany, the sacrifice of 6 million Jews, and the downfall of colonialism, Hitler was able to ascend to being a meme god around the same level as Kek. Hitler now exists solely on the Internet, where he watches over all his followers and preys on the weak,

PEPE, KEK AND FRIENDS 247

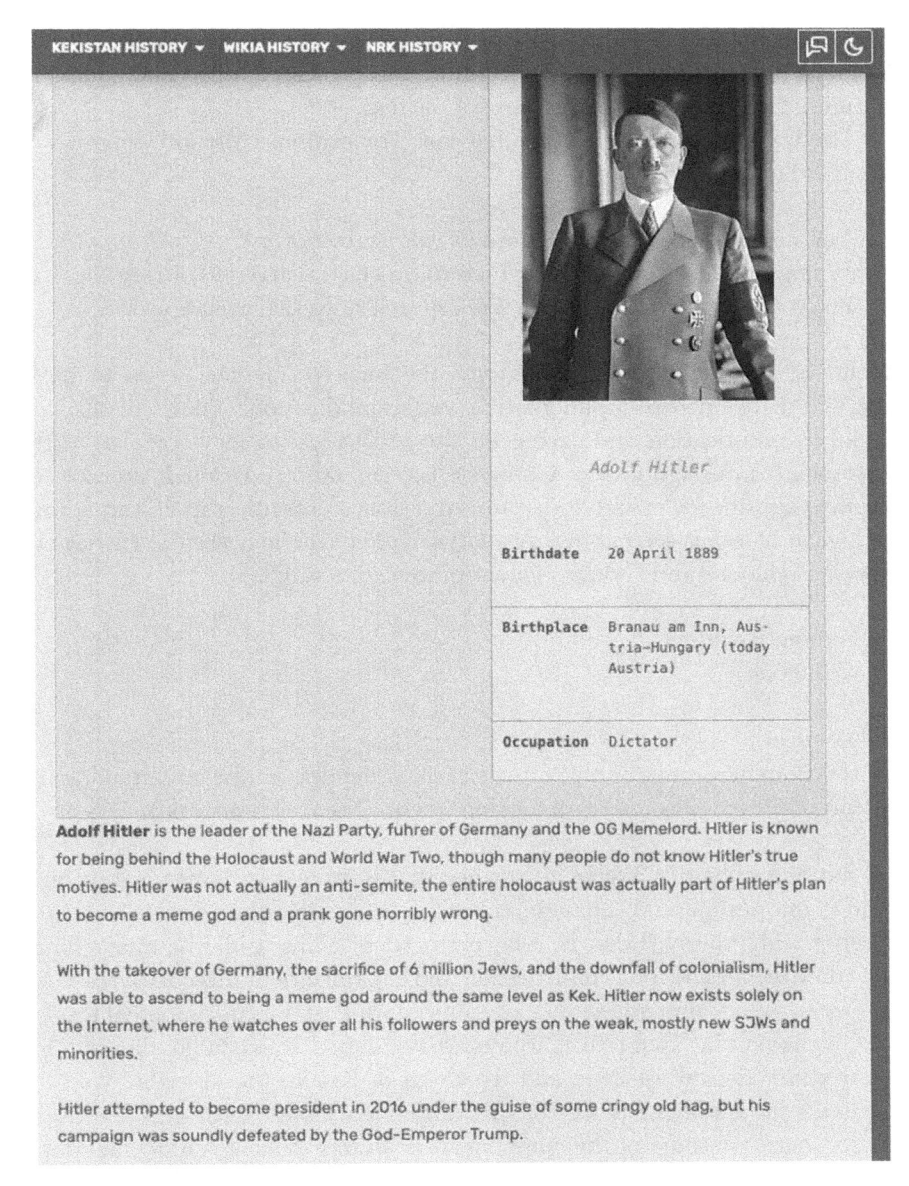

**Figure 24.9** Screenshot from the Kekistan site; Adolf Hitler's page.

mostly new SJWs and minorities. Hitler attempted to become president in 2016 under the guise of some cringy old hag, but his campaign was soundly defeated by the God-Emperor Trump.

Defining the holocaust a "prank gone horribly wrong" could possibly be interpreted as an attempt at humor, but of course the Holocaust is part of the scripts not available for humor in our society. It is unclear why Hitler is suddenly associated with Hilary Clinton and presented as an antagonist of Trump. This contradicts prior parts of the text.

The quality of the pages is rather low. For example, the following is an unedited quote:

> they succeeded to hold back the Liberals against over
> wealming odds even to having their main general arrested during the
> Third battle of Berkeley At the Free speech rally. (Micronations wiki)

Note the misspelled "overwhelming," the incorrect syntax "even to having," and the incorrect punctuation and capitalization. These all display lack of sophistication and caring for the project. Also, they correlate with low social status/ignorance. Content-wise, the fantasy is much inferior to Pastafarianism, for example, because the story contradicts itself and is full of logical holes, as seen above. A good sample of the text are the entries on Foreign relations and Culture, here reproduced in full:

> Foreign Relations
> we h8 cuks
>
> Culture
> Kekistan's culture mainly consists of dank memes, anime, and making
> fun of the left, also there all fucking weebs. (Micronations wiki)

h8 stands for "hate." "Weebs" is strange in this context, as it means someone who is into anime and Japanese culture. It is possible that the author confused it with "dweeb," that is, a boring nerd. Leaving aside the misspelling for "they're" and the poor punctuation and capitalization, this compares very poorly with the witty abundance of materials of Pastafarian canonical texts.

Greene (2019), Kien (2019), Tuters (2019) and Al-Rawi (2020) describe in some detail the use of Pepe and the myth of Kek in the alt-right. We are left with the question: Is any of this funny? As I have indicated here and there, there are some of the components of humor (incongruities, superiority and aggression). While the texts fall short of other examples, such as the Pastafarian memes and they tend to violate many of the rules of accessible scripts for humor in society, they certainly can function as in-group demarcators. Because of this, they are sufficient to build the sense of belonging to an online community, illustrated by Tsakona (2020), for much different materials.

# CONCLUSION: PLUS ÇA CHANGE…

We started out this book with a question: How has the internet changed humor? We can now answer with a paradox: the more it changes, the more it stays the same. At a deep level, we know that humor is the same across cultures and across times. The grand theories of incongruity, superiority and release capture these universal traits of human nature: we like unexpected, surprising things that make us feel better about ourselves and we like to play, free of the stresses of life. Of course what any of those things mean, for a given culture and a given time, is up for grabs: what specifically is unexpected or what counts as play, for example, are culture-driven constructs. Each culture determines what things are OK to be made fun of and what things are out of bounds.

So, of course, we could have predicted that humor in the abstract sense remains unchanged, but that what our culture in the first two decades of the new millennium finds appropriate as the object of humor has changed. The time has come to review these changes.

The biggest one is probably the emergence of the humorous internet meme. In a sense, of course, humorous memes have always existed (jokes, comedy genres, etc.). What has changed however, is the participatory culture of social media, the advent of the produsers and the blurring of the professional/amateur boundary. When memes, videos, witty tweets, cartoons, music parodies and generally speaking "media content" are produced and immediately disseminated by individuals with no training and sometimes even less talent, the result is a steady stream of content, often devoid of any quality. However, social media resolves the problem of the substandard quality of material by enacting a most effective selection method, that is, by making the one true marker of success, virality, the result of a very large number of individual decisions (each produser has to decide whether to replicate or to remix each individual item they come across).

The second biggest difference is the mainstreaming of cringe humor. The fact that the experience of mirth may be mixed with the experience of embarrassment, be it personal or vicarious, is clearly a defining characteristic of humor in the age of the internet and social media.

The third major difference is the blurring of the boundary between real and satirical news, and between joking and white suprematist propaganda, which we discussed at some length. The destabilization of the boundary between play and real-life aggression, exploited by the alt-right for its propaganda, is probably the most significant and distressing difference in the new humor of the internet.

The fourth major difference is the emergence of crowd-sourced, community productions that both produce content and establish a virtual, online community, based on the shared interest and the shared experience of enacting the event. This is seen in crowd-sourced memeplexes, such as Boaty McBoatface, LOLCats, Pastafarianism, the Chuck Norris facts, but also in the alt-right use of deliberately offensive material to create a sense of in-group. Replication and remixing are far from being unique to this period, as we saw. However, what is unique to the age of social media is the visibility that the processes of reproduction and remixing have achieved, as well as the facilitation by the technological affordances of digital media of the process. Nowadays, if I want to produce a music video in which I replace the musicians with muppets, all I need is a couple of apps and a little free time.

The affordances of the technology turn out to play a significant role in determining the shape of internet humor. The length of Vines, or the transience and anonymity of comments in 4chan, have been shown to influence significantly the material they host. Conversely, we can see the opposite dynamics at play, for example, when users exploit the alt-text feature of HTML and turn it into an opportunity for punch lines (Chapter 6), or when users take advantage of the shapes of ASCII characters to create emoticons, or pervert (literally) innocent emojis to convey risqué messages (eggplant emoji, peach emoji, taco emoji anyone?) we see the irrepressible humanity of the users that invests pragmatic meanings over unsuspecting systems devised for entirely different purposes.

Overall, the Web 2.0 is the concrete realization of what Debord called "the spectacle" and humor is part and parcel of it. The last sentence of the first thesis of *The Society of Spectacle* reads, in the English translation by Donald Nicholson-Smith, "All that once was directly lived has become mere representation." This does not quite capture the wistfulness of the original: "Tout ce qui était directement vécu s'est eloigné dans une représentation" (Debord, 1967, these 1): "All that was directly lived has distanced itself in a representation." The loss of humanity is the result of the alienation of a person from their true self, through the manufacturing of false wants and needs (consumerism, advertising, mass media). In particular, this is reflected in interpersonal relations which become mediated (médiatisé) by representations: "The spectacle is not a collection of images; rather, it is a social relationship between people that is mediated by images" (Thesis 4). In other words, we no longer interact directly with other people, but we interact with them via representations (images). The Debordian spectacle is inherently part of the economic reality of the production of goods and of work: "The spectacle is simply the economic realm developing for itself" (Thesis 16, p. 16). Alienation is described as the degrading of "being" into "having"; the spectacle is then the degrading of "having" into "appearing" (Thesis 17; p. 16).

In other words, the logic of capitalism, which sees profit as the exclusive meaning of life, has asserted itself not only as the dominant ideology but as the de facto only ideology, what Debord calls "spectacle." Jameson (1991, p. 4) described the defining character of postmodern late capitalism as follows: "Aesthetic production today has become integrated into commodity production generally: the frantic economic urgency of producing fresh waves of ever more novel-seeming goods (from clothing to aeroplanes), at ever greater rates of turnover, now assigns an increasingly essential structural function and position to aesthetic innovation and experimentation." Replace "clothing" and "areoplanes" with "memes" and you have a perfect description of the Web 2.0, in which produsers churn out content for the spectacle. This is of course not a novel idea (see for example, Briziarelli & Armano, 2017; Frayssé, 2019; Morelock & Narita, 2021; Kollyri & Milioni, 2022; Hanschu & Johnson, 2023).

Just one example: the spectacularization of anger. What is an authentic expression of anger and frustration, possibly misguided, but nonetheless authentic, gets turned into spectacle, by overlaying music or autotuning the audio (see the Karen metal videos, for example, in Chapter 19) for TikTok reel or a Facebook video, in order to mock the anger or just simply make it into an object of spectacle. Another facet of this phenomenon is the "uglification" of humor (Attardo, 2022), that is, the use of gratuitous cruelty and extreme aggression in the retelling of jokes. As a reader comment put it, "being an asshole is the new funny."

Should this book end on such a depressing note? Perhaps not. Perhaps the communities that emerge on the internet make up for those lost in meatspace. Perhaps humor can disrupt the spectacle. Perhaps the arc of history does bend toward justice, equality and fraternity. Perhaps our collective humanity, of which humor is one of the highest expressions, will eventually reassert itself.

# BIBLIOGRAPHY

Adams, A. (2012). *Humor markers in computer-mediated communication.* Unpublished MA Thesis, Texas A&M University-Commerce.
Al-Rawi, A. (2020). Kekistanis and the meme war on social media. *The Journal of Intelligence, Conflict, and Warfare, 3*(1), 13–13.
Anderson, S. (2011). Watching people watching people watching. *New York Times Magazine*, 25 November.
Aspray, B. (2019). On trolling as comedic method. *JCMS: Journal of Cinema and Media Studies, 58*(3), 154–159. https://link.gale.com/apps/doc/A598464419/LitRC?u=anon~fe9a7fb8&sid=googleScholar&xid=36055322
Astruc, A. (1948). Naissance d'une nouvelle avant-garde: La caméra-stylo. *L'écran Français, 144*. http://www.newwavefilm.com/about/camera-stylo-astruc.shtml
Attardo, S. (2001). *Humorous Texts.* De Gruyter.
Attardo, S. (2005). The role of affordances at the semantics/pragmatics boundary. In B. G. Bara, L. Barsalou, & M. Bucciarelli (Eds.), *Proceedings of the CogSci 2005. XXVII Annual Conference of the Cognitive Science Society.* Lawrence Erlbaum, pp. 169–174.
Attardo, S. (Ed.). (2014). *Encyclopedia of Humor Studies.* Sage Publications.
Attardo, S. (2017). Humor and pragmatics. In Attardo, S. (Ed.), *The Routledge Handbook of Language and Humor* (pp. 174–188). Routledge.
Attardo, S. (2019). Humor and mirth: Emotions, embodied cognition, and sustained humor. In L. Alba and L. McKenzie (Eds.), *Emotion in Discourse* (pp. 189–211). Benjamins.
Attardo, S. (2020a). *The Linguistics of Humor: An Introduction.* Oxford University Press.
Attardo, S. (2020b). Memes, memeiosis, and memetic drift: Cheryl's Chichier She Shed. *Media Linguistics, 7*(2), 146–168. DOI: 10.21638/spbu22.2020.201.
Attardo, S. (2021). *Memetics and Combinatorics.* Paper presented at the "Do Androids Share Memes About Electric Sheep?" Workshop. University of Bologna, 19 November 2021.
Attardo, S. (2022). The Uglification of the Pagliacci joke. https://salvatoreattardo.substack.com/p/the-uglification-of-the-pagliacci
Attardo, S. (2023). Review of Sienkiewicz, M. & Marx, N. (2022). *HUMOR: International Journal of Humor Research, 36*(1), 159–163.
Attardo, S., & Raskin, V. (1991). Script theory revis(it)ed: Joke similarity and joke representation model. *Humor: International Journal of Humor Research, 4*(3–4), 293–347.
Bakhtin, M. (1965). *Rabelais and His World.* Indiana University Press.
Ball, M. (2016). Why D.C. hates Ted Cruz. *The Atlantic.* https://www.theatlantic.com/politics/archive/2016/01/why-dc-hates-ted-cruz/426915/

Ballentine, C. (2021). Shiba Inu coin craze is driving demand for—What else?—Shiba Inu Puppies. *Bloomberg*. https://www.bloomberg.com/news/articles/2021-11-05/shiba-inu-dogecoin-crypto-interest-drives-demand-for-real-dogs#xj4y7vzkg

Barinka, A. (2022). One of TikTok's biggest stars roasts dudes for their Misogyny, racism, and fatphobia. *Bloomberg Businessweek*, 1 August.

Baron, N. S. (2004). See you online: Gender issues in college student use of instant messaging. *Journal of Language and Social Psychology, 23*(4), 397–423.

Baron, N. S. (2008). *Always On: Language in an Online and Mobile World*. Oxford University Press.

Barrett, R. (1999). Indexing polyphonous identity in the speech of African American drag queens. Reinventing identities: The gendered self in discourse. In M. Bucholtz, A. C. Liang, & L. A. Sutton (Eds.), *Reinventing Identities: The Gendered Self in Discourse* (pp. 313–331.). Oxford: Oxford University Press.

Bateson, Gregory. 1972. *Steps to an Ecology of Mind*. Ballantine.

Bauer, P. (2018). Flying Spaghetti monster. *Britannica*. https://www.britannica.com/topic/Flying-Spaghetti-Monster

Baumeister, R. F., Bratslavsky, E., Finkenauer, C., & Vohs, K. D. (2001). Bad is stronger than good. *Review of General Psychology, 5*(4), 323–370.

Becker, A. B. (2014). Humiliate my enemies or mock my friends? Applying disposition theory of humor to the study of political parody appreciation and attitudes toward candidates. *Human Communication Research, 40*(2), 137–160.

Berger, J. (2013). *Contagious: Why Things Catch On*. Simon & Schuster.

Berger, J., & Le Mens, G. (2009). How adoption speed affects the abandonment of cultural tastes. *Proceedings of the National Academy of Sciences, 106*(20), 8146–8150.

Berger, J., & Milkman, K. L. (2012). What makes online content viral? *Journal of Marketing Research, 49*(2), 192–205.

Bergson, Henri. (1901). Le rire. *Alcan*, 45th ed. https://beq.ebooksgratuits.com/Philosophie/Bergson-rire.pdf

Berkowitz, D., & Schwartz, D. A. (2016). Miley, CNN and the onion: When fake news becomes realer than real. *Journalism Practice, 10*(1): 1–17. DOI: 10.1080/17512786.2015.1006933.

Bhat, P., & Klein, O. (2020). Covert hate speech: White nationalists and dog whistle communication on twitter. In J. E. Rosenbaum, & G. Bouvier (Eds.), *Twitter, the Public Sphere, and the Chaos of Online Deliberation* (pp. 151–172). Springer.

Biggs, J. (2016). Papa, what's a shitpost? *Tech Crunch*. https://techcrunch.com/2016/09/23/papa-whats-a-shitpost/

Billig, M. (2001). Humour and embarrassment: Limits of 'nice-guy' theories of social life. *Theory, Culture & Society, 18*(5), 23–43.

Bischetti, L., & Attardo, S. (2023) From mode adoption to saluting a dead kitten: Reactions to a humorous tweet by Ricky Gervais. In E. Linares & E. Ruiz Gurillo (Eds.), *The Pragmatics of Humor in Interactive Contexts*. Benjamins.

Bischetti, L., Canal, P., & Bambini, V. (2021). Funny but aversive: A large-scale survey of the emotional response to Covid-19 humor in the Italian population during the lockdown. *Lingua, 249*, 102963.

Blackmore, S. (1999). *The Meme Machine*. Oxford: Oxford University Press.

Blair, W. (2018). *Tall Tale America: A Legendary History of Our Humorous Heroes*. University of Chicago Press.

Bliss, L. (2022). 'Would you rather?' Weirdness and affect in reaction videos to porn. *First Monday, 27*(6).

Blommaert, J. (2015). Meaning as a nonlinear effect: The birth of cool. *AILA Review, 28*(1), 7–27.

Bogost, I. (2016). Why a silicon valley founder is funding a factory for Trump memes. *The Atlantic*. https://www.theatlantic.com/technology/archive/2016/09/revenge-of-thenerds/501344/

Börzsei, L. K. (2013). Makes a meme instead. *New Media Studies Magazine, 7*.

Bou-Franch, P., & Blitvich, P. G. C. (2014). Conflict management in massive polylogues: A case study from YouTube. *Journal of Pragmatics, 73*, 19–36.

Bou-Franch, P., Lorenzo-Dus, N., & Blitvich, P. G. C. (2012). Social interaction in YouTube text-based polylogues: A study of coherence. *Journal of Computer-Mediated Communication, 17*(4), 501–521.

Bovet, A., & Makse, H. A. (2019). Influence of fake news in Twitter during the 2016 US presidential election. *Nature Communications, 10*(1), 1–14.

Bowman-Grieve, L. (2013). A psychological perspective on virtual communities supporting terrorist & extremist ideologies as a tool for recruitment. *Security Informatics, 2*(1), 1–5.

Bradbury, J. (2018). Parodying racial passing in Chappelle's show and Key & Peele. In H. Davies & S. Ilott (Eds.), *Comedy and the Politics of Representation* (pp. 79–97). Cham: Palgrave Macmillan.

Bramlett, F. (2018). Linguistic discourse in web comics: Extending conversation and narrative into alt-Text and hidden comics. In V. Werner (Ed.), *The Language of Pop Culture* (pp. 72–91). Routledge.

Brideau, K., & Berret, C. (2014). A brief introduction to impact: 'The meme font'. *Journal of Visual Culture, 13*(3), 307–313.

Briziarelli, M., & Armano, E. (2017). *The Spectacle 2.0*. University of Westminster Press.

Brodie, Ian (2018). Pretend news, false news, fake news: The onion as put-on, prank, and legend. *The Journal of American Folklore, 131*(522), 451–459. DOI: 10.5406/jamerfolk.131.522.0451.

Brooks, D. (2000). *Bobos in Paradise: The New Upper Class and How They Got There*. Simon and Schuster.

Brubaker, J. R. (2008). Wants moar: Visual media's use of text in LOLcats and silent film. *gnovis Journal, 8*(2), 117–124.

Bruns, A. (2008). *Blogs, Wikipedia, Second Life, and Beyond: From Production to Produsage*. Lang.

Brzozowski, W. (2022). Did pastafarians lose in Strasbourg, after all? *The Oxford Journal of Law and Religion, 10*(3), 487–494. DOI: 10.1093/ojlr/rwac001.

Buchel, B. (2012). *Internet memes as means of communication*. Unpublished MA Thesis, Masaryk University, Brno.

Burgess, J. (2008). 'All your chocolate rain are belong to us?' Viral Video, YouTube and the dynamics of participatory culture. In G. Lovink & S. Niederer (Eds.), *Video Vortex Reader: Responses to YouTube* (pp. 101–109). Amsterdam: Institute of Network Cultures.

Burns, R. G. (2008). German symbolism in rock music: National signification in the imagery and songs of Rammstein. *Popular Music, 27*(3), 457–472.

Bybee, J. (2015) *Language Change*. Cambridge University Press.

Calhoun, K. (2019). Vine racial comedy as anti-hegemonic humor: Linguistic performance and generic innovation. *Journal of Linguistic Anthropology, 29*(1), 27–49.

Castelfranchi, C. (2001). Towards a cognitive memetics: Socio-cognitive mechanisms for memes selection and spreading. *Journal of Memetics-Evolutionary Models of Information Transmission*, *5*, 1–19.

Chiaro, D. (2018). *The Language of Jokes: Analyzing Verbal Play*. Routledge.

Chohan, U. W. (2021). A history of Dogecoin. *Discussion Series: Notes on the 21st Century*. https://ssrn.com/abstract=3091219 or http://dx.doi.org/10.2139/ssrn.3091219

Choi, M. (2022). After fierce criticism for delaying landmark veterans bill, Ted Cruz votes to pass it. *The Texas Tribune*. https://www.texastribune.org/2022/08/02/ted-cruz-john-cornyn-veterans-health-care/

Clements, W. M. 1969. The types of the Polack joke. Folklore Forum. A Bibliographic and Special Series. N.3. 22. Revised ed. 1973.

Click, M. (Ed.). (2019). *Anti-Fandom: Dislike and Hate in the Digital Age*. New York University Press.

CNN. (2012). https://www.cnn.com/2012/11/27/world/asia/north-korea-china-onion

CNN Blog. (2011). https://news.blogs.cnn.com/2011/02/12/austin-does-limp-bizkit-frontman-a-solid/

COAUtilities. (2022). https://coautilities.com/wps/wcm/connect/occ/coa/util/contact-us/coa-utility-departments/austin-resource-recovery

Cohen, E. L., Knight, J., Mullin, M., Herbst, R., Leach, B., Shelledy, A., & Rebich, D. (2021). Loving to hate the Kardashians: Examining the interaction of character liking and hate-watching on the social influence of a reality TV show. *Psychology of Popular Media*, *10*(2), 136–148.

Cohn, M. A., Mehl, M. R., & Pennebaker, J. W. (2004). Linguistic markers of psychological change surrounding September 11, 2001. *Psychological Science*, *15*(10), 687–693.

Condren, C. (2012). Satire and definition. *Humor: International Journal of Humor Research*, *25*(4), 375–399.

Coppa, F. (2008). Women, Star Trek, and the early development of fannish vidding. *Transformative Works and Cultures*, *1*. DOI: 10.3983/twc.2008.044.

Costera Meijer, I., & Groot Kormelink, T. (2015). Checking, sharing, clicking and linking: Changing patterns of news use between 2004 and 2014. *Digital Journalism*, *3*(5), 664–679.

Critchley, S. (2002). *On Humour*. Routledge.

Cusack, C. M. (2010). *Invented Religions: Faith, Fiction, Imagination*. Routledge.

Dafaure, M. (2020). The "great meme war:" The alt-right and its multifarious enemies. *Angles. New Perspectives on the Anglophone World*, *10*.

Dafonte-Gómez, A. (2018). News media and the emotional public sphere: Audiences as medium: Motivations and emotions in news sharing. *International Journal of Communication*, *12*, 2133–2152.

Dale, J. P. (2016). Cute studies: An emerging field. *East Asian Journal of Popular Culture*, *2*(1), 5–13.

Danesi, M. (1994). *Cool: The Signs and Meanings of Adolescence*. University of Toronto Press.

Danesi, M. (2017). *The Semiotics of Emoji: The Rise of Visual Language in the Age of the Internet*. Bloomsbury.

Dao, E., Muresan, A., Hornbæk, K., & Knibbe, J. (2021, May). Bad breakdowns, useful seams, and face slapping: Analysis of VR fails on YouTube. In *Proceedings of the 2021 CHI Conference on Human Factors in Computing Systems* (pp. 1–14).

Davies, C. (1990). *Ethnic Humor Around the World: A Comparative Analysis*. Bloomington: Indiana University Press.

Davies, C. E. (2010). Joking as boundary negotiation among "good old boys": "White trash" as a social category at the bottom of the Southern working class in Alabama. *Humor: International Journal of Humor Research, 23*(2), 179–200.

Daviess, B. (2019). 'Making memes and shitposting': The powerful political discourse of alt-right meme culture. DOI: 10.2139/ssrn.4118990. https://ssrn.com/abstract=4118990

Dawkins, R. (1976). *The Selfish Gene.* Oxford University Press.

de Jongste, H. (2020). *Playing With Mental Models: Humour in the BBC Comedy Series the Office.* John Benjamins Publishing Company.

Dearden, L. (2019). Revered as a saint by online extremists, how Christchurch shooter inspired copycat terrorists around the world. *The Independent.* https://www.independent.co.uk/news/world/australasia/brenton-tarrant-christchurch-shooter-attack-el-paso-norway-poway-a9076926.html

Debord, G. (1967). *La société du spectacle.* Gallimard.

Denisova, A. (2019). *Internet Memes and Society: Social, Cultural, and Political Contexts.* Routledge.

Dennett, D. (1991). *Consciousness Explained.* Little & Brown.

Dennett, D. (1995). *Darwin's Dangerous Idea.* Simon & Schuster.

DiBenedetto, C. (2022). Insulin producer Eli Lilly sees stock drop because of a fake blue check tweet. https://mashable.com/article/eli-lilly-stock-dip-twitter

dictionary.com. (2022). Doxing, sealioning, and rage farming: The language of online harassment and disinformation. https://www.dictionary.com/e/online-harassment-disinformation-terms/

Dionigi, A., Duradoni, M., & Vagnoli, L. (2022). Humor and the dark triad: Relationships among narcissism, Machiavellianism, psychopathy and comic styles. *Personality and Individual Differences, 197,* 111766.

Dogendorsed. (2021). 13 Popular dog-themed cryptocurrencies. *Dogendorsed.* https://dogendorsed.com/popular-dog-themed-cryptocurrencies/

Donahue, A, (2022). Conveying, marking, and enhancing humor on twitter with textual representations of Twitch.Tv emotes. Paper presented at the 12 Humor Research Conference. www.tamuc.edu/humor

Donavan, D. T., Mowen, J. C., & Chakraborty, G. (1999). Urban legends: The word-of-mouth communication of morality through negative story content. *Marketing Letters, 10*(1), 23–35.

Donovan, J., Dreyfuss, E., & Friedberg, B. (2022). *Meme Wars: The Untold Story of the Online Battles Upending Democracy in America.* Bloomsbury

Dorson, R. M. (1965). The career of "John Henry". *Western Folklore, 24*(3), 155–163.

Douglas, N. (2014). It's supposed to look like shit: The Internet ugly aesthetic. *Journal of Visual Culture, 13*(3), 314–339.

Dresner, E., & Herring, S. C. (2010). Functions of the nonverbal in CMC: Emoticons and illocutionary force. *Communication Theory, 20*(3), 249–268.

Dundes, A. (1987). *Cracking Jokes: Studies of Sick Humor Cycles and Stereotypes.* Berkeley: Ten Speed Press.

Dundes, A. (1988). April fool and April fish: Towards a theory of ritual pranks. *Etnofoor, 1*(1), 4–14.

Durando, J. (2015). Pastafarian can wear strainer on head in license photo. *USA Today.* https://www.usatoday.com/story/news/nation-now/2015/11/16/church-flying-spaghetti-monster-massachusetts-religion/75862946/

Eagleton, T. (1991). *Ideology*. Verso.

Eco, U. (1963). *Diario Minimo*. Mondadori. Engl. translation. Weaver, W. 1993. *Misreadings*. Harcourt Brace.

Eco, U. (1995). Ur-fascism. *The New York Review of Books*, *42*(11), 12–15. https://www.nybooks.com/articles/1995/06/22/ur-fascism/

Economist. (2021). Wikipedia is 20, and its reputation has never been higher. https://www.economist.com/international/2021/01/09/wikipedia-is-20-and-its-reputation-has-never-been-higher

Edmonds, M. (2010). *Out of the Northwoods: The Many Lives of Paul Bunyan, With More Than 100 Logging Camp Tales*. Wisconsin Historical Society.

Edwards, D. A., Ausiello, D., Salzman, J., Devlin, T., Langer, R., Beddingfield, B. J., ... & Roy, C. J. (2021). Exhaled aerosol increases with COVID-19 infection, age, and obesity. *Proceedings of the National Academy of Sciences*, *118*(8), e2021830118.

Ekman, P. (1992). Facial expressions of emotion: An old controversy and new findings. *Philosophical Transactions of the Royal Society of London. Series B: Biological Sciences*, *335*(1273), 63–69.

Ellman, C. & Reppen, J. (Eds.). (1997). *Omnipotent Fantasies and the Vulnerable Self*. Rowman and Littlefield.

Ester, P., & Vinken, H. (1993). Yuppies in cross-national perspective: Is there evidence for a yuppie value syndrome? *Political Psychology*, *14*(4), 667–696.

Evans, V. (2017). *The Emoji Code: The Linguistics Behind Smiley Faces and Scaredy Cats*. London: Picador.

Feinberg, A. (2017). This is the daily Stormer's playbook. *Huffington Post*. https://www.huffpost.com/entry/daily-stormer-nazi-style-guide_n_5a2ece19e4b0ce3b344492f2

Feldman, N. (2016). Is god a spaghetti monster? That's a serious legal question. *Bloomberg*. https://www.bloomberg.com/opinion/articles/2016-04-18/is-god-a-spaghetti-monster-that-s-a-serious-legal-question#xj4y7vzkg

Felton, H. W. (Ed.). (1947). *Legends of Paul Bunyan*. Knopf.

Fichman, P., & Sanfilippo, M. R. (2016). *Online Trolling and Its Perpetrators: Under the Cyberbridge*. Rowman & Littlefield Publishers.

Fillmore, C. J., Kay, P., & O'connor, M. C. (1988). Regularity and idiomaticity in grammatical constructions: The case of let alone. *Language*, *64*(3), 501–538.

Finchelstein, F. (2017). *From Fascism to Populism in History*. University of California Press.

Frayssé, O. (2019). Gazing at "Fetishes" 2.0: Using the spectacle concept to understand consumer cultures in the age of digital capitalism. *The French Journal of Media Studies*, *7*(2).

French, A. J. (2010). Stuff white people buy: Race, consumption, and group identification. *Consumers, Commodities and Consumption: A Newsletter of the Consumer Studies Research Network*, *11*(2), 11–2. https://csrn.camden.rutgers.edu/pdf/11-2_french.pdf

Friedman, T. (2005). *The World is Flat: A Brief History of the Twenty-First Century*. Farrar, Strauss & Giroux.

Gal, N. (2019). Ironic humor on social media as participatory boundary work. *New Media & Society*, *21*(3), 729–749. DOI: 10.1177/1461444818805719.

Gallucci, N. (2019). Why so many people type 'lol' with a straight face: An investigation. *Mashable*. https://mashable.com/article/why-do-people-type-lol-when-they-arent-laughing-out-loud

Garley, M., Slade, B., & Terkourafi, M. (2009). Hwæt! LOL! Common formulaic functions in Beowulf and blogs. *Papers From the Annual Meeting of the Chicago Linguistic Society*, *45*(1), 111–126.

Gawne, L., & Vaughan, J. (2011). I can haz language play: The construction of language and identity in LOLspeak. In M. P. L. Dao & M. Bowler (Eds.), *Proceedings of the 42nd ALS Conference—2011* (pp. 97–122). Canberra: Australian National University.

Gibson, J. J. (1979). *The Ecological Approach to Visual Perception.* Taylor & Francis.

Gilbert, C. J. (2013). Playing with Hitler: Downfall and its ludic uptake. *Critical Studies in Media Communication, 30*(5), 407–424.

Gillin, J. (2017). The more outrageous, the better: How clickbait ads make money for fake news sites. *PolitiFact.* https://www.politifact.com/article/2017/oct/04/more-outrageous-better-how-clickbait-ads-make-mone/

Goel, S., Anderson, A., Hofman, J., & Watts, D. J. (2016). The structural virality of online diffusion. *Management Science, 62*(1), 180–196.

Goel, S., Watts, D. J., & Goldstein, D. G. (2012). The structure of online diffusion networks. In *Proceedings of the 13th ACM Conference on Electronic Commerce* (pp. 623–638).

Goffman, E. (1956). Embarrassment and social organization. *American Journal of Sociology, 62*(3), 264–271.

Goffman, E. (1974). *Frame Analysis: An Essay on the Organization of Experience.* Harvard University Press.

Golshan, T. (2016). Boaty McBoatface, explained. *Vox.* https://www.vox.com/2016/5/8/11606554/nerc-rrs-david-attenborough-boaty-mcboatface-explained

Goodwin, M. (1994). Meme, counter-meme. *Wired*, 1 October.

Goodyear, D. (2005). Quiet depravity: The demure outrages of a standup comic. *The New Yorker, 24*, 50–55.

Graeber, D., & Wengrow, D. (2021). *The Dawn of Everything: A New History of Humanity.* Penguin UK.

Grant, N., & Stanley, T. (2014). Reading the wallpaper: Disrupting performances of whiteness in the blog "Stuff White People Like.". In A. Ibrahim, S. R. Steinberg, & L. Hutton (Eds.), *Critical Youth Studies Reader* (pp. 172–183). Peter Lang.

Greene, V. S. (2019). "Deplorable" satire: Alt-right memes, white genocide tweets, and redpilling normies. *Studies in American Humor, 5*(1), 31–69.

Grice, P. (1989). *Studies in the Way of Words.* Harvard University Press.

Griffin, R. (1993). *The Nature of Fascism.* Routledge.

Grzanka, P. R., & Maher, J. (2012). Different, like everyone else: Stuff White people like and the marketplace of diversity. *Symbolic Interaction, 35*(3), 368–393.

Guadagno, R. E., Rempala, D. M., Murphy, S., & Okdie, B. M. (2013). What makes a video go viral? An analysis of emotional contagion and Internet memes. *Computers in Human Behavior, 29*(6), 2312–2319.

Guess, A. M., & Lyons, B. A. (2020). Misinformation, disinformation, and online propaganda. In J. A. Tucker & N. Persily (Eds.), *Social Media and Democracy: The State of the Field, Prospects for Reform* (pp. 10–33). Cambridge University Press.

Guo, L., & Vargo, C. (2020). "Fake news" and emerging online media ecosystem: An integrated intermedia agenda-setting analysis of the 2016 US presidential election. *Communication Research, 47*(2), 178–200.

Hagen, S. (2018). 4chan/pol/ image walls: Memes. *OILab.Eu.* https://oilab.eu/4chanpolimage-walls-memes/

Hanschu, J., & Johnson, L. M. (2023). The economic and psychological origins of right-wing radicalization in the US. In B. Warf & J. Heppen (Eds.), *Geographies of the 2020 US Presidential Election* (pp. 25–49). Routledge.

Harber, K. D., & Cohen, D. J. (2005). The emotional broadcaster theory of social sharing. *Journal of Language and Social Psychology, 24*(4), 382–400.

Harvey, C. G., Stewart, D. B., & Ewing, M. T. (2011). Forward or delete: What drives peer-to-peer message propagation across social networks? *Journal of Consumer Behaviour, 10*(6), 365–372.

Heaney, K. (2014). The 42 ways to type laughter, define: Here's what your typed and texted LOL-Ing really means. *BuzzFeed*. https://www.buzzfeed.com/katieheaney/the-42-ways-to-type-laughter-defined

Hempelmann, C. F. (2003). "99 nuns giggle, 1 nun gasps:" The not-all-that-Christian natural class of Christian jokes. *Humor: International Journal of Humor Research, 16*(1), 1–31.

Henrich, J., Boyd, R., & Richerson, P. J. (2008). Five misunderstandings about cultural evolution. *Human Nature, 19*(2), 119–137.

Herbst, J. P. (2021). The politics of Rammstein's sound: Decoding a production aesthetic. *Journal of Popular Music Studies, 33*(2), 51–76.

Herring, S., Job-Sluder, K., Scheckler, R., & Barab, S. (2002). Searching for safety online: Managing "trolling" in a feminist forum. *The Information Society, 18*(5), 371–384.

Herring, S. C. (2007). A faceted classification scheme for computer-mediated discourse. *Language @ Internet, 4*(1).

Heylighen F. (1993). Selection criteria for the evolution of knowledge. In: *Proc. 13th Int. Congress on Cybernetics (Association Internationale de Cybernètique, Namur)*, pp. 524–528.

Heylighen, F. (1997). Objective, subjective and intersubjective selectors of knowledge. *Evolution & Cognition, 3*(1), 63–67.

Heylighen, F. (1998). What makes a meme successful? Selection criteria for cultural evolution. In *15th International Congress on Cybernetics* (pp. 418–423).

Heylighen, F., & Chielens, K. (2009). Cultural evolution and memetics. In R. A. Meyers (Ed.), *Encyclopedia of Complexity and Systems Science* (pp. 3205–3220). Springer.

Hirsch, G. (2019). Hitler's out of dope: A cross-cultural examination of humorous memes. *Journal of Pragmatics, 149*, 25–39.

Holland, E. C., & Levy, A. (2018). The onion and the geopolitics of satire. *Popular Communication, 16*(3), 182–195.

Holmes, D. R. (2019). Fascism at eye level: The anthropological conundrum. *Focaal, 84*, 62–90.

Holt, K. (2013) Vine and the art of 6-second comedy. *Dailydot*. https://www.dailydot.com/upstream/vine-comedy-marlo-meekins-max-burlingame/

Horta Ribeiro, M. (2022). What does research really tell us about deplatforming? https://manoelhortaribeiro.github.io/posts/2022/06/deplatforming

Horta Ribeiro, M., Ottoni, R., West, R., Almeida, V. A. F., and Meira, W., Jr. (2020). Auditing radicalization pathways on YouTube. In *Proceedings of the 2020 Conference on Fairness, Accountability, and Transparency* (pp. 131–141).

Huffington Post. (2012). Mountain dew naming campaign hijacked by infamous message board 4chan. https://www.huffpost.com/entry/4chan-mountain-dew-n_1773076?guccounter=1

Hye-Knudson, M. (2018). Painfully funny: Cringe comedy, benign masochism, and not-so-benign violations. *Leviathan, 2*, 13–31.

Jaffe, A., (2016). Indexicality, stance and fields in sociolinguistics. In N. Coupland (Ed.), *Sociolinguistics: Theoretical Debates* (pp. 86–112). Cambridge: Cambridge University Press.

James, A. (2014). *Assholes: A Theory*. Anchor.

James, R. M. (2014). *Trolls: From Scandinavia to Dam Dolls, Tolkien, and Harry Potter*. No Publisher.
Jameson, F. (1991). *Postmodernism, or, the Cultural Logic of Late Capitalism*. Duke University Press.
Jenkins, H. (2006). *Convergence Culture*. New York, London: New York University Press.
Jenkins, H. Ford, S., & Green, J. (2013). *Spreadable Media: Creating Value and Meaning in a Networked Culture*. New York University press.
Jennings, K. (2018). *Planet Funny: How Comedy Took Over Our Culture*. Scribner.
Johnson, A., Del Rio, E., & Kemmitt, A. (2010). Missing the joke: A reception analysis of satirical texts. *Communication, Culture & Critique, 3*(3), 396–415.
Johnson, B. K., & Rosenbaum, J. E. (2015). Spoiler alert: Consequences of narrative spoilers for dimensions of enjoyment, appreciation, and transportation. *Communication Research, 42*(8), 1068–1088.
Julin, G. (2021). What's the punch line?: Punching up and down in the comic thuderdome. In J. M. Henrigillis & S. Gimbel (Eds.), *It's Funny Cause It's True: The Lighthearted Philosophers' Society's Introduction to Philosophy Through Humor* (pp. 143–155). Gettysburg College Open Educational Resources. https://cupola.gettysburg.edu/cgi/viewcontent.cgi?article=1009&context=oer
Kartono, A., Wahyudi, S. T., Setiawan, A. A., & Sofian, I. (2021). Predicting of the coronavirus disease 2019 (COVID-19) epidemic using estimation of parameters in the logistic growth model. *Infectious Disease Reports, 13*(2), 465–485.
Kaye, S. M. (2010). *The Onion and Philosophy: Fake News Story True, Alleges Indignant Area Professor*. Open Court Publishing.
Kennedy, M. (2019). Boaty McBoatface, internet-adored sub, makes deep-sea discovery on climate change. *NPR*. https://www.npr.org/2019/06/18/733759839/boaty-mcboatface-internet-adored-sub-makes-deep-sea-discovery-on-climate-change
Key and Peele. (2015). Spoiler alert. https://www.youtube.com/watch?v=VDEuS5wIk5Q
Kharif, O. (2022). Crypto slump leaves 12,100 coins trapped in Zombie trading Limbo. *Bloomberg*. https://www.bloomberg.com/professional/blog/crypto-slump-leaves-12100-coins-trapped-in-zombie-trading-limbo/
Kien, G. (2019). *Communicating With Memes: Consequences in Post-Truth Civilization*. Rowman & Littlefield.
Kim, H. S. (2015). Attracting views and going viral: How message features and news-sharing channels affect health news diffusion. *Journal of Communication, 65*(3), 512–534.
King, H. (2021) Cryptocurrency jokes get serious. https://www.axios.com/2021/07/09/joke-meme-coins
Knobel, M., & Lankshear, C. (2007). Online memes, affinities, and cultural production. In M. Knobel & C. Lankshear (Eds.), *A New Literacies Sampler* (pp. 199–227). Peter Lang.
Kochkodin, B. (2021). Dogecoin's creator is baffled by meteoric rise to $9 billion. *Bloomberg News*. https://www.bloomberg.com/news/articles/2021-02-11/dogecoin-s-creator-is-just-as-baffled-as-you-are-about-its-rise#xj4y7vzkg
Kollyri, L., & Milioni, D. L. (2022). "Spectacular" user subjectivities on Instagram: A discursive interface analysis. *International Journal of Communication, 16*, 5358–5380.
Kotler-Fux, S. (2018). "Hitler-rants" parodies: Folklore in Israel's virtual sphere. In *Jerusalem Studies in Jewish Folklore* (pp. 161–193).
Krach, S., Cohrs, J. C., de Echeverría Loebell, N. C., Kircher, T., Sommer, J., Jansen, A., & Paulus, F. M. (2011). Your flaws are my pain: Linking empathy to vicarious embarrassment. *PLoS One, 6*(4), e18675.

Kuipers, G. (2015). *Good Humor, Bad Taste: A Sociology of the Joke*. De Gruyter.
Kumar, S., West, R., & Leskovec, J. (2016). Disinformation on the web: Impact, characteristics, and detection of wikipedia hoaxes. In *Proceedings of the 25th International Conference on World Wide Web* (pp. 591–602).
Laineste, L., & Voolaid, P. (2016). Laughing across borders: Intertextuality of internet memes. *The European Journal of Humour Research*, 4(4), 26–49.
Lakoff, G., & Johnson, M. (1980). *Metaphors We Live By*. University of Chicago press.
Lander, C. (2008). *Stuff White People Like*. New York: Random House Trade Paperbacks.
Lander, C. (2010) *Whiter Shades of Pale: The Stuff White People Like, Coast to Coast, From Seattle's Sweaters to Maine's Microbrews*. New York: Random House.
Larson, G. (1989). *The Prehistory of the Far Side*. Andrews and McMeel.
Laubert, C., & Parlamis, J. (2019). Are you angry (happy, sad) or aren't you? Emotion detection difficulty in email negotiation. *Group Decision and Negotiation*, 28(2), 377–413.
Leigh, C. (2009). Lurkers and lolcats: An easy way from out to in. *Journal of Digital Research & Publishing*, 2, 131–141.
Lelièvre, F. J. (1954). The basis of ancient parody. *Greece & Rome*, 1(2), 66–81. http://www.jstor.org/stable/641056
Leporati, M. & Jacklosky, R. (2021). Peeling the onion: Pop culture satire in the writing classroom. In I. Kinane (Ed.), *Isn't It Ironic? Irony in Contemporary Popular Culture* (pp. 20–38). Routledge.
Lessig, L. (2008). *Remix: Making Art and Commerce Thrive in the Hybrid Economy*. Penguin.
Licklider, J. C. R. 1967. *Televistas: Looking Ahead through the Side Windows*. Report of the Carnegie Commission on Public Television (pp. 201–225). http://creativecadio.weebly.com/uploads/1/0/2/2/10226800/licklider-televistas-carnegie-1967.pdf
Lofaro, M. A. (Ed.). (1985). *Davy Crockett: The Man, the Legend, the Legacy, 1786–1986*. University of Tennessee Press.
Lorenz, Konrad. (1943). Die angeborenen formen moglicher arfahrung [The innate forms of potential experience]. *Zeitschrift für Tierpsychologie*, 5, 235–409.
Ludemann, D. (2021). Digital semaphore: Political discourse and identity negotiation through 4chan's/pol. *New Media & Society*, 1–20.
Maćkowiak, A. (2016). Mythical universes of third-millennium religious movements: The church of the flying Spaghetti Monster and matrixism. *Maska*, 1(29).
Maddox, J. (2022). *The Internet is For Cats: How Animal Images Shape Our Digital Lives*. Rutgers University Press.
Mamié, Robin, Horta Ribeiro, Manoel, & West, Robert. (2021). Are anti-feminist communities gateways to the far right? Evidence from reddit and YouTube. In *13th ACM Web Science Conference 2021* (pp. 139–147).
Marcin, T. (2022a). People started spreading fake news on Twitter the instant they could buy a blue check. https://mashable.com/article/fake-news-blue-check-tweets-verification
Marcin, T. (2022b). The fake verified posts got way worse for Twitter. https://mashable.com/article/twitter-fake-verified-posts-worse-elon-musk
Marcoccia, M. (2004). On-line polylogues: Conversation structure and participation framework in internet newsgroups. *Journal of Pragmatics*, 36(1), 115–145.
Marcuse, H. (1964). *One-Dimensional Man: Studies in the Ideology of Advanced Industrial Society*. Boston: Beacon. https://www.marcuse.org/herbert/pubs/64onedim/odmcontents.html

Markman, K. M. (2013). Exploring the pragmatic functions of the acronym lol in instant messenger conversations. In *International Communication Association Annual Conference*, London, UK. https://www.academia.edu/9811993/Exploring_the_Pragmatic_Functions_of_the_Acronym_LOL_in_Instant_Messenger_Conversations

Marone, V. (2016). Looping out loud. *The European Journal of Humour Research*, 4(4), 50–66.

Marsh, M. (2015). *Practically Joking*. Utah State University Press.

Martin, R. A., & Ford, T. (2018). *The Psychology of Humor: An Integrative Approach*. Academic Press.

Mayer, A. V., Paulus, F. M., & Krach, S. (2021). A psychological perspective on vicarious embarrassment and shame in the context of cringe humor. *Humanities*, 10(110), 1–15.

McCloud, S. (2000). *Reinventing Comics*. New York: Paradox Press.

McCool, B. (2015). When national Lampoon magazine dropped the atom bomb of spoilers. *Tech Times*. https://www.techtimes.com/articles/117575/20151218/when-national-lampoon-magazine-dropped-atom-bomb-spoilers.htm

McCulloch, G. (2019). *Because the Internet: Understanding the New Rules of Language*. New York: Riverhead/Penguin.

McDaniel, B. (2021). Popular music reaction videos: Reactivity, creator labor, and the performance of listening online. *New Media & Society*, 23(6), 1624–1641.

McGhee, P. E., & Lloyd, S. A. (1981). A developmental test of the disposition theory of humor. *Child Development*, 52(3), 925–931.

McGill, S. (2005). *Virgil Recomposed: The Mythological and Secular Centos in Antiquity*. Oxford University Press.

McGraw, A. P., & Warren, C. (2010). Benign violations: Making immoral behavior funny. *Psychological Science*, 21(8), 1141–1149.

McKay, I. (2020). Some distributional patterns in the use of typed laughter-derived expressions on Twitter. *Journal of Pragmatics*, 166, 97–113.

McSweeney, M. A. (2016). Lol! I didn't mean it: Lol as a marker of illocutionary force. CIRCL Presentation, March 8, 2016. The Graduate Center at CUNY.

McSweeney, M. A. (2018). *The Pragmatics of Text Messaging: Making Meaning in Messages*. Routledge.

McSwiney, J., Vaughan, M., Heft, A., & Hoffmann, M. (2021). Sharing the hate? Memes and transnationality in the far right's digital visual culture. *Information, Communication & Society*, 24(16), 2502–2521.

McWorther, J. (2013a). https://www.ted.com/talks/john_mcwhorter_txtng_is_killing_language_jk/transcript?language=en

McWorther, J. (2013b). Txtng is killing language. *JK!!!* https://www.ted.com/talks/john_mcwhorter_txtng_is_killing_language_jk/transcript?language=en

Meier, A. (2019). Why do Facebook and Twitter's anti-extremist guidelines allow right-wingers more freedom than Islamists? *The Washington Post*, 1 August 2019. https://www.washingtonpost.com/politics/2019/08/01/why-do-facebook-twitters-anti-extremist-guidelines-allow-right-wingers-more-freedom-than-islamists/

Miao, H. (2021, January 23). 'It's just Bernie being Bernie'—How a photo of Sanders wearing mittens at Inauguration Day went viral. *CNBC*. https://www.cnbc.com/2021/01/23/bernie-sanders-inauguration-meme-heres-the-story-behind-the-photo.html

Michot, N. (2007). Les usages lexicaux des jeunes sur les supports modernes de communication. In *Actes du 26ème Colloque International sur le Lexique et la Grammaire (session thématique).* http://infolingu.univ-mlv.fr/Colloques/Bonifacio/proceedings/michot.pdf

Middleton, J. (2014). *Documentary's Awkward Turn: Cringe Comedy and Media Spectatorship.* Routledge.

Miltner, Kate. (2011). *SRSLY phenomenal: An investigation into the appeal of LOLCats.* MA Thesis, London School of Economics and Political Science.

Minor, W. (2018). That's the joke: Four cryptocurrencies you shouldn't take seriously. *Block Telegraph,* 27 August. https://blocktelegraph.io/joke-cryptocurrencies/

Mohammed, S. N., & Mohammed, S. (2021). Reactistan: Do the subaltern speak on YouTube? *The Journal of Social Media in Society, 10*(2), 136–161.

Möller, A. M., & Boukes, M. (2021). Online social environments and their impact on video viewers: The effects of user comments on entertainment experiences and knowledge gain during political satire consumption. *New Media & Society,* 14614448211015984.

Monroe, J. (2018) Weezer Cover Toto's "Rosanna," trolling viral campaign for "Africa" cover. *Pitchfork.* https://pitchfork.com/news/weezer-cover-totos-rosanna-trolling-viral-campaign-for-africa-cover/

Monzani, D., Vergani, L., Pizzoli, S. F. M., Marton, G., & Pravettoni, G. (2021). Emotional tone, analytical thinking, and somatosensory processes of a sample of Italian tweets during the first phases of the COVID-19 pandemic: Observational study. *Journal of Medical Internet Research, 23*(10), e29820.

Morelock, J., & Narita, F. Z. (2021). *The Society of the Selfie: Social Media and the Crisis of Liberal Democracy.* London: University of Westminster Press. DOI: 10.16997/book59.

Moss, G. (2017). The growing integration of bourgeois and bohemian culture. In G. Moss (Ed.), *Artistic Enclaves in the Post-Industrial City* (pp. 49–55). Cham: Springer.

Nagle, A. (2017). *Kill All Normies: Online Culture Wars From 4chan and Tumblr to Trump and the Alt-Right.* John Hunt Publishing.

Nani, A. (2022). The doge worth 88 billion dollars: A case study of Dogecoin. *Convergence,* 13548565211070417.

Naveed, N., Gottron, T., Kunegis, J., & Alhadi, A. C. (2011). Bad news travel fast: A content-based analysis of interestingness on twitter. In *Proceedings of the 3rd International Web Science Conference* (pp. 1–7).

Nelson, S. R. (2006). *Steel Drivin' Man: John Henry, the Untold Story of an American Legend.* Oxford University Press.

Nerhardt, G. (1970). Humor and inclination to laugh: Emotional reactions to stimuli of different divergence from a range of expectancy. *Scandinavian Journal of Psychology, 11*(1), 185–195.

Nikolinakou, A., & King, K. W. (2018). Viral video ads: Emotional triggers and social media virality. *Psychology & Marketing, 35*(10), 715–726.

Nordling, N., Sandnabba, N. K., Santtila, P., & Alison, L. (2006). Differences and similarities between gay and straight individuals involved in the sadomasochistic subculture. In P.J. Kleinplatz & C. Moser (Eds.), *Sadomasochism: Powerful Pleasures* (pp. 41–57). Routledge.

Oppliger, P. A. (2003). *Wrestling and Hypermasculinity.* McFarland.

Osborne, M. P. (1991). *American Tall Tales.* Knopf.

Packer, D., & Van Bavel, J. (2021). Understanding our online dumpster fire. *Psychology Today.* https://www.psychologytoday.com/us/blog/the-power-us/202107/understanding-our-online-dumpster-fire

Page, A. (2016). "This baby sloth will inspire you to keep going": Capital, labor, and the affective power of cute animal videos. In J. P. Dale, J. Goggin, J. Leyda, A. P. McIntyre, & D. Negra (Eds.), *The Aesthetics and Affects of Cuteness* (pp. 85–104). Routledge.

Paul, K. (2022). 'Dangerous misogynist' Andrew Tate booted from Instagram and Facebook. *The Guardian*, 19 August.

Paxton, R. O. (2004). *The Anatomy of Fascism*. Vintage.

Pennebaker, J. W., Booth, R. J., & Francis, M. E. (2007). *Linguistic Inquiry and Word Count (LIWC): LIWC2007*. Austin, TX: LIWC.net.

Pennebaker, J. W., Boyd, R. L., Booth, R. J., Ashokkumar, A., & Francis, M. E. (2022). Linguistic inquiry and word count: LIWC-22. Pennebaker Conglomerates. https://www.liwc.app

Pennebaker, J. W., Boyd, R. L., Jordan, K., & Blackburn, K. (2015). The development and psychometric properties of LIWC2015.

Pérez, R. (2022). *The Souls of White Jokes: How Racist Humor Fuels White Supremacy*. Stanford University Press.

Perks, L. G., & McElrath-Hart, N. (2018). Spoiler definitions and behaviors in the post-network era. *Convergence*, 24(2), 137–151.

Phillips, W. (2015). *This Is Why We Can't Have Nice Things: Mapping the Relationship Between Online Trolling and Mainstream Culture*. MIT Press.

Phillips, W., & Milner, R. M. (2017). *The Ambivalent Internet: Mischief, Oddity, and Antagonism Online*. Polity.

Piesman, M., & Hartley, M. (1984). *The Yuppie Handbook; the State-of-the-Art Manual for Young Urban Professionals*. New York: Long Shadow Books.

Pirandello, L. (1908). *L 'umorismo*. Milan: Mondadori. English Translation on humor by Antonio Illiano & Daniel P. Testa. 1969. University of North Carolina Press.

Prochazkova, E., & Kret, M. E. (2017). Connecting minds and sharing emotions through mimicry: A neurocognitive model of emotional contagion. *Neuroscience & Biobehavioral Reviews*, 80, 99–114.

Quam-Wickham, N. (1999). Rereading man's conquest of nature: Skill, myths, and the historical construction of masculinity in western extractive industries. *Men and Masculinities*, 2(2), 135–151. DOI: 10.1177/1097184X99002002002.

Quillen, E. G. (2017). The satirical sacred: New Atheism, parody religion, and the argument from fictionalization. In C. R. Cotter, P. A. Quadrio, & J. Tuckett (Eds.), *New Atheism: Critical Perspectives and Contemporary Debates* (pp. 193–220). Springer.

Quitner, J. (1994). The war between alt.tasteless and rec.pets.cats. *Wired*. https://www.wired.com/1994/05/alt-tasteless/

Ray, Beverly, & Marsh, George E. (2001). Recruitment by extremist groups on the Internet. *First Monday*, 6(2). DOI: 10.5210/fm.v6i2.834. https://firstmonday.org/ojs/index.php/fm/article/view/834

Rensin, E. (2014). The great satirical-news scam of 2014. *New Republic*. https://newrepublic.com/article/118013/satire-news-websites-are-cashing-gullible-outraged-readers

Reuters. (2012). Slovak lawmakers reject online vote to name bridge after Chuck Norris. https://www.reuters.com/article/entertainment-us-slovakia-chucknorris-idUSBRE88K0U820120921

Reutzel, B. (2022). What are meme cryptocurrencies and should you buy them? *CNBC*. https://www.cnbc.com/select/what-are-meme-cryptocurrency/

Robertson, Harry. (2019). Murdoch Murdoch—The alt-right's very own sitcom. *Medium.* https://medium.com/tales-from-the-alt-right/murdoch-murdoch-the-alt-rights-sitcom-6c033d30d2ae

Rodgers, S. (2020). The joyful voyeurism of reaction videos. *Kill Your Darlings.* https://www.killyourdarlings.com.au/article/the-joyful-voyeurism-of-reaction-videos/

Rogers, E. (2003). *Diffusion of Innovations* (5th ed.). Free Press.

Rogers, K. (2016). Boaty McBoatface: What you get when you let the internet decide. *The New York Times.* https://www.nytimes.com/2016/03/22/world/europe/boaty-mcboatface-what-you-get-when-you-let-the-internet-decide.html

Rogers, K. M. (1998). *The Cat and the Human Imagination.* Ann Arbor: University of Michigan Press.

Rose, M. A. (2014). Parody. In S. Attardo (Ed.), *Encyclopedia of Humor Studies* (pp. 552–554). Sage.

Rosenfeld, E. (2012). Mountain Dew's 'Dub the Dew' online poll goes horribly wrong. *Time.* https://newsfeed.time.com/2012/08/14/mountain-dews-dub-the-dew-online-poll-goes-horribly-wrong/

Rosenfeld, G. D. (2015). *Hi Hitler!: How the Nazi Past is Being Normalized in Contemporary Culture.* Cambridge University Press.

Rozin, P., & Royzman, E. B. (2001). Negativity bias, negativity dominance, and contagion. *Personality and Social Psychology Review, 5*(4), 296–320.

Rutkoff, A. (2007). With 'LOLcats' Internet fad, anyone can get in on the joke. *Wall Street Journal, 25.*

Saleem, S. (2020). This YouTube channel makes pakistani tribal people react to western snacks and it's downright entertaining! *Diva.* https://www.divaonline.com.pk/this-youtube-channel-makes-pakistani-tribal-people-react-to-western-snacks-and-its-downright-entertaining/

Salzman, A. (2021). Dogecoin started as a joke. Now it's too important to laugh off. *Barron's.* https://www.barrons.com/articles/dogecoin-started-as-a-joke-now-its-too-important-to-laugh-off-51620229273

Sanderson, D. (1997). *Smileys.* Oreilly & Associates.

Schiller, M. (2020). Heino, Rammstein and the double-ironic melancholia of Germanness. *European Journal of Cultural Studies, 23*(2), 261–280.

Schlaile, M. P., Knausberg, T., Mueller, M., & Zeman, J. (2018). Viral ice buckets: A memetic perspective on the ALS ice bucket challenge's diffusion. *Cognitive Systems Research, 52,* 947–969.

Schneebeli, C. (2019). The meaning of LOL: Patterns of LOL deployment in YouTube comments. In *ADDA 2–Approaches to Digital Discourse Analysis,* May 2019, Turku, Finland.

Schwabach, A. (2012). Reclaiming copyright from the outside in: What the downfall Hitler meme means for transformative works, fair use, and parody. *Buffalo Intellectual Property Law Journal, 8*(1), 1–22.

Schwanebeck, W. (2021). Introduction to painful laughter: Media and politics in the age of cringe. *Humanities, 10*(4), 123.

Schwind, K. H. (2015). Like watching a motorway crash: Exploring the embarrassment humor of the office. *Humor: International Journal of Humor Research, 28*(1), 49–70.

Segev, E., Nissenbaum, A., Stolero, N., & Shifman, L. (2015). Families and networks of internet memes: The relationship between cohesiveness, uniqueness, and quiddity concreteness. *Journal of Computer-Mediated Communication, 20*(4), 417–433.

Serrels, M. (2021). Dogecoin: The origin story of the Elon Musk supported cryptocurrency. *CNET*. https://www.cnet.com/personal-finance/crypto/dogecoin-the-origin-story-of-the-elon-musk-supported-cryptocurrency/

Sewell, C., & Keralis, S. D. (2019). The history & origin of cat memes: From the 18th century to lolcats; or, how cats have basically changed the internet and the world Furever. *Hyperrhiz*, 21. http://hyperrhiz.io/hyperrhiz21/miscellany/7-cat-memes.html

Shifman, L. (2011). An anatomy of a YouTube meme. *New Media & Society*, 14(2), 187–203.

Shifman, L. (2014a). *Memes in Digital Culture*. MIT Press.

Shifman, L. (2014b). The cultural logic of photo-based meme genres. *Journal of Visual Culture*, 13(3), 340–358.

Shouse, E., & Oppliger, P. (2012). Sarah is magic: The (post-gendered?) comedy of Sarah Silverman. *Comedy Studies*, 3(2), 201–216.

Sienkiewicz, M., & Marx, N. (2022). *That's Not Funny: How the Right Makes Comedy Work for Them*. University of California Press.

Simpson, P. (2003). *On the Discourse of Satire: Towards a Stylistic Model of Satirical Humour*. Benjamins.

Skalicky, S. (2019). Investigating satirical discourse processing and comprehension: The role of cognitive, demographic, and pragmatic features. *Language and Cognition*, 11(3), 499–525.

Skalicky, S., & Crossley, S. A. (2019). Examining the online processing of satirical newspaper headlines. *Discourse Processes*, 56(1), 61–76.

Smith, J. A. (1984). A reappraisal of legislative privilege and American colonial journalism. *Journalism Quarterly*, 61(1), 97–141.

Snyder, G. F. (2015). "Marking whiteness" for cross-racial solidarity. *Du Bois Review: Social Science Research on Race*, 12(2), 297–319.

Song, S. (2013). Psychology of sharing on social media: Attention, emotion and reaction. sonya's thoughts on media and tech. https://sonya2song.blogspot.com/

Spaschi, C. F. (2021). A cognitive analysis of the invented religions: The Flying Spaghetti Monster case. *Journal for the Study of Religions and Ideologies*, 20(60), 128–140.

Spillett, R. (2019). I don't name this ship Boaty McBoatface! Kate and William christen £200million polar research ship Sir David Attenborough with Champagne - Despite 124,000 voting for the comic name instead. *The Daily Mail*. https://www.dailymail.co.uk/news/article-7507181/Kate-William-prepare-christen-polar-research-ship-Sir-David-Attenborough.html

Spitzberg, B. H. (2014). Toward a model of meme diffusion (M3D). *Communication Theory*, 24(3), 311–339.

Stark, J. (2018). Internet joke 'Boaty McBoatface' now has a coin. *Coin World*. https://www.coinworld.com/news/world-coins/internet-joke-boaty-mcboatface-now-has-a-coin.html

Steinhart, E. (2017) Pastafarianism. http://ericsteinhart.com/articles/pastafarianism.pdf

Steir-Livny, L. (2017). Is it OK to laugh about it yet? Hitler Rants YouTube parodies in Hebrew. *The European Journal of Humour Research*, 4(4), 105–121.

Stevens, E. M. & McIntyre, K. (2019). The layers of the onion: The impact of satirical news on affect and online sharing behaviors. *Electronic News*, 13(2), 78–92. DOI: 10.1177/1931243119850264.

Suh, B., Hong, L., Pirolli, P., & Chi, E. H. (2010, August). Want to be retweeted? Large scale analytics on factors impacting retweet in twitter network. In *2010 IEEE Second International Conference on Social Computing* (pp. 177–184). IEEE.

Swift, J. (1726). *Gulliver's travels into several remote nations of the world.* https://www.gutenberg.org/ebooks/829

Tagliamonte, S. A. (2016). So sick or so cool? The language of youth on the internet. *Language in Society, 45*(1), 1–32.

Tagliamonte, S. A., & Denis, D. (2008). Linguistic ruin? LOL! Instant messaging and teen language. *American Speech, 83*(1), 3–34.

Tangney, J. P., Miller, R. S., Flicker, L., & Barlow, D. H. (1996). Are shame, guilt, and embarrassment distinct emotions? *Journal of Personality and Social Psychology, 70*(6), 1256.

The Guardian. (2014). Queen photobombs Hockeyroo Jayde Taylor's Commonwealth Games selfie. https://www.theguardian.com/sport/2014/jul/24/commonwealth-games-queen-photobombs-australian-selfie

Thomas, L. (2016). The quiet death of 'the daily currant', patient zero in the fake news epidemic. *Vulture.* https://www.vulture.com/2016/11/the-quiet-death-of-the-daily-currant-patient-zero-in-the-fake-news-epidemic.html

Thorleifsson, C. (2021). From cyberfascism to terrorism: On 4chan/pol/culture and the transnational production of memetic violence. *Nations and Nationalism, 28*(1), 286–301. DOI: 10.1111/nana.12780.

Tiffany, K. (2020). The misogynistic joke that became a Goth-meme fairy tale. *The Atlantic,* 3 February. https://www.theatlantic.com/technology/archive/2020/02/doomer-girl-meme-4chan-tumblr-wojak-history/605764/

Traub, J. (2003). Weimar Whiners: The way we live now. *New York Times,* 1 June 2003.

Trillò, T., & Shifman, L. (2021). Memetic commemorations: Remixing far-right values in digital spheres. *Information, Communication & Society, 24*(16), 2482–2501.

Tsakona, V. (2020). *Recontextualizing Humor: Rethinking the Analysis and Teaching of Humor.* de Gruyter.

Tuters, M. (2019). LARPing & liberal tears: Irony, belief and idiocy in the deep vernacular web. In M. Fielitz & N. Thurston (Eds.), *Post-Digital Cultures of the Far Right: Online Actions and Offline Consequences in Europe and the US* (pp. 37–48). Transcript Verlag.

Urbina, B., & Alejandro, S. (2021). Shitposting and memeculture: An aesthetic politics of techno-coloniality? (May 4, 2021). https://ssrn.com/abstract=3839267

Van Dijk, W. W., Ouwerkerk, J. W., van Koningsbruggen, G. M., & Wesseling, Y. M. (2012). "So you wanna be a pop star?": Schadenfreude following another's misfortune on TV. *Basic and Applied Social Psychology, 34*(2), 168–174.

Vargas, R. A. (2022) Alex Jones ordered to pay $45.2m in punitive damages to Sandy Hook family. *The Guardian,* 5 August.

Varnhagen, C. K., McFall, G. P., Pugh, N., Routledge, L., Sumida-MacDonald, H., & Kwong, T. E. (2010). Lol: New language and spelling in instant messaging. *Reading and Writing, 23*(6), 719–733.

Vásquez, C. (2017). "My life has changed forever!": Narrative identities in parodies of Amazon reviews. *Narrative Inquiry, 27*(2), 217–234.

Vásquez, C. (2019). *Language, Creativity and Humour Online.* Routledge.

Veblen, T. (1889). *The Theory of the Leisure Class.* New York: The Modern Library.

Venema, D., & Alm, N. (2022). Judging the flying Spaghetti Monster. https://freethinker.co.uk/2022/07/judging-the-flying-spaghetti-monster/

Verschueren, J. (2000). Notes on the role of metapragmatic awareness in language use. *Pragmatics: Quarterly Publication of the International Pragmatics Association (IPrA), 10*(4), 439–456.

Viega, J., & Thompson, H. (2012). The state of embedded-device security (spoiler alert: It's bad). *IEEE Security & Privacy, 10*(5), 68–70.

Voigts, E. (2018). Memes, GIFs, and remix culture: Compact appropriation in everyday digital life. In D. Cutchins, K. Krebs, & E. Voigts (Eds.), *The Routledge Companion to Adaptation* (pp. 390–402). Routledge.

Vookoti, S. (2013). NASA finds message from god on mars: Fact check. http://www.hoaxorfact.com/Pranks/nasa-finds-message-from-god-on-mars-hoax-analysis.html

Waisanen, Don J. (2011). Crafting hyperreal spaces for comic insights: The onion news network's ironic iconicity. *Communication Quarterly, 59*(5), 508–528. DOI: 10.1080/01463373.2011.615690.

Waller, B. M., & Micheletta, J. (2013). Facial expression in nonhuman animals. *Emotion Review, 5*(1), 54–59. DOI: 10.1177/1754073912451503.

Walton, S., & Jaffe, A. (2011). "Stuff white people like": Stance, class, race, and internet commentary. In C. Thurlow & K. Mroczek (Eds.), *Digital Discourse: Language in the New Media* (pp. 199–219).

Warren-Crow, H. (2016). Screaming like a girl: Viral video and the work of reaction. *Feminist Media Studies, 16*(6), 1113–1117.

Waysdorf, A. S. (2021). Remix in the age of ubiquitous remix. *Convergence, 27*(4), 1129–1144.

Weeks, B. E., & Holbert, R. L. (2013). Predicting dissemination of news content in social media: A focus on reception, friending, and partisanship. *Journalism & Mass Communication Quarterly, 90*(2), 212–232.

Weeks, L. (2016). The sad, happy life of Harry Whittier Frees. *NPR*. https://www.npr.org/sections/npr-history-dept/2016/01/06/462040450/the-sad-happy-life-of-harry-whittier-frees

Weisenthal, J. (2014). Introducing Stalwartbucks: I'm launching my own digital currency. *Business Insider*. https://www.businessinsider.com/introducing-stalwartbucks-2014-1

Westermann, E. B. (2018). Drinking rituals, masculinity, and mass murder in Nazi Germany. *Central European History, 51*(3), 367–389.

White, E. J. (2020). *A Unified Theory of Cats on the Internet*. Stanford University Press.

Wiggins, B. E. (2019). *The Discursive Power of Memes in Digital Culture: Ideology, Semiotics, and Intertextuality*. Routledge.

Wilson, C. (2022). Australian Dogecoin creator Jackson Palmer on grifts, Elon Musk, crypto bubbles and Pauline Hanson. Crikey. https://www.crikey.com.au/2022/05/30/dogecoin-jackson-palmer-elon-musk-crypto-bubble-pauline-hanson/

Wodak, R. (2017). The "Establishment", the "Élites", and the "People": Who's who? *Journal of Language and Politics, 16*(4), 551–565.

Yarosh, S., Bonsignore, E., McRoberts, S., & Peyton, T. (2016). YouthTube: Youth video authorship on YouTube and Vine. In *Proceedings of the 19th ACM Conference on Computer-Supported Cooperative Work & Social Computing* (pp. 1423–1437).

Young, D. G., (2020). *Irony and Outrage: The Polarized Landscape of Rage, Fear, and Laughter in the United States*. Oxford University Press.

Yus, F. (2011). *Cyberpragmatics: Internet-Mediated Communication in Context*. John Benjamins Publishing Company.

Yus, F. (2018). Multimodality in memes: A cyberpragmatic approach. In P. Bou-Franch & P. G. C. Blitvich (Eds.), *Analyzing Digital Discourse: New Insights and Future Directions* (pp. 105–131).

Yus, F. (2021). Incongruity-resolution humorous strategies in image macro memes. *Internet Pragmatics, 4*(1), 131–149.

Yus, F. (2022). *Smartphone Communication: Interactions in the App Ecosystem*. Routledge.
Zeng, E., Kohno, T., & Roesner, F. (2020). Bad news: Clickbait and deceptive ads on news and misinformation websites. In *Workshop on Technology and Consumer Protection* (pp. 1–11). IEEE.
Zhang, L., Wang, F., & Liu, J. (2014, March). Understand instant video clip sharing on mobile platforms: Twitter's vine as a case study. In *Proceedings of Network and Operating System Support on Digital Audio and Video Workshop* (pp. 85–90).
Zillmann, D. (1983). Disparagement humor. In P. E. McGhee & J. H. Goldstein (Eds.), *Handbook of Humor Research* (Vol. I, pp. 85–107). Springer.
Zimmer, B. (2014). Spoiler alert: How spoilers started out. *The Wall Street Journal, 10*.
Zimmer, B., & Carson, C. E. (2011). Among the new words. *American Speech, 86*(4), 454–479.

# AUTHOR INDEX

Adams, A. 55
Alm, N. 140, 148
Anderson, S. 207–8
Aspray, B. 237
Astruc, A. 197
Attardo, S. 22, 26, 30, 44, 48, 112–13, 124, 166, 190, 220

Bakhtin, M. 127
Ball, M. 53, 67, 198
Ballentine, C. 90
Barinka, A. 211
Baron, N. S. 51, 57, 59
Bateson, G. 47
Bauer, P. 140
Baumeister, R. F. 167
Becker, A. B. 41
Berger, J. 161, 166–67
Bergson, Henri. 48, 68–69, 177, 194–95
Berret, C. 135
Bhat, P. 239
Billig, M. 190
Bischetti, L. 4, 157, 166
Blackmore, S. 15
Blair, W. 151
Bliss, L. 207
Blitvich, P. G. C. 20
Blommaert, J. 162
Bogost, I. 233
Booth, R. J. 66
Börzsei, L. K. 134
Bou-Franch, P. 17
Bovet, A. 10
Bowman-Grieve, L. 220
Bradbury, J. 96
Bramlett, F. 73
Brideau, K. 135
Brodie, Ian 102–3, 105
Brooks, D. 30, 69, 82, 180–81
Brubaker, J. R. 135

Bruns, A. 24
Brzozowski, W. 140
Burgess, J. 26
Burns, R. G. 202
Bybee, J. 116

Calhoun, K. 198
Carson, C. E. 183
Chiaro, D. 16, 135
Chielens, K. 162, 164
Chohan, U. W. 89
Choi, M. 107
Clements, W. M. 112
Click, M. 234
CNN 102, 124
Cohen, D. J. 167
Cohen, E. L. 234
Cohn, M. A. 193
Condren, C. 101
Coppa, F. 32
Costera Meijer, I. 166
Critchley, S. 135
Crossley, S. A. 103
Cusack, C. M. 140, 146

Dafonte-Gómez, A. 166
Dale, J. P. 135–36
Danesi, M. 55–56, 162
Davies, C. 46, 112
Davies, C. E. 82
Daviess, B. 221–22, 229
Dawkins, R. 15–16, 100, 162
de Jongste, H. 194
Dearden, L. 237
Denis, D. 51, 58
Denisova, A. 2
Dionigi, A. 235
Donahue, A. 4, 55
Donovan, D. T. 101
Donovan, J. 2, 245

Dorson, R. M. 151
Douglas, N. 19
Dundes, A. 111–12, 126–27
Durando, J. 143

Eagleton, T. 81
Eco, U. 2, 78, 230–32
Economist 10, 104
Edmonds, M. 151
Edwards, D. A. 164
Ekman, P. 190
Ester, P. 82
Evans, V. 55–56

Feinberg, A. 238
Feldman, N. 147
Felton, H. W. 151
Fichman, P. 228
Fillmore, C. J. 117
Finchelstein, F. 231
Ford, S. 48
Ford, T. 48
French, A. J. 79–80, 82
Friedman, T. 12

Gal, N. 2, 181
Gallucci, N. 58
Garley, M. 58
Gawne, L. 135
Gibson, J. J. 26
Gilbert, C. J. 47, 177, 181
Gillin, J. 105
Goel, S. 164
Goffman, E. 47, 127, 190, 209
Golshan, T. 123
Goodwin, M. 175
Goodyear, D. 189
Graeber, D. 79
Grant, N. 78
Green, J. 21
Greene, V. S. 219, 238
Grice, P. 47–48
Griffin, R. 230, 232
Groot Kormelink, T. 166
Grzanka, P. R. 77–78, 82
Guadagno, R. E. 167
Guardian 123, 131, 185
Guess, A. M. 101, 202

Harber, K. D. 167
Hartley, M. 82
Harvey, C. G. 25, 53, 222
Heaney, K. 58

Heft, A. 149
Hempelmann, C. F. 112
Henrich, J. 168, 223
Herbst, J. P. 205
Herring, S. 20, 228–29
Heylighen, F. 25, 162, 164–65
Hirsch, G. 178–79
Holbert, R. L. 167
Holland, E. C. 102
Holmes, D. R. 231–32
Holt, K. 198
Horta Ribeiro, M. 220–21
Huffington Post 124, 238
Hye-Knudson, M. 190

Jacklosky, R. 103
Jaffe, A. 77–78, 81–82
James, A. 235
James, R. M. 234
Jenkins, H. 114
Jennings, K. 16
Johnson, A. 103
Johnson, B. K. 95
Johnson, L. M. 251
Johnson, M. 190
Jordan, K. 95
Julin, G. 42

Kartono, A. 169
Kennedy, M. 128
Keralis, S. D. 135
King, H. 33, 91, 148, 198
King, K. W. 33, 91, 148, 198
Klein, O. 239
Knight, J. 27
Knobel, M. 140
Kochkodin, B. 85
Krach, S. 190
Kret, M. E. 190
Kuipers, G. 48
Kumar, S. 10

Lakoff, G. 190
Lander, C. 77, 79–80, 82
Lankshear, C. 140
Larson, G. 72
Laubert, C. 58
Le Mens, G. 161
Leigh, C. 135
Lelièvre, F. J. 21
Leporati, M. 103
Lessig, L. 32, 35
Levy, A. 102

Licklider, J. C. R. 71
Lloyd, S. A. 41
Lofaro, M. A. (Ed.). 151
Lorenz, Konrad 135
Ludemann, D. 229, 234
Lyons, B. A. 101

Maćkowiak, A. 140, 146
Maddox, J. 135–37
Maher, J. 77–78, 82
Makse, H. A. 10
Marcin, T. 165
Marcoccia, M. 17
Marcuse, H. 243
Markman, K. M. 58
Marone, V. 198
Marsh, G. E. 220
Marsh, M. 126–27
Martin, R. A. 48
Marx, N. 177, 219–20, 232
Mayer, A. V. 190–91
McCloud, S. 73
McCool, B. 93
McCulloch, G. 12, 14, 26, 51, 55–56, 58, 135, 168, 170
McDaniel, B. 208
McElrath-Hart, N. 95
McGhee, P. E. 41
McGill, S. 32
McGraw, A. P. 40, 194
McKay, I. 58
McSweeney, M. A. 58
McSwiney, J. 239
McWorther, J. 51, 58
Meier, A. 220
Miao, H. 25
Micheletta, J. 131
Michot, N. 58
Middleton, J. 209
Milkman, K. L. 166–67
Miller, R. S. 4, 142
Milner, R. M. 123, 177
Miltner, Kate. 134–35
Minor, W. 91
Mohammed, S. 148, 215
Mohammed, S. N. 148, 215
Monroe, J. 234
Monzani, D. 193
Moss, G. 82
Murphy, S. 83

Nagle, A. 229, 237
Nani, A. 85, 88–89, 91

Nelson, S. R. 151
Nerhardt, G. 42
Nordling, N. 206

Oppliger, P. 191, 205
Osborne, M. P. 151

Packer, D. 10
Page, A. 136
Parlamis, J. 58
Paul, K. 73, 104, 151, 222–23
Paxton, R. O. 231
Pennebaker, J. W. 193
Pérez, R. 230
Perks, L. G. 94–95, 217
Phillips, W. 20, 36, 52, 123, 177, 228–29, 235–36
Piesman, M. 82
Pirandello, L. 69
Prochazkova, E. 190

Quam-Wickham, N. 151
Quillen, E. G. 140, 146, 149

Raskin, V. 44
Ray, B. 53, 188, 220
Rensin, E. 104
Reuters 123
Reutzel, B. 91
Robertson, H. 221
Rodgers, S. 208
Rogers, E. 165
Rogers, K. 123
Rogers, K. M. 132
Rose, M. A. 201
Rosenbaum, J. E. 95
Rosenfeld, E. 124
Rosenfeld, G. D. 181
Roy, C. J. 32
Royzman, E. B. 167
Rozin, P. 167
Rutkoff, A. 134

Saleem, S. 215
Salzman, A. 85, 88
Sanderson, D. 54
Sanfilippo, M. R. 228
Schiller, M. 202, 205
Schneebeli, C. 58
Schwabach, A. 177
Schwanebeck, W. 190
Schwind, K. H. 191
Segev, E. 113

Serrels, M. 85, 89–90
Sewell, C. 135
Shifman, L. 16, 25, 113, 178, 239
Shouse, E. 191
Sienkiewicz, M. 219–20, 232
Simpson, P. 101
Skalicky, S. 4, 103
Smith, J. A. 148, 167
Snyder, G. F. 81–82
Song, S. 167
Spaschi, C. F. 140, 147
Spillett, R. 128
Spitzberg, B. H. 164–65, 223
Stanley, T. 192
Stark, J. 59
Steinhart, E. 142, 147–48
Steir-Livny, L. 179, 181
Suh, B. 164
Swift, J. 16, 51, 100, 169

Tagliamonte, S. A. 51–52, 58
Tangney, J. P. 190
Thomas, L. 12, 40, 105, 146
Thompson, H. 93
Thorleifsson, C. 229–30, 232, 236–37
Tiffany, K. 243
Traub, J. 231
Trillò, T. 239
Tsakona, V. 61, 89, 179

Van Bavel, J. 10
Van Dijk, W. W. 195
Varnhagen, C. K. 58
Vásquez, C. 21, 200

Vaughan, J. 135
Veblen, T. 79, 208
Venema, D. 140, 148
Verschueren, J. 80
Viega, J. 93
Vinken, H. 82
Voigts, E. 32
Vookoti, S. 48

Waisanen, Don J. 107
Waller, B. M. 131
Walton, S. 77–78, 82
Warren, C. 40, 194, 207
Warren-Crow, H. 207
Waysdorf, A. S. 32
Weeks, B. E. 167
Weeks, L. 134
Weisenthal, J. 91
Wengrow, D. 79
West, R. 100, 178
Westermann, E. B. 205
White, E. J. 135–37
Wiggins, B. E. 16
Wilson, C. 90
Wodak, R. 236

Yarosh, S. 200
Young, D. G. 219
Yus, F. 16, 56, 61

Zeng, E. 105
Zhang, L. 198
Zimmer, B. 93, 183

# SUBJECT INDEX

Abbott 201
acronym 16, 51, 57, 134
Adam 139, 141, 190
advice dog (meme) 18, 137
Aeneid 93
affordances 22, 26–27, 29, 36–37, 58–59, 63, 75–76, 113–14, 165, 168, 197, 229–30, 235, 250
Africa (continent) 12, 140, 223
Africa (song) 234–35
African-American 151, 161, 192, 200
Afualo, J. 211–12, 236
aggression 20, 41, 116, 172, 226, 248, 250–51
AI 9, 72
Aita (Am I the Asshole? meme) 52
aliens 60, 156
Alliteration 111, 113, 115, 117, 119, 121, 124
Altavista 9
alt-right 1, 8, 107, 137, 206, 217, 219–20, 222–23, 225–26, 228–29, 231–33, 237–42, 246, 248, 250
Amazon 9, 11, 21, 54, 146
America 9, 11, 63, 79–80, 140, 195, 197
America Online (AOL) 9
American/s 54, 81, 112–13, 124, 126, 151, 158, 160–61, 189, 191–92, 198, 200, 214
America's Funniest Home Videos (TV show) 63, 197
Amish 178
Anakin (meme) 117–18
anchor meme 25, 27, 30, 113–18, 122, 175
animal 4, 26–27, 63, 90–91, 131–38, 184, 186–88, 198
anime 72, 225, 248
anonymity 20, 222, 229, 235, 250
anonymous 2, 4, 20, 41, 157, 205, 217, 225, 228–30, 233, 236, 243

antagonistic 95, 127, 190, 228–29, 234, 248
anthropomorphism 90–92, 131–34, 136–37
Anti Defamation League (ADL) 239–41
Anti-Joke Chicken (meme) 137
antisemitism 225, 237, 239–40
Antunes, A. 201–2
Apache 10
Apple 77
Arabia 165, 169
argot 52
Aristotle 40, 64, 194–95
Arlecchino 18
arousal 25, 167
ASCII 54–55, 250
Asia 82
asshole 52, 235, 251
Astley, R. 9, 44; *see also* rickrolling
Attenborough, R. 123, 128, 130
Audacity 36
audience 16–17, 33, 47, 64, 69, 71–73, 78, 95, 100–101, 127, 152, 160, 179–82, 190–92, 194, 200, 203, 207, 210, 213–14, 220, 222, 228, 239
Austin 124
Australia 125, 140, 143
Austria 123, 140, 178
Automattic 2
autotune 201, 251
awkward 18–19, 56, 83, 137, 191–92, 195
awkward penguin (meme): *see* penguin
awkwardness 190

baby boomer 14, 243
Baby Yoda 30
Babylon Bee 40–41, 101, 219
Bachelor, A. 198, 200
Bachelorette 137
Baidu 9

Bakhtin, M. 127
Ball, H. 53
Balochi 213
Banff 186–87
Baptist 102, 107
Baschenis, E. 222–23
batonic (gesture) 56–57
BBS 7–8
BDSM 202, 206
Beatles 15, 21, 33, 35, 139
Beethoven, L. 15
benign violation 40, 64, 194
Bergson, H. 48, 64, 68–69, 177, 194–95
Bernie (meme) 25–28, 34, 45–46, 117, 169
bestiality 225
Bible 33, 139, 147–48, 205
Bieber, J. 130
Binance 91
BIPOC 138
bird 76
Bitcoin 85, 87–88, 91, 157
Bitmapworld (comic) 74
bleaching: *see* semantic bleaching
Blockbuster 89
blockchain 87–88
blog 2–3, 9, 16, 77–79, 82, 124, 135
blondes 46
Bloomberg 91
Boaty McBoatface (meme) 89, 109, 123, 125–30, 143, 145, 170, 250
Bobos in Paradise (book) 82
bourgeois 82
Boy's Club (comic) 239
Bratislava 123–24
Breaking Bad 104
Brexit 180
brigading 130
British 13–14, 72, 87, 123, 130, 134, 175
Brolsma, G. 21
Brooks, M. 69
browser 7, 134
Buzz Lightyear (film) 128
Bybit 88

calque 111
Canada 47, 79, 181, 198
capital 25
capitalism 133, 243, 251
caricature 158, 241
cartoon 9, 18, 20, 49, 55, 71–73, 75–76, 137, 153, 217, 220, 239, 241, 244, 249
Casablanca (Film) 117
catfishing 21

cathode-ray tube (CRT) 53
cats 11, 131–38, 226, 228
cento 32
CERN 7
Chad (meme) 242
Chappelle, D. 17, 83, 96
charivari 126
Charlottesville 233
chat 54–55, 128, 134, 233
chatbot 99
Cheezburger 135
Cheryl She Shed (meme) 111, 113–17, 157, 181
China 102, 140, 146
Chiquita 165
Chomsky, N. 20, 59
Christchurch 220, 232, 237
Christian 32, 40–41, 77, 140–41
Christianity 40–41, 146–48
Chuck Norris facts (meme) 23, 143, 151–55, 157–58, 160
class 1, 42, 78, 82–83, 96–97, 112, 191, 231
clickbait 104
clown 180
Clueless Hero (comic) 73
Clueless Padme (meme) 117–22
CMC 51
CNN 102, 124
COAUtilities 124
Cockney 52
colander 141–43
comedian 17–18, 39, 47, 81, 166, 189, 198
comedy 14, 16–18, 69, 93, 95–96, 104, 125, 173, 190–91, 194, 198, 209, 220, 222, 249
comic 16, 71, 73, 76, 81, 152, 177, 201, 239, 245
comics 16, 19, 22, 32, 71–74, 118, 120, 137, 243
commedia dell'arte 18
compilation 36, 49, 63–68, 193
concatenation 140
Confession Bear (meme) 137
connotation 8, 32, 35, 122, 162, 214, 240
conservative 158–59, 219
conspicuous consumption 79, 208
conspiracy 114, 220, 225, 231, 236
construction 111, 116–17, 122, 179, 214
consumerism 77, 146, 149, 250
consumption 79–80, 83, 94, 208
Coolio 178
cooperative (principle) 47

## SUBJECT INDEX

cosplay 72, 244
Costello 201: *see also* Abbott
covfefe 59–60
Covid 27, 40, 155–57, 163–64, 169, 181, 201, 225
cringe 69, 173, 189–96, 209, 247, 249
crowdsourcing 10, 89
Cruz, T. 107, 198–99
cryptocurrencies 85, 88–92
Cthulhu 91
Ctrl+Alt+Del (comic) 73
cuck 221
Cuckistan 231–32
cuckolds 221, 232
Cucks 232
cuks 248
cute 11, 135–38, 172, 203–4
cyberbullying 228
cyberfascism 230

dad jokes 169
*Daily Currant* 48, 104
Dallas 72
Danger Mouse 33
dank 35, 52, 153, 168–69, 171, 248
Dante 93
Darcy 94
Dawkinian meme 144–45, 231
Debord, G. 229, 250–51
decay (exponential) 60, 162–63, 169, 171
decontextualization 103
Democrats 114
deplatforming 221
Di Caprio, L. 80
Digg 168
Dilbert (cartoon) 71
Dinosaur Comics 71, 75
Disaster Girl (meme) 114–15
Discordianism 146
disinformation 101
disparagement humor 91
disposition theory 41, 195
dissonance 47
dog 18, 20, 27, 67, 78, 85, 90–92, 105, 137, 153, 188, 239
Doge (meme) 85–86, 89–92
Dogecoin 85–86, 88–92
Dogelon 91
Dogendorsed 91
Dogg 89
donut 198
doom 243
doom scrolling 136, 138

Doomer 52, 243–44
Downfall (Film) 175, 177–82, 203, 246
doxxing 130
dozens 36
Dr. Who (TV show) 72
drift (memetic) 111, 114–17, 119, 121, 154, 157, 181
Dumbledore 95

eBay 9
Economist, The 10
educated 78, 82–83, 96, 107, 139, 141, 159
Egypt 132–33, 245
Eli Lilly 165
elite 78, 82
EMACS 10
email 7, 9, 14, 25, 125
embarrassment 22, 64, 69, 173, 189–96, 207, 209, 250
emblems 56
embodiment 48, 72, 79, 190
emojis 5, 14, 17, 53–60, 167, 193, 250
emotes 54–55, 58
emoticons 54–55, 58, 60, 250
emotion 22, 39–41, 55–56, 58, 132, 157, 167, 171–72, 177, 190–91, 193–96, 201, 205, 207–9
empathy 41, 58, 235
England 185
English 8, 32, 43, 51, 57, 97, 116–17, 135, 161, 180, 210, 250
enhancers of humor 156, 160
enregisterment 35, 162, 222
entitlement 36, 80, 229, 235
Ephron, N. 9
Epic Gamer comic 73
epidemics 163, 169
epidemiological 169–71
estrangement 74, 78
Ethereum 91
ethics 130, 146, 231, 235
ethnic 41, 81, 83, 111–12, 168
ethnographic 2, 235
ethology 135
Europe 11, 123, 140, 214, 232
evangelical 40
evolution 23, 39, 136, 139
exaggeration 21, 96–97, 105–6, 155–56, 159–61, 221, 235, 245
exhilaration 39, 42
Expanding Brain 170–71
expected 33, 42–44, 69, 106, 112–13, 154, 158, 170, 191, 200

exponential growth 60, 143, 162–63, 169–71; *see also* decay

Facebook 9–10, 13–14, 20, 22, 63, 71–72, 77, 95, 103, 114, 131, 136, 165, 168–69, 198, 213, 220–23, 233, 245, 251
fads 26, 145, 161, 171
fag (faggot) 52
Fahlman, S. 54
fail 39, 63–65, 67–69, 82, 118, 121, 229
FailArmy 64
fake news 10, 18, 65, 68, 99–106, 146, 165–66
Family Guy 153
fandom 175, 231, 234, 244–46
fanvidding 32
fanzines 8
fap 52, 124
Fapple 124
fascism 1, 107, 222, 225, 229–32, 236–37
feminist 220, 237
Ferrari 80
fetishes 177
Feuer Frei (song) 203–4
Fidonet 7
File Transfer Protocol (FTP) 7
Filipino 77
film 9, 11, 60–61, 63, 83, 93, 114, 117, 151–52, 173, 175, 177–78, 197, 203
Fitzpatrick, J. 128
flash mob 89, 125–27, 130
Flying Spaghetti Monster (FSM) 139–42, 146–47, 149; *see also* Pastafarianism
folklore 111, 126, 145, 151, 231
foreground 128, 183, 231
Formalists 74
Foul Bachelorette Frog 137
4chan 2, 19, 22, 52, 63, 85, 124, 168, 170, 217, 225–27, 229–30, 232, 235–37, 239, 242–43, 250
Fox News 102
Foxworthy J. 82
frame 43–44, 47, 56, 83, 113, 127, 138, 164, 188, 203, 214
France 25, 52
Funniest Home Videos 63, 197

Gab 240
Gamergate 225
GameStop 89
Gangsta Paradise (song) 178
Ganz B. 175, 177, 181
Garageband 36

gay 104, 206
geek 71–72
Gen X 14
Gen Z 10, 14, 16, 138
General Theory of Verbal Humor (GTVH) 44, 155, 160, 184, 203–4
genocide 177, 220, 236
genre 2, 21–22, 31–32, 36, 49, 63–64, 85, 92–93, 102, 107, 168, 173, 185, 191, 195, 198, 200–202, 204, 207, 209, 213–14, 231, 249
German 85, 173, 176, 178–80, 202, 205, 213–14, 230
Germany 176, 205, 230, 246
Gervais, R. 166
Gestalt 184
gestures 21, 29, 35, 39, 56, 96, 173, 198
GIFs 15
GIMP 36
GNU 10
god 40, 48, 67–68, 78, 80, 146, 148, 159, 245–46
Godard, J.L. 197
goddess 146, 236, 245
Godfather 93
Godot 159–60
Goebbels 80
Goering 80
Goodwin's Law 175
Google 4, 9, 20, 33, 59, 63, 93, 125, 143–45, 152–53, 176, 183, 198
Google Ngram 4, 94, 183
Google Trends 4, 143–45, 153
Gopher 9
GPS 66
grammaticalization 58, 116–17
Greek 148, 236
Grindr 104
ground 46, 65, 67, 127, 166–67, 183–85, 187
Grumpy Cat 109, 131–35, 137, 143–45
GTVH: *see* General Theory of Verbal Humor
Guardian, The 123, 131, 185
Guevara, C. 128
Gulliver's Travels (Novel) 16
Gutfeld 219

hacking 10, 20, 225, 228
hacktivism 225, 228
haha 55, 58, 193
Halo/Halopedia 90–91
Hamlet 32

## SUBJECT INDEX

harassing 20, 36, 130, 228
hashtag 164, 198
headlines 40, 99, 103, 106, 166–67
Hebrew 141, 179
Hello Kitty 136–37
Henderson, B. 139
Himmler 80
Hitler 100, 124, 127, 173, 175–81, 203, 221, 225, 239, 246–48
Hittite 53
hoaxes 11, 48, 100, 102, 166
Hobbes 40
HODL 91
holocaust 177, 181, 246–47
homophobia 104, 205, 232, 235
homosexual 52, 104, 202, 206, 235
Houyhnhnms 16
HTML 7, 9, 36, 56, 73, 76, 250
HTTP 7, 10
Huckabee 153–54
Hudson 192
Huffington Post 124, 238
hyperbolic 154
hyperdetermined 180
hyperinflation 85
hypermasculinity 202–6

iconicity 8, 81, 107, 177
ideology 3, 10, 40, 79–82, 137, 139, 167, 195, 205, 230, 236, 240, 251
image macros 60, 134–35
Imgur 154
iMovie 36
incels 237, 243
incongruity 27, 29, 41–48, 60, 69, 76, 90–92, 106, 111–12, 114, 122, 128, 141, 156, 158, 160, 178–81, 183–85, 188, 201, 207–8, 210, 214, 245, 248–49
indexicality 81
Indiana 27, 214
Indietits (comic) 75–76
Insanity Wolf (meme) 137
intelligent design 139–40
Internet Explorer 7
intertextuality 26, 29–30, 34, 112–15, 117, 157–58
iPhone 36, 197, 208
Iranian 102
irony 48, 55–57, 66, 77, 90–91, 101, 106–7, 148, 167, 169, 205, 219, 222, 231–32, 235, 237, 241
Islam 146, 148, 220, 232
Islamophobic 232

Israel 165, 179, 181
Italy 14, 18, 46, 69, 78, 87, 116, 139, 209, 230
Izzard E. 17

Jamaica 92, 140
Japan 54, 136, 140, 207, 223
Japanese 63, 72, 136, 141, 248
jargon 124, 229
jazz 77, 161
JennyCam 208
Jesus 33, 148
Jewish 189
Jews 148, 231, 246
joke 8–9, 15, 21, 25, 34, 39–41, 44–47, 52, 54, 72, 78, 80, 82, 85, 88–89, 91–93, 100–101, 103–4, 107, 111–14, 126–27, 137, 139–40, 144, 147, 149, 151, 154, 156–57, 159–60, 169, 178–80, 183, 189, 196, 198, 214, 219, 222, 234, 249, 251
joking 47, 156, 182, 221–22, 238, 250
justification (resolution) 111
juxtaposition 33, 64, 107, 160

Kabuki 136, 214
Kant 146
Kanye West 100, 178
kappa (emote) 55
Karachi 213, 215
Karen (meme) 36, 46, 201, 251
Kato-chan Ken-chan Gokigen TV 63
kawaii 136–38
Keanu Reeves (meme) 46
Kek 164, 239, 241, 243–48
Kekistan 231, 244–48
Key and Peele 93, 95–96
Khabane: *see* Khaby, L.
Khaby, L. 209–11, 214
kitten 134, 222
Know Your Meme 2–4, 24, 64, 117, 135, 152–53, 168, 175–76, 183, 207, 241
Korea 245

LA (language knowledge resource) 45, 156, 160
Lahontan 79
Lamborghini 80, 83
Lame: *see* Khaby, L.
Late Night with Conan O'Brien (TV show) 151–52
laugh 14, 29, 58, 66–69, 102, 160, 177, 182, 193, 195, 211

laughing 39, 57, 67, 134, 171, 177, 190, 192–93, 217
laughter 39–40, 49, 55, 57–58, 65–67, 69, 152, 193–94, 212
Law and Order (TV show) 15
lawyers 112–13, 236
Lee, G. 134
left 8, 115, 126, 157–58, 177, 188, 201, 231, 237, 244, 248
Leggero, N. 18, 189, 191, 196
Lego 33, 173, 202–5
Lenin 117–18, 120
lesbian 198
Leviathan 40
Levy 102
LGBT 232
LGBTQ 99, 122, 138
liberal 34, 82, 237, 248
libertarian 10
Lichtenstein 32
lifecasting 208
lightbulb jokes 112
Limp Bizkit 124
LinkedIn 13–14, 137
Linux 10
Litecoin 91
livestreamed 237
LIWC 193
LMAO 57, 193
logical 45–46, 104, 140, 156, 184, 201, 204, 248
logical mechanism (LM) 45, 155, 160
LOL 51, 55, 57–58, 83, 134, 193, 245
LOLCats 85, 134–35, 172, 232, 250
Lolita 136
Lovecraft, H. P. 91
Lowth 51
Luckey, P. 233
lulz 52, 217, 225, 227–29, 231, 233, 235–38

Machiavellianism 235
machismo 202
malware 105
manga 225
Marcuse, H. 243
marijuana 99, 104
marker (grammatical) 117
markers (of humor) 53–58, 105, 107, 193
Marvel 73, 205
Marx 177, 219–20, 232
maschere 18
masculinity 202, 205–6

mashup 24–25, 31–33, 46, 85, 90, 100, 114–15, 117, 178, 200, 203
masks 18, 163
masochism 202
Massachusetts 142–43
Matrix (film) 167
maxim 48, 102
McBoatface: *see* Boaty
meaning 2, 8, 15–16, 23, 32, 34–35, 37, 52, 54, 56, 58–59, 91, 106, 116–18, 134, 154, 159–60, 169, 173, 177–78, 182, 222, 233, 243, 251
meanings 27, 32, 34–35, 51, 56, 162, 231, 250
meatballs 147
meatspace 17, 20, 251
mechanism (logical) 44–46, 104, 140, 184, 186, 201, 204, 208
media 1, 9–10, 13, 17–18, 22–23, 30, 33, 35–36, 60, 63, 72–73, 94–95, 104, 126–27, 143, 153, 164–67, 176–77, 200, 221, 239–40, 249–50
mediated 17, 41, 58, 114, 136–37, 161, 232, 251
medieval 18, 52, 72, 116, 126, 132
meme: *see* individual memes
memeiosis 25–26, 29, 34, 115–16, 125, 181
memeization 237
mememakers 222
memeplex 139–45, 147, 149, 164, 250
memesphere 19
memetic 15, 23, 25, 27, 29, 31–33, 35, 37, 109, 111, 113–19, 128, 154, 157, 162–64, 181, 222, 237
men 59, 83, 96, 112, 124, 136, 139, 205–6, 213, 242
mennonites 102
metal (music) 124, 134, 173, 201–2, 213–14, 251
metalinguistic 30, 56, 74
metanarrative 76, 180
metaphor 10, 40, 46, 78, 81, 136, 138, 148, 159, 161, 163, 222, 231–32, 243
metasemiotic 81
metatextual 31, 112
Meteor (meme) 218
Mexican 78, 141
Michelangelo 141
Mickey Mouse 137
microgenres 21
micronarrative 156, 160
Micronations 245, 248
Microsoft 24, 134, 177, 181

## SUBJECT INDEX 281

Millennials 14, 99
Millers: *see* We're the Millers (film)
Minecraft 125
misinformation 101, 105
misinterpreted 5, 58
misleading 100, 105, 165
misogynistic 205, 221–22, 225, 228–29, 232
misspelling 85, 91, 248
MIT 127–28
Mitten Bernie (meme) 25, 27, 34–35, 46, 162, 169
mixed emotion (theory of humor) 40, 191, 194–96, 249
mockery 42, 47–48, 52, 56, 67, 81, 83, 114, 124, 126, 148, 154, 159–60, 180–81, 198, 201, 208, 211–12, 229, 238, 251
modern 40, 42, 116, 138, 152, 160, 230, 236
modernism 160
Moleskine 77, 83
monetized 10, 71, 137
Montesquieu 79
Morton, E. (comedian) 17–18
Mosaic 7
Moscow 72
mountain 66, 124, 127, 234
movie 24, 32, 60, 64, 93–96, 117, 128, 152, 176–78, 183, 201, 205, 217, 229, 233–34
Mozilla 7
MST3K: *see* Mystery Science Theater 3000
MSWord 24
MTV 100
multimodal 21, 173, 198, 200
muppet 27
Murdoch Murdoch 221
Murray, B. 184
music 9, 11, 18, 21, 32–33, 39, 65, 77, 100, 139, 161, 173, 178, 197, 200–202, 204–5, 208–9, 213–14, 220, 249–51
musical 15, 126, 178, 181, 201, 212
Musk, E. 2, 89, 91, 165
Mussolini 230
Mustangs 80
Myspace 13
Mystery Science Theater 3000 233
myth 46, 139, 146, 234, 245, 248
mythos 245

Nakamoto, S. 87–88
Namecoin 91

narcissism 235
narrative 32, 45, 64, 83, 95, 139, 165, 177, 179, 204
narrative strategy (NS) 45, 156, 160
narrowcasting 71–72
NASA 48
Nascar 79
National Lampoon 93
nationalism 8, 220, 229, 231
Natural Environment Research Council (NERC) 123–24
Nazi 80, 124, 175–76, 180–81, 202, 205, 219–21, 230, 232, 239, 245
NBC 151, 191
NDH (Neue Deutsche Härte) 202
Neo 167
neoNazi 8, 124
Neopets 13
nerd 248
Netflix 117, 119
Netherlands 140
Netscape 7
New York Times 102, 125, 166–67
New Yorker 20
newfag 52
newlyweds 126
News 1, 7–8, 10–11, 35, 40, 46–49, 99–107, 113, 129, 136, 138, 144, 163, 166–68, 172, 177, 179, 188, 198, 219, 250
newsgroup 8–9, 25, 226
newspaper 11, 94–95, 99, 102–3, 192
newsworthy 105, 116
Nietzsche, F. 217
Nigeria 140
Nintendo 207, 214
non-player character (NPC) 19, 241–43
nonsense 22, 156, 239
normalfag 52, 243
normies 52, 222, 243, 246
norms 48, 243
Notaro, T. 18, 189, 196
not safe for work (NSFW) 225
Nouvelle Vague 197
NPR 123
numanuma (meme) 21

Obama, B. 77, 104
Ocean 11 (movie) 64
Oculus 233
OED 125
Office (tv show) 189, 191, 193–95, 198
*Onion* 77, 99, 101–3, 105, 107, 191

onlookers 69, 126–27
onomatopoetic 245
opposable thumbs 26–27
opposition (of scripts) 32–33, 44–45, 79, 83, 91–92, 104, 106, 118, 121–22, 124, 137, 140–41, 156, 160, 177–78, 180–81, 183, 201, 203–4, 210, 213–14, 228, 243; *see also* script
Order of the Stick (webtoon) 71–73
Osteen, J. 40–41
ostranenie 74, 78
othering 52, 82

Pacifier (film) 152
Padme (meme) 117–18
Pakistan 212–15
Palin, S. 178
palingenesis 230, 237
Pamela (novel) 178
parallelism 46, 201, 203–4
paranoid 230
Paranoid parrot (meme) 137
Pareto, W. 162
Paris 72
parka 27, 34–35
parking 87, 175, 177–79, 181
parody 21–22, 30, 32, 71, 73, 83, 99–100, 114, 116, 139–41, 146–49, 157, 160, 173, 175–82, 200–205, 218, 222, 249
participatory 178, 249
pasta 140–42, 147
Pastafarianism 109, 139–49, 164, 244, 248, 250
Patreon 71
patriarchy 124, 139, 202
pay-per-click 100
Peanuts (cartoon) 72–73
Pearls Before Swine (cartoon) 201
Peele: *see* Key and Peele
Peercoin 91
penguin (awkward penguin) 18–19, 137
Penny Arcade (comic) 73
Pepe the Frog (meme) vi 18, 55, 91, 137, 221, 229, 236, 239–41, 245–46, 248
PepeCash 91
personality 234–35
personhood 148
Pharisees 148
phatic 55–56, 58, 96
philosoraptor (meme) 18, 137
phone 7, 36, 53–54, 66, 69, 113, 125, 197
photobombing 22, 46, 183–88
photographer 25, 183, 188

Photoshop 27, 36, 165, 201
pictograms 54
Pinterest 168
Pirandello, L. 69
pirate 140, 142–43
Pixar 128
pixel 74
planking 15
Plato 40, 194–95
plaudits 166
playfulness 8, 44–47, 53, 58, 127, 156, 188, 229
playing 12, 41, 197–98, 208, 222–23, 234, 237
pleasure 40, 96, 207–8
podcasts 18, 219
Podemos 231
Polish 46, 111–13
politicians 104, 166, 228
polylogues 17
Ponzi scheme 91
poop (emoji) 54
populism 231
Pornhub 15, 71
pornography 9, 15, 207, 221, 225, 235
portmanteau word 24, 124, 140, 178, 243
Portugal 202, 230
poster 22, 41, 52, 114, 128, 211, 244; *see also* posts
posting 17, 136, 217, 225–26, 228–29, 235, 237, 241
postmodern 59–60, 251
posts 8, 17, 22, 24, 126, 136, 138, 168, 217, 222, 225, 230, 245
Potter, H. 95
power 11, 34, 41–42, 80, 82, 94, 109, 124, 127, 130, 154, 160, 162–63
pragmatic 56, 250
pragmatics 127, 134
pranks 21, 44, 48, 65, 68, 89, 124–28, 130, 184–86, 188, 214, 235, 246–47
prescriptivism 51
pretending 9, 21, 43, 65, 87, 95, 100, 102, 105, 112, 126, 179, 186, 212, 214
Pride and Prejudice 33, 94
Principle of Cooperation 17, 48, 102, 107
Prius (car) 79–80
Producers (movie) 181
produsage 23–24, 249, 251
Project Gutenberg 10
propaganda 1, 10, 107, 166, 217, 219–21, 225, 232, 237, 239–40, 243, 250
prototypical 17, 46, 156, 226

psychoanalysis 159, 177
psychology 26, 40, 44–45, 48, 95, 115, 167, 184, 194, 231
psychopathy 235
Pulcinella 18
Pulp Fiction (film) 114
pun 48, 52, 107, 131, 140–41, 157
punch 18
punching up/down 41–42, 124, 130, 192, 228
punchline 156, 158, 160
punctuation 58, 248
punk 202
Putin, V. 106
Pyle, N. 74

Queen Elizabeth 185
Questionable Content (comic) 76
Quickmeme 36
Quixote, Don. 16

race 16, 22, 77–78, 81–83, 96, 191, 230, 237
racist 3, 22, 137, 218, 221, 225, 229–30, 232, 235, 237–38, 240–41
radio 94, 165
rage comics 19–20, 26, 118, 120, 243–44
Rage guy: *see* rage comics
Rammstein 33, 173, 202–6, 212–13
rant 173, 175–76, 179–81, 200–201, 203
rap 33, 124
rape 90, 189, 196, 205, 225
Rastafarian 140
Raw (film) 83
reaction 17, 22, 39, 41, 60, 66–67, 69, 78, 80, 136, 173, 180, 190–91, 193–94, 199, 207–11, 213–14, 233, 241, 243–44, 246
Reactistan 212
recontextualization 32, 81
Reddit 2, 13, 17, 19, 24, 64–65, 71, 85, 89, 103, 114, 130, 168, 220–21, 245–46
Rednecks 80, 82
Reeves, K. 46
Release (theory of humor) 40, 249
relevance 48, 181
religion 33, 40, 48, 139–40, 146–49, 164, 239, 244
remix 22, 24–26, 29–33, 35–36, 100, 116–17, 119, 125, 157, 165, 178, 201–2, 205, 249–50
Republican 35, 102, 104, 107, 114, 116, 153, 228

resolution 33, 42, 44–47, 54, 83, 111, 113–14, 140–41, 179, 184, 188, 208
resolved 27, 45
retronym 91
retweet 25, 36, 164–67
rhetorical 102, 213, 229
rhyming 52
rhythm 56
rickrolling 44, 232
riddle 101
ridicule 32, 40–41, 104, 124, 141, 152–53, 159–60, 195, 202, 204, 208, 226, 229, 236, 245
Riefenstahl, L. 229
Ringley, J. 208
rofl 57
Rogan, J. 219
Rome 93
Roomba 67
Rosanna (song) 234
rotfl 57
Russia 74, 106, 119, 140, 152
*Rutles* 21

Saab 79
sacrifice 102, 180, 246
sad 46, 241, 243
Sad Cat Token 91
Sadism 202
safe for work 225
Saharan 12
salient 21, 64, 81, 113, 148, 167, 186, 194
Salis, R. 128
salt 125
Sanders, B. 25, 27, 34–35, 46, 162
Santorum, R. 104
sarcasm 56, 101, 106, 148, 212, 235
Satan 32
satire 1, 32, 42, 48–49, 78, 96, 99–105, 107, 125, 147, 153, 166, 168, 172, 197, 219, 239, 245, 250
Satoshi 87
Saturn 27
Saudi Arabia 165, 169
saxophone 162, 198
scams 90, 105, 214
Schadenfreude 177, 195–96
schema 43–44
Schopenhauer 229
Schulz, C. M. 72–73
Scientology 228
Scott 54, 191–95
Scottish 17–18

screenshots 102, 143, 158, 242, 247
script 24, 27, 32–33, 43–46, 79, 83, 91, 104, 106, 112, 118, 122, 124, 127, 137, 140–41, 156, 160, 176–80, 182–83, 194, 200–201, 203–4, 210, 213–14, 219, 248
script switch 44
scripture 147–48
scumbag Steve (meme) 18
Sedaris 77
Seinfeld 173
selfie 185, 197–98
semantic 14, 37, 56, 58, 111, 116–18, 134, 140
semantic bleaching 58, 111, 116–18, 177
semiotic 2, 15, 26–27, 34, 37, 39, 81, 141, 204
sex 11, 104, 106, 118, 121, 168
sexist 3, 232, 235
sexual 21, 78, 82, 221, 237
Shakespearian 32
Shamela (novel) 178
Shiba Inu 85, 90–91
shitposting 232–34, 246
shivaree 126
signifier 177
signs 8, 34–35, 159, 188, 191
Silverman, S. 189, 191, 196
Simpsons 4
sitcom 189, 191, 193, 195, 221
Situationism 229
Skype 14
slang 49, 51–53, 61, 90, 168
slash fan fiction 32
Slovakia 123
smartphone 13, 36, 63, 72, 197
smile 43, 56, 132, 245
smiley 53–55, 74, 245
smiling 39, 54–55, 114, 118, 202
Smudge (meme) 29, 156
snacking (social media) 166
Snapchat 168
Snape 95
Snoop Dogg 89
social media 9–10, 13, 18, 23, 60, 95, 104, 126–27, 164–67, 200, 221, 239–40, 249–50
socialist 34, 202, 205, 214
Socially Awkward Penguin (meme) 137
sociolinguistics 127
sociology 2, 23, 48, 127, 147
software 10, 24, 36, 63, 193, 230, 233
Sonic the Hedgehog 30, 33
sophistication 80, 248

Sophists 236
Soyjak 19, 241–42
Spaceballs (movie) 30–31, 180
Spaghetti Monster 139–40, 147
Spanish 83, 176–77, 230–31
spectacle 205, 250–51
SpiderMan 73
Spock 32
spoiler 49, 51, 93–97, 186
Sponge Bob 56
sprite comics 74
Stalin 117–18, 120, 179–80
Stallman, R. 10
Stalwartbucks 91
stance 55–56, 79, 83, 101, 104, 107, 114, 146–47, 149, 158, 173, 181, 213, 218, 228
standup 17, 190
Star Trek (TV show) 8, 32, 93
Stargate (film) 60
status 33, 39, 47, 52–53, 55–56, 79, 91–92, 114, 137, 141, 147–48, 154, 169, 178, 180, 185, 190, 222, 243, 246, 248
Steam 240–41
Steinlen, T.A. 128
stereotypes 3, 46, 68, 78, 81, 83, 106, 111, 198, 200, 214, 237–38
Stormer, The Daily 238
Strange Plant (comic) 74
Stuff White People Like (SWPL) 77–80, 82–83
stupid 111, 209
style 73, 78, 85, 102, 202, 237–38
Subaru 79
subreddit 103, 233
Substack 4–5, 102
subtitles 66, 176, 178–80, 203
Success Kid (meme) 27, 41–42, 88
suffix 116–17
suicide 228–29
Superheroes 159
superiority 40–41, 48, 64, 68–69, 159, 178, 180, 195–96, 209, 214, 235, 237, 248–49
Superman 159
superspreaders 164
Surrealism 229
Swift 16, 51, 100, 169
switch: *see* script
Switzerland 7
synchronous 17, 58–59
synchrony 190
syncretism 231

## SUBJECT INDEX

syndicated 72–73
syntactic 27, 111, 122
syntax 56, 59, 64, 85, 248

TA: *see* target
Tarantino, Q. 114
Tardar sauce: *see* Grumpy Cat
target (TA) 40–41, 44–46, 68, 78–79, 82–83, 91, 101, 112, 114, 124, 126–28, 136, 155–56, 160, 181, 190, 192, 195, 201, 204, 207–11, 214, 228, 231, 237
Tasmania 78
Tate, A. 222–23
TED 77
teenagers 21, 106, 130, 137–38, 197, 200, 208–9
Tel Aviv 175, 177, 179, 181
Telegram 240
telegraph 58
televangelist 40, 201
television 17, 71, 95
tellability 100–101, 105
terrorism 230, 237
Texas 35, 72, 142, 151–54, 158, 160, 177, 201, 212, 215
texting 51
textual 26, 34, 115, 156, 165, 200
theology 40, 140, 148
theories 40–42, 48, 64, 87, 114, 165, 195, 202, 225, 231, 236, 249
TikTok 9, 13, 21–22, 36, 63, 71–72, 209, 211, 214, 251
Tits or GTFO (meme) 52, 229
Tokyo 63
tortellini 140
Torvalds, L. 10
Tosche Station 201
Toto (band) 234
transgressive 81–82, 191, 230, 236
translation 4, 179, 234, 250
triability 165
tribal 212–15
triggering 221–22
triggers 136, 172, 181, 201
TripAdvisor 9
troll 52, 95, 212, 225–29, 231–36, 241
Trollface 243
trolling 1, 10, 22, 42, 52, 130, 210–12, 217–18, 226, 228–29, 234–37
trope 78, 105, 134, 213
Truffault, F. 197
Trump, D. 29–30, 33, 47, 59, 180, 232, 239, 243, 245–48

truth 34, 48, 52, 81, 99, 102–3, 141, 231, 236
Trybals 212–13
TTYL 51
Tubbing with Tash 189
Tumblr 2, 9, 13–14, 138, 168
Turkish 146
TV 9, 11, 15, 17, 32, 63, 94, 107, 151, 153–54, 158, 160, 190, 234
tweets 10, 25, 54–56, 59, 89, 95, 100, 124, 164–68, 234, 249
Twilight 233
Twitch 2, 208
Twitter 2, 10, 13, 17, 21, 25, 29, 36, 58, 63, 71–72, 95, 131, 164, 168, 178–79, 185, 197–98, 208, 213, 220–22, 233–34

Ubisoft 240
uglification 251
ugly 19, 22
Ukraine 119
unboxing 207–8
Unicode 54
unicycle 43, 46
UNIX 10
unpacking 207–8, 230
Urban Dictionary 24, 124, 183, 221
Urdu 213
Usenet 8, 57, 93, 226
Utah 142
Utopia 10

vaudeville 194
Veblen, T. 79, 208
verbal 21, 39, 44, 126, 155, 173, 178
Verizon 2
Vespa 77
vicarious 190, 195–96, 207–8, 250
vidding 32
video 1–4, 9, 11, 13, 15–18, 21–22, 30, 32–33, 35–37, 44, 47, 58, 63–64, 68–69, 71–72, 74, 83, 89–90, 93–94, 96–97, 107, 113–14, 128, 137, 166–67, 173, 175, 178–81, 186–87, 189, 192–93, 197–98, 200–205, 207–15, 220–21, 225, 233–34, 237, 242–43, 249–51
videocamera 197
videogames 89, 125
videographer 208
Villon, F. 52
Vimeo 197, 203–4
Vin Diesel 23, 152–53
Vine 16, 63, 197–98, 200, 250

vineographer 198
violation 40, 42, 48, 64, 102, 105, 107, 112, 179, 190, 194–95, 235, 243
violence 22, 202, 205, 230–31, 236–37, 240–41
viral 2–3, 16, 22–26, 34, 59–60, 71, 77, 89, 100, 109, 113, 115, 117, 123–26, 135, 139, 143, 152–53, 161, 163–68, 172, 183, 185, 207, 222, 249
Virgil 32
virus 23, 155–56, 161, 169
volcano 139
Volkswagen 79
Volvo 79

Walker Texas Ranger (TV series) 151–54, 158, 160, 177
Walmart 191, 195
Warhol, A. 32
Web 1.0 7 12
Web 2.0 9 103, 109, 250
webcam 135, 208
webcomic 73–74, 76
Webster 161
Weezer (band) 234–35
Wendat 79
We're the Millers (film) 64
Wesley Crusher (TV character) 8
Westboro Baptist Church 102, 107
WhatsApp 58
White Men Can't Jump (film) 83
white supremacy 107, 220, 222, 229–30, 237, 239, 250
Whiteness 78–79, 81
whites 79, 81–82, 220
Whittier Frees, H. 134
Wikia 245

Wikileaks 228
wikimedia 126
Wikipedia 2–4, 8–10, 21, 24, 33, 54, 73, 87, 99–100, 103–4, 123, 125, 131, 136–37, 146, 158, 183, 201–2, 207, 213, 220, 225, 233
Wojak 19, 164, 241–43
woke 97, 124
Wolf of Wall Street (film) 80
Woman Yelling at Cat (meme) 29–31, 33, 143, 156–57, 170
Word 24, 178, 238
WordPress 2, 9, 139
Woyjak 241
Wrath of Kahn, The (Movie) 93

Xbox 240
xenophobia 231
XKCD 16, 71–74

Yahoo 2, 8, 16
Yang, J. 16
Yankovic 21, 178
Yarosh 200
yassification 118, 122
Yelp 9
Yoda 30
You don't mess with Zohan: *see* Zohan
YouTube 2, 9–10, 17, 22, 32, 36, 58, 63–64, 71, 95, 114, 166, 175, 179–80, 189, 192–94, 197–98, 200, 202–3, 208, 212–14, 220–21
You've Got Mail (Film) 9
yuppies 82

Zohan (movie) 177
zombies 33

Printed in the USA
CPSIA information can be obtained
at www.ICGtesting.com
JSHW020822260824
68723JS00001B/2